BEYOND THE FAR STARS

STARBORN

STAN LEE

CHRIS ROBERSON

KHARY RANDOLPH

VOLUME ONE

Ross Richie - Chief Executive Officer

Matt Gagnon - Editor-in-Chief

Adam Fortier - VP-New Business

Wes Harris - VP-Publishing

Lance Kreiter - VP-Licensing & Merchandising

Chip Mosher - Marketing Director

Bryce Carlson - Managing Editor

Ian Brill - Editor

Dafna Pleban - Editor

Christopher Burns - Editor

Shannon Watters - Assistant Editor

Eric Harburn - Assistant Editor

Adam Staffaroni - Assistant Editor

Brian Latimer - Lead Graphic Designer

Stephanie Gonzaga - Graphic Designer

Phil Barbaro - Operations

Ivan Salazar - Marketing Manager

Devin Funches - Marketing Assistant

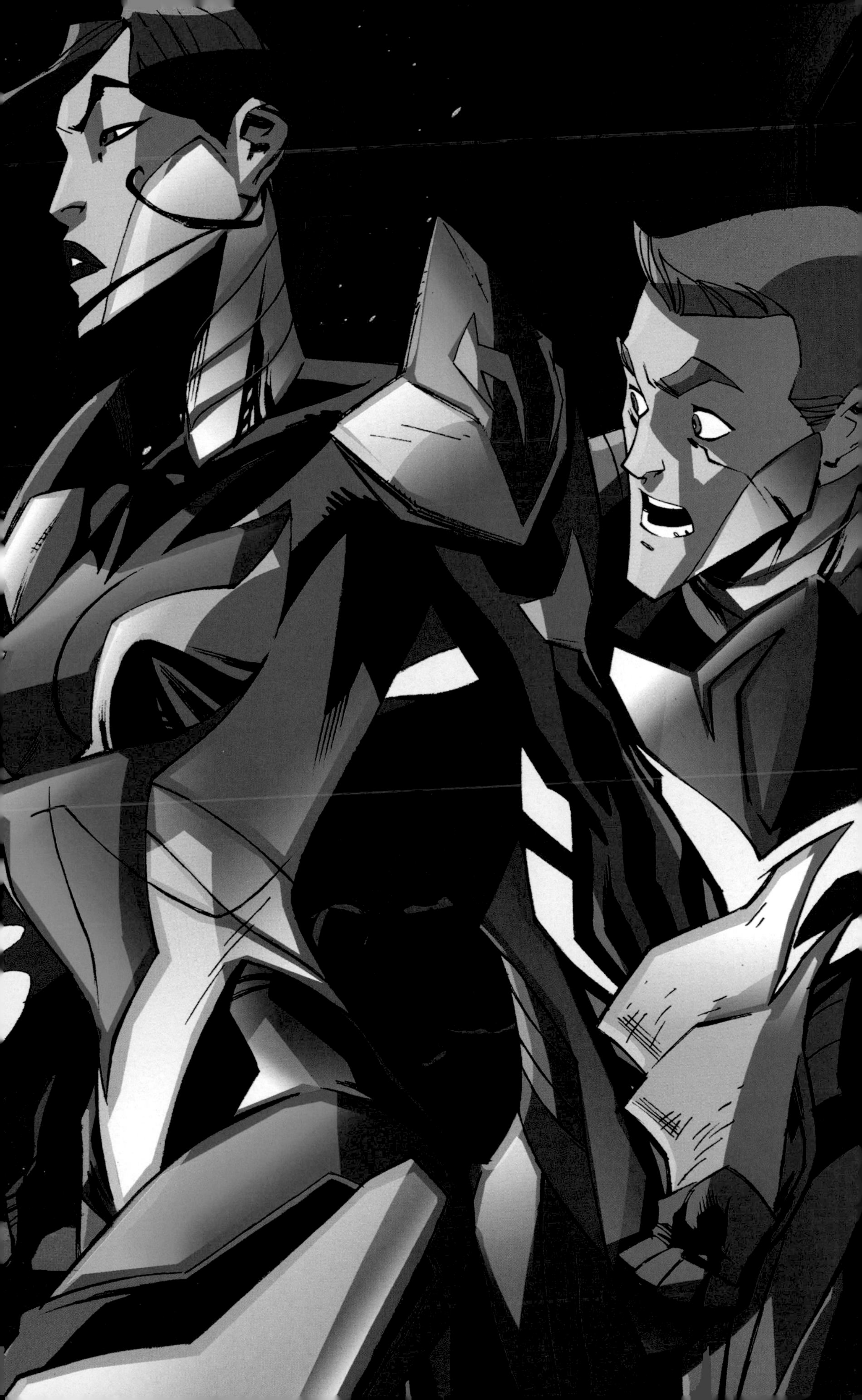

GRAND POOBAH
STAN LEE

WRITTEN BY
CHRIS ROBERSON

ART BY
KHARY RANDOLPH

COLORS BY
MITCH GERADS

LETTERS BY
ED DUKESHIRE

COVER
HUMBERTO RAMOS
WITH EDGAR DELGADO

GRAPHIC DESIGNER
BRIAN LATIMER

EDITOR
BRYCE CARLSON

EDITOR-IN-CHIEF
MATT GAGNON

PUBLISHER
ROSS RICHIE

SPECIAL THANKS
GILL CHAMPION

BOOM! STUDIOS

Stan Lee's POW! ENTERTAINMENT

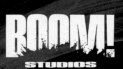

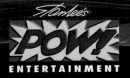

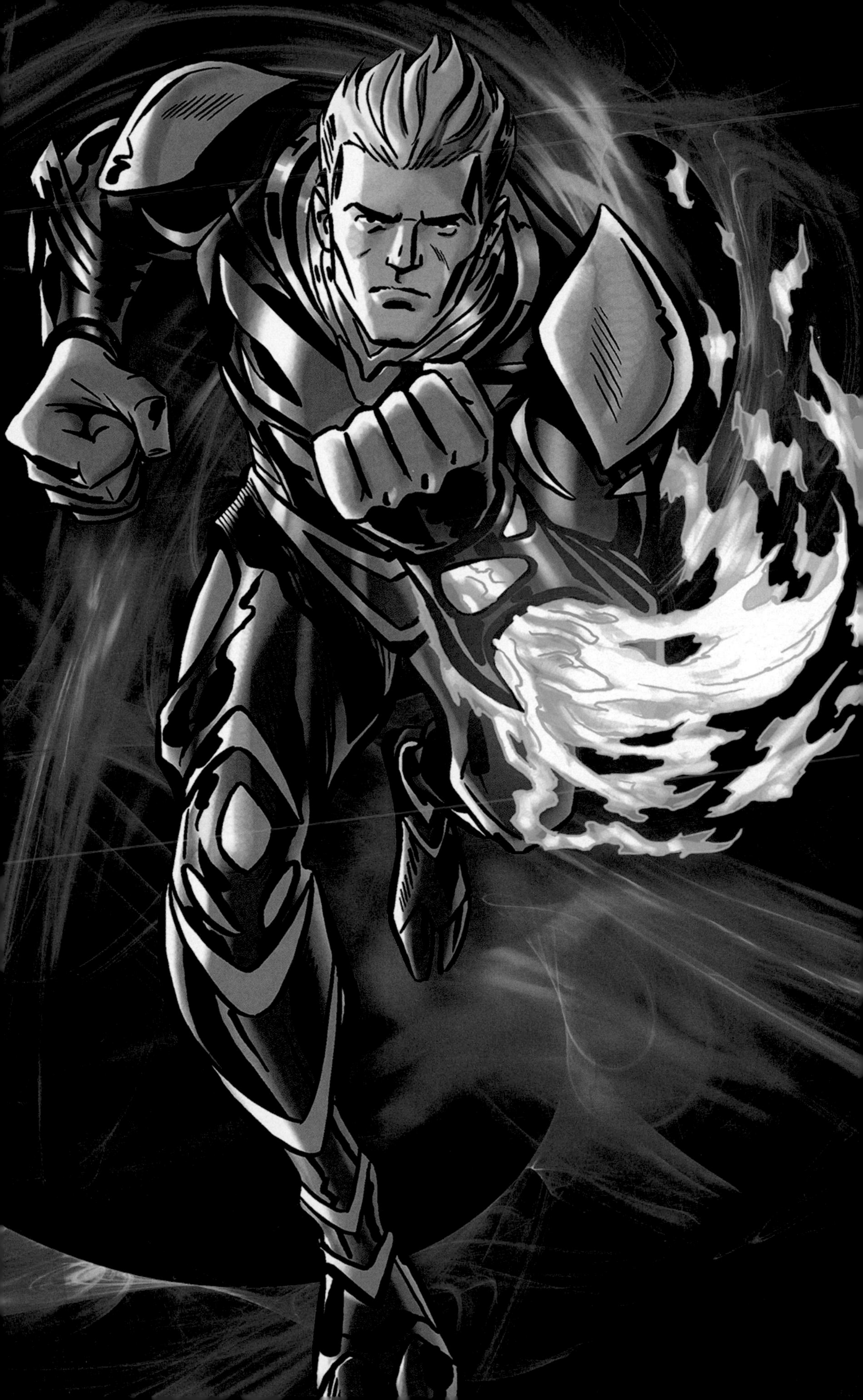

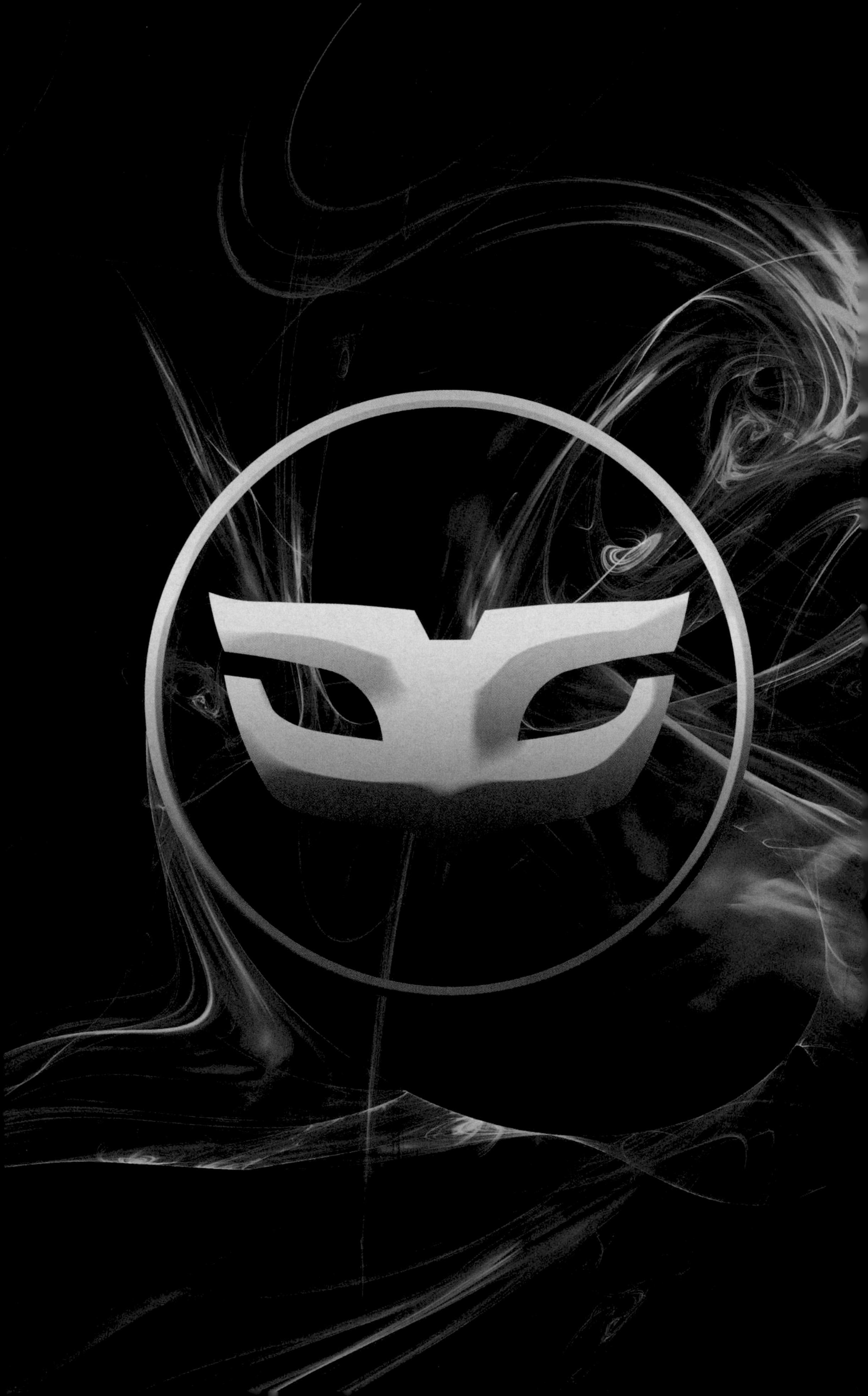

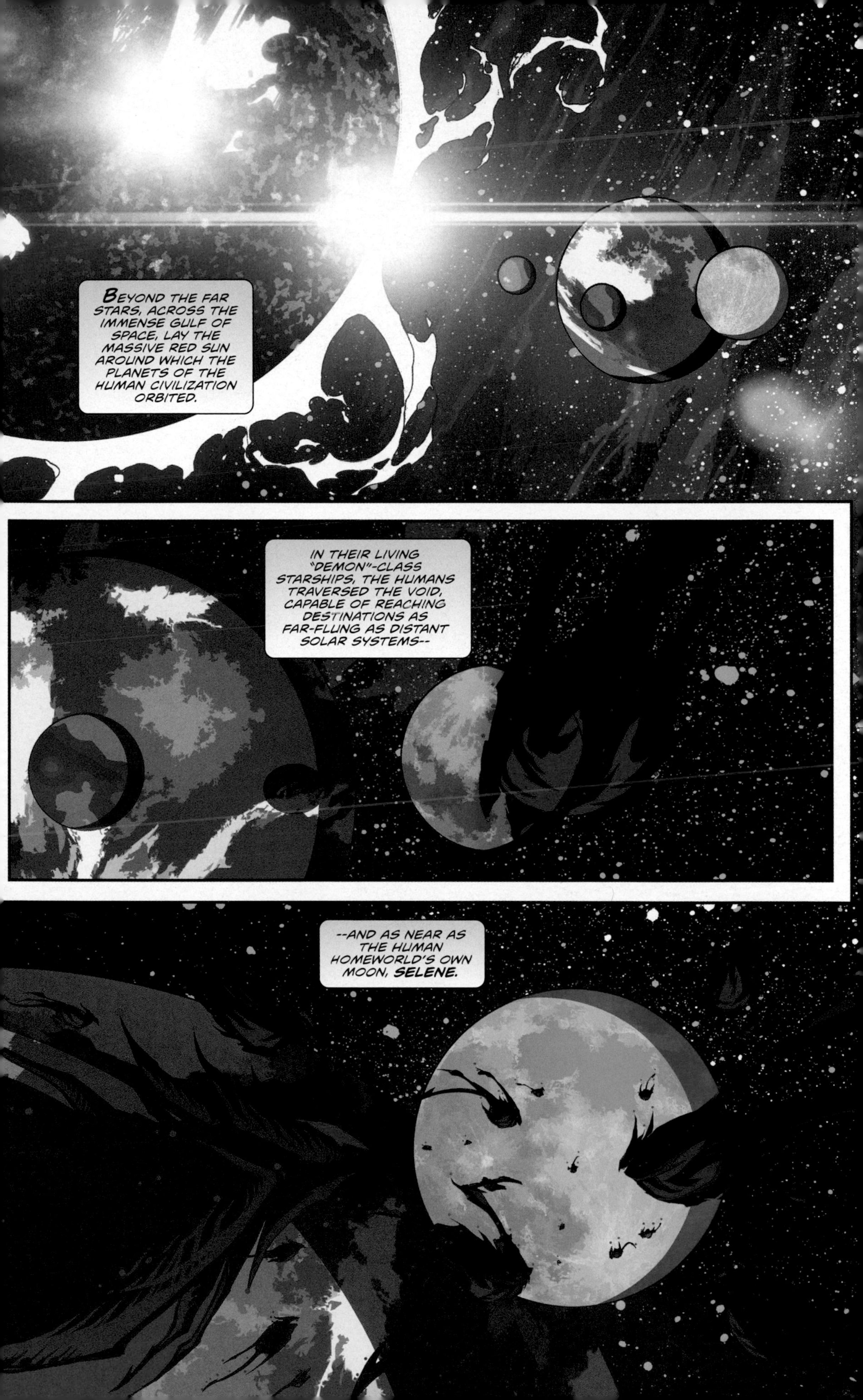
BEYOND THE FAR STARS, ACROSS THE IMMENSE GULF OF SPACE, LAY THE MASSIVE RED SUN AROUND WHICH THE PLANETS OF THE HUMAN CIVILIZATION ORBITED.
IN THEIR LIVING "DEMON"-CLASS STARSHIPS, THE HUMANS TRAVERSED THE VOID, CAPABLE OF REACHING DESTINATIONS AS FAR-FLUNG AS DISTANT SOLAR SYSTEMS--
--AND AS NEAR AS THE HUMAN HOMEWORLD'S OWN MOON, SELENE.

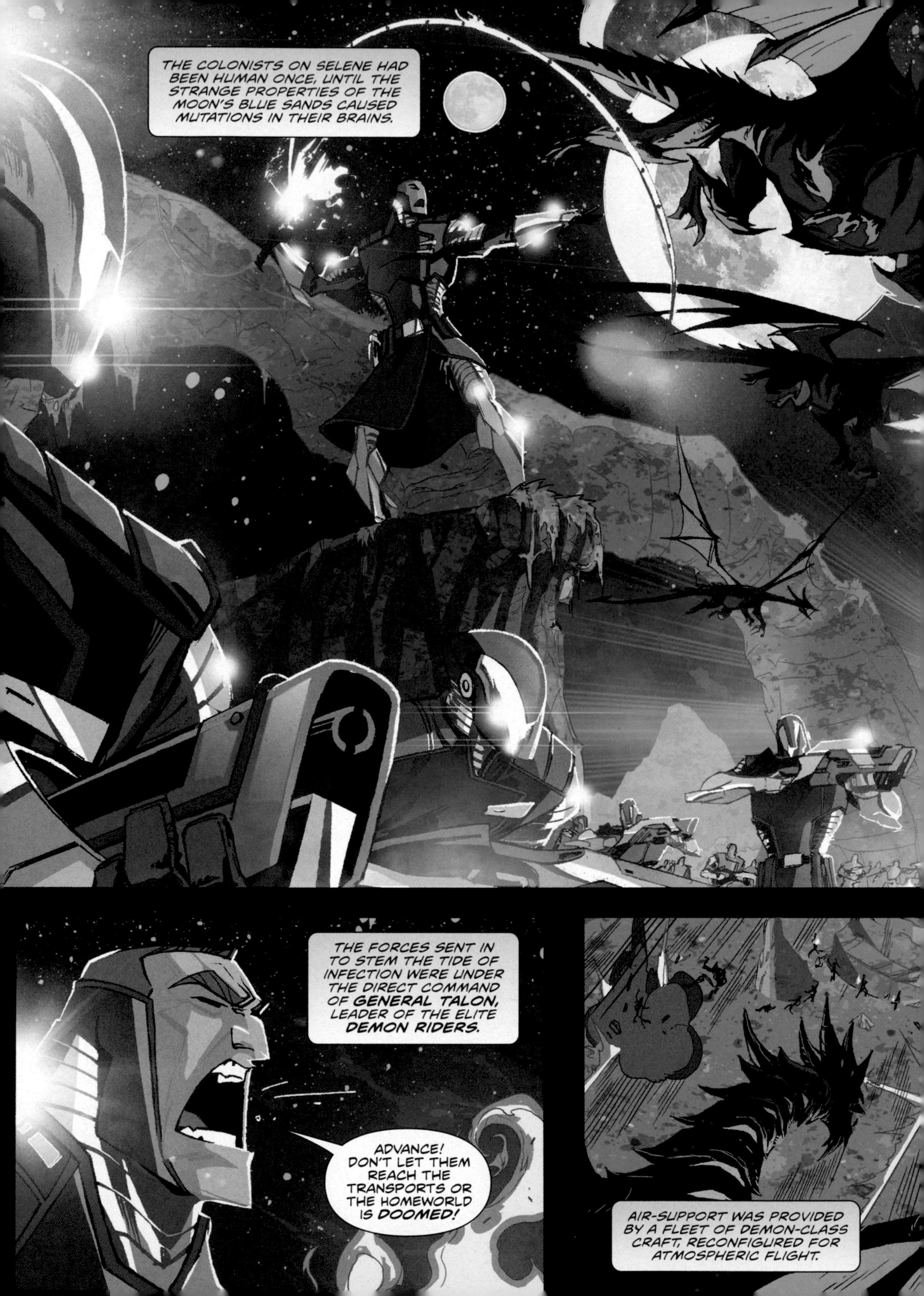
THE COLONISTS ON SELENE HAD BEEN HUMAN ONCE, UNTIL THE STRANGE PROPERTIES OF THE MOON'S BLUE SANDS CAUSED MUTATIONS IN THEIR BRAINS.
THE FORCES SENT IN TO STEM THE TIDE OF INFECTION WERE UNDER THE DIRECT COMMAND OF GENERAL TALON, LEADER OF THE ELITE DEMON RIDERS.
ADVANCE! DON'T LET THEM REACH THE TRANSPORTS OR THE HOMEWORLD IS DOOMED!
AIR-SUPPORT WAS PROVIDED BY A FLEET OF DEMON-CLASS CRAFT, RECONFIGURED FOR ATMOSPHERIC FLIGHT.

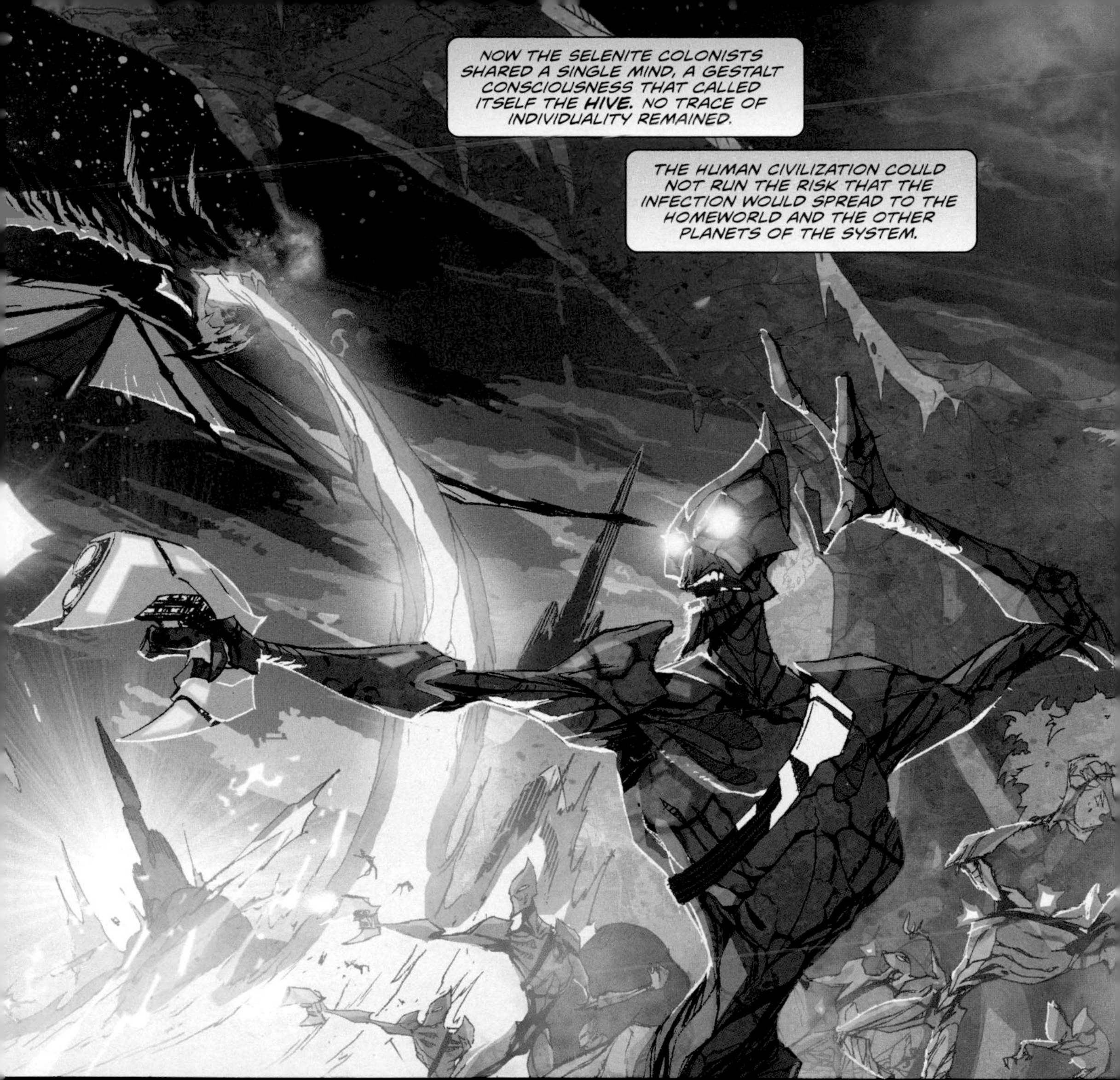
NOW THE SELENITE COLONISTS SHARED A SINGLE MIND, A GESTALT CONSCIOUSNESS THAT CALLED ITSELF THE **HIVE.** NO TRACE OF INDIVIDUALITY REMAINED.
THE HUMAN CIVILIZATION COULD NOT RUN THE RISK THAT THE INFECTION WOULD SPREAD TO THE HOMEWORLD AND THE OTHER PLANETS OF THE SYSTEM.

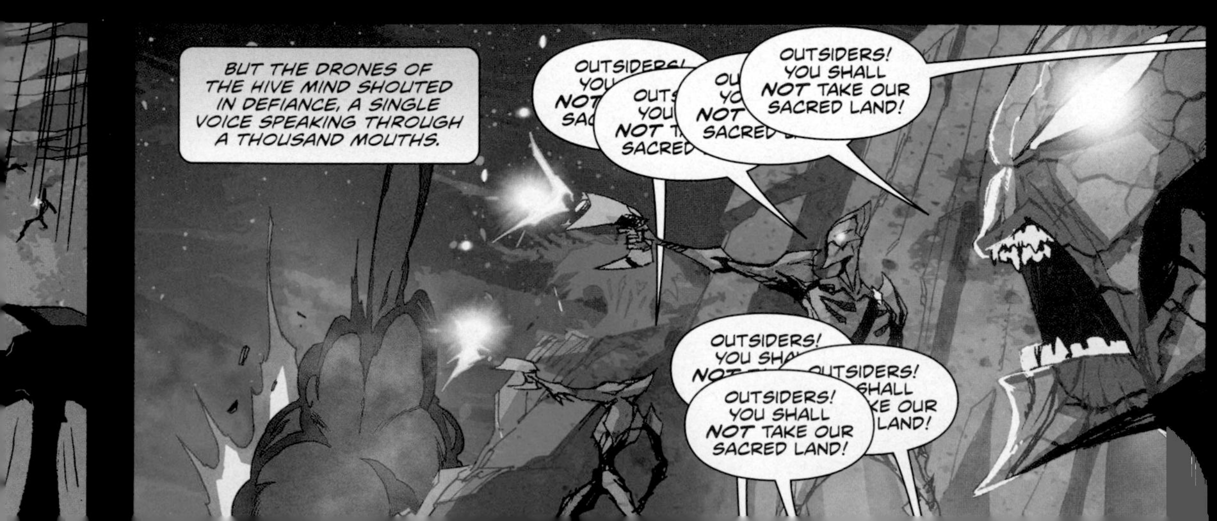
BUT THE DRONES OF THE HIVE MIND SHOUTED IN DEFIANCE, A SINGLE VOICE SPEAKING THROUGH A THOUSAND MOUTHS.
OUTSIDERS! YOU SHALL **NOT** TAKE OUR SACRED LAND!
OUTSIDERS! YOU SHALL **NOT** TAKE OUR SACRED LAND!

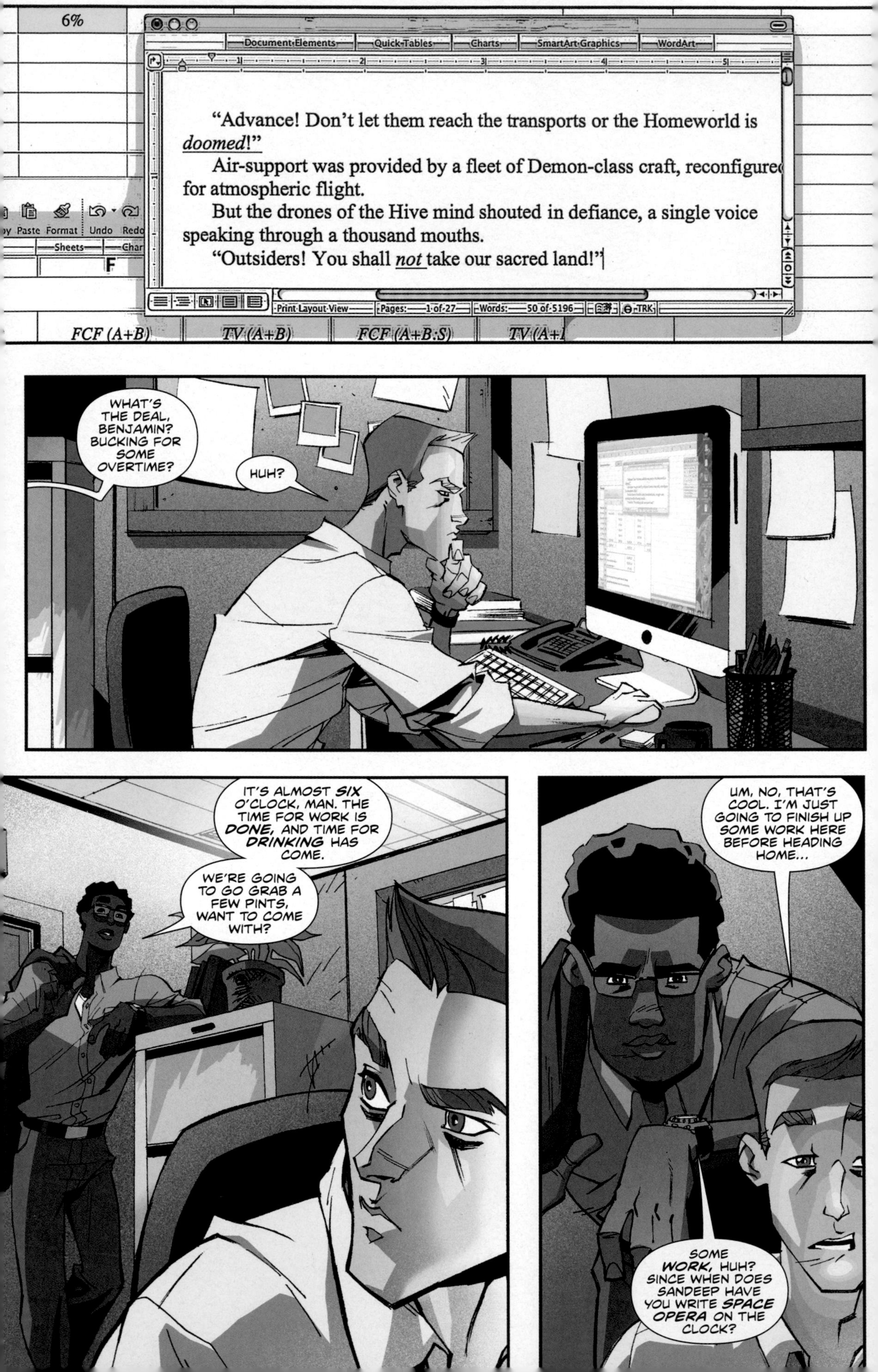
6%
Document Elements
Quick Tables
Charts
SmartArt Graphics
WordArt
"Advance! Don't let them reach the transports or the Homeworld is *doomed*!"
Air-support was provided by a fleet of Demon-class craft, reconfigured for atmospheric flight.
But the drones of the Hive mind shouted in defiance, a single voice speaking through a thousand mouths.
"Outsiders! You shall *not* take our sacred land!"
Paste Format Undo Redo
Sheets
F
Print Layout View
Pages: 1 of 27
Words: 50 of 5196
TRK
FCF (A+B)
TV (A+B)
FCF (A+B:S)
WHAT'S THE DEAL, BENJAMIN? BUCKING FOR SOME OVERTIME?
HUH?
IT'S ALMOST *SIX* O'CLOCK, MAN. THE TIME FOR WORK IS *DONE*, AND TIME FOR *DRINKING* HAS COME.
WE'RE GOING TO GO GRAB A FEW PINTS, WANT TO COME WITH?
UM, NO, THAT'S COOL. I'M JUST GOING TO FINISH UP SOME WORK HERE BEFORE HEADING HOME...
SOME *WORK*, HUH? SINCE WHEN DOES SANDEEP HAVE YOU WRITE *SPACE OPERA* ON THE CLOCK?

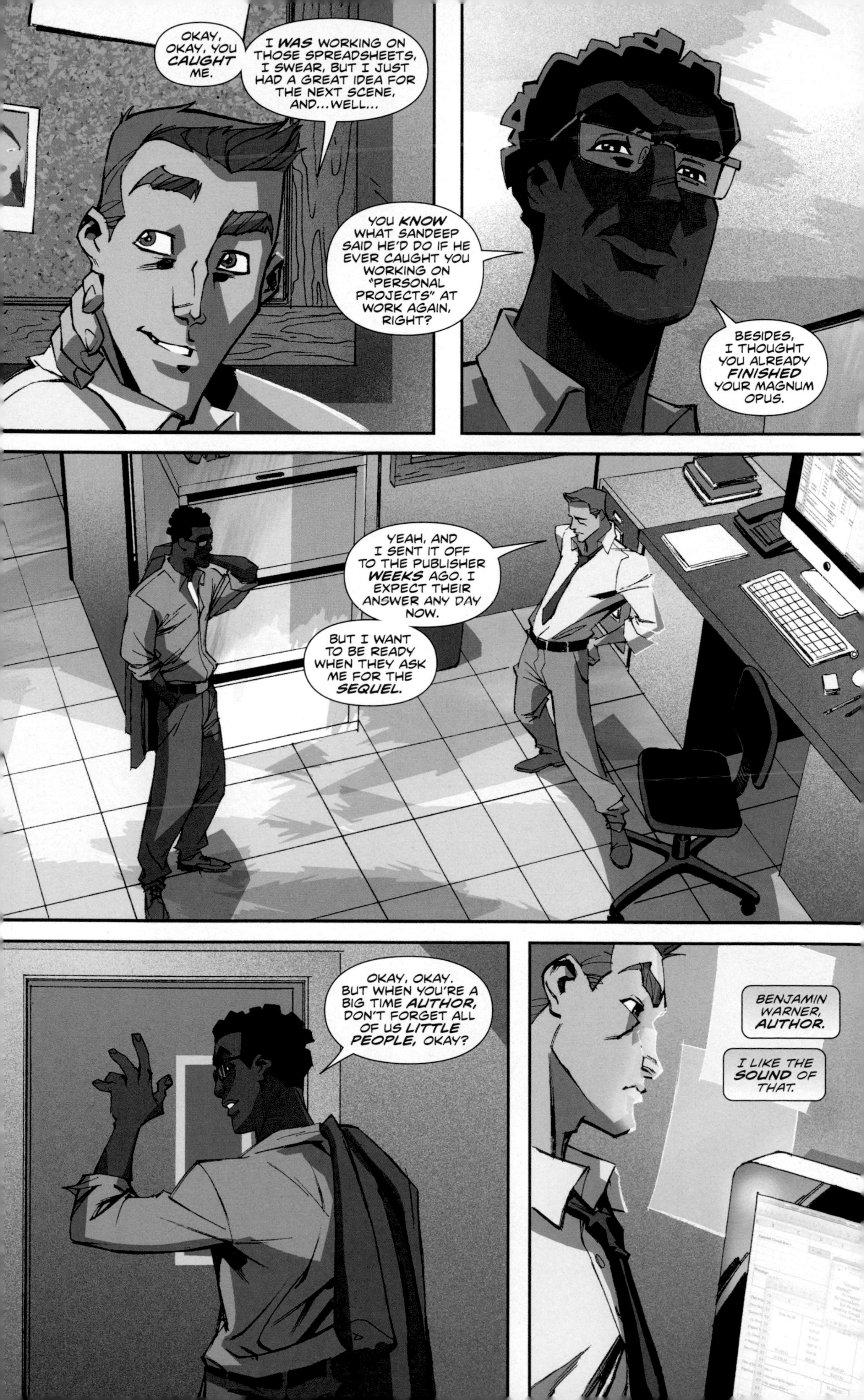
OKAY, OKAY, YOU CAUGHT ME.
I WAS WORKING ON THOSE SPREADSHEETS, I SWEAR, BUT I JUST HAD A GREAT IDEA FOR THE NEXT SCENE, AND...WELL...
YOU KNOW WHAT SANDEEP SAID HE'D DO IF HE EVER CAUGHT YOU WORKING ON "PERSONAL PROJECTS" AT WORK AGAIN, RIGHT?
BESIDES, I THOUGHT YOU ALREADY FINISHED YOUR MAGNUM OPUS.
YEAH, AND I SENT IT OFF TO THE PUBLISHER WEEKS AGO. I EXPECT THEIR ANSWER ANY DAY NOW.
BUT I WANT TO BE READY WHEN THEY ASK ME FOR THE SEQUEL.
OKAY, OKAY. BUT WHEN YOU'RE A BIG TIME AUTHOR, DON'T FORGET ALL OF US LITTLE PEOPLE, OKAY?
BENJAMIN WARNER, AUTHOR.
I LIKE THE SOUND OF THAT.

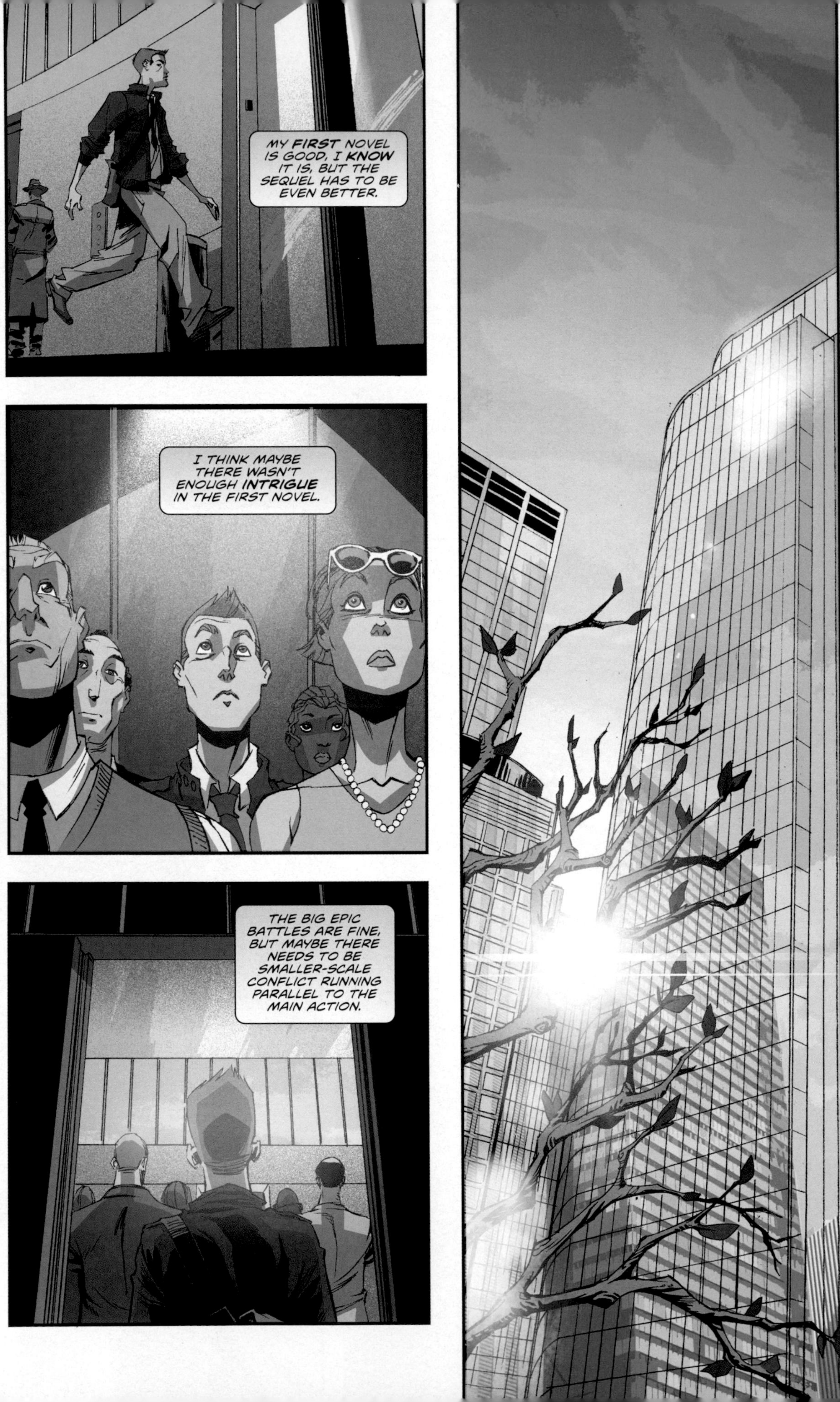
MY FIRST NOVEL IS GOOD, I KNOW IT IS, BUT THE SEQUEL HAS TO BE EVEN BETTER.
I THINK MAYBE THERE WASN'T ENOUGH INTRIGUE IN THE FIRST NOVEL.
THE BIG EPIC BATTLES ARE FINE, BUT MAYBE THERE NEEDS TO BE SMALLER-SCALE CONFLICT RUNNING PARALLEL TO THE MAIN ACTION.

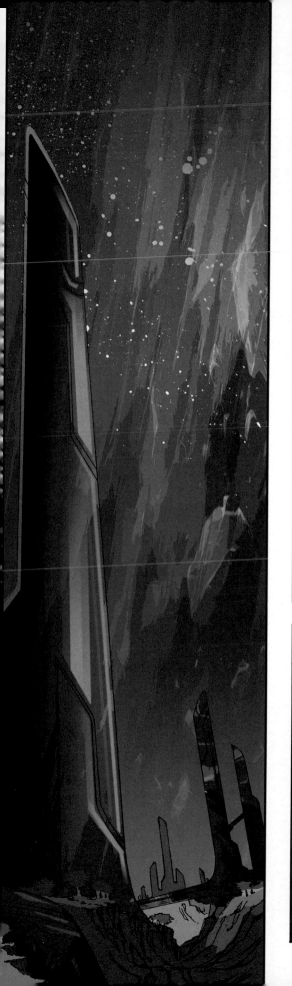

LIKE, MAYBE THE EMPEROR'S FAVORITE WIFE IS ALL ALONE IN HER PRIVATE CHAMBERS, UNAWARE THAT A TEAM OF HIVE ASSASSINS HAS INFILTRATED THE OBSIDIAN PALACE.

WHAT THE ASSASSINS DON'T REALIZE, THOUGH, IS THAT ONE OF THEM *ISN'T* A MEMBER OF THE HIVE, BUT IS ONE OF THE EMPEROR'S PERSONAL GUARDS.

ONE OF THE SHAPE-SHIFTING *CRIMSON HAND.*

BY THE TIME THE HIVE MEMBERS REALIZE THEIR MISTAKE, IT IS *TOO LATE,* AND...

BUT WAIT, THAT DOESN'T WORK. THE HIVE MEMBERS ARE TELEPATHIC. WOULDN'T THEY KNOW *IMMEDIATELY* THAT THE *CRIMSON HAND* WASN'T ONE OF THEM?

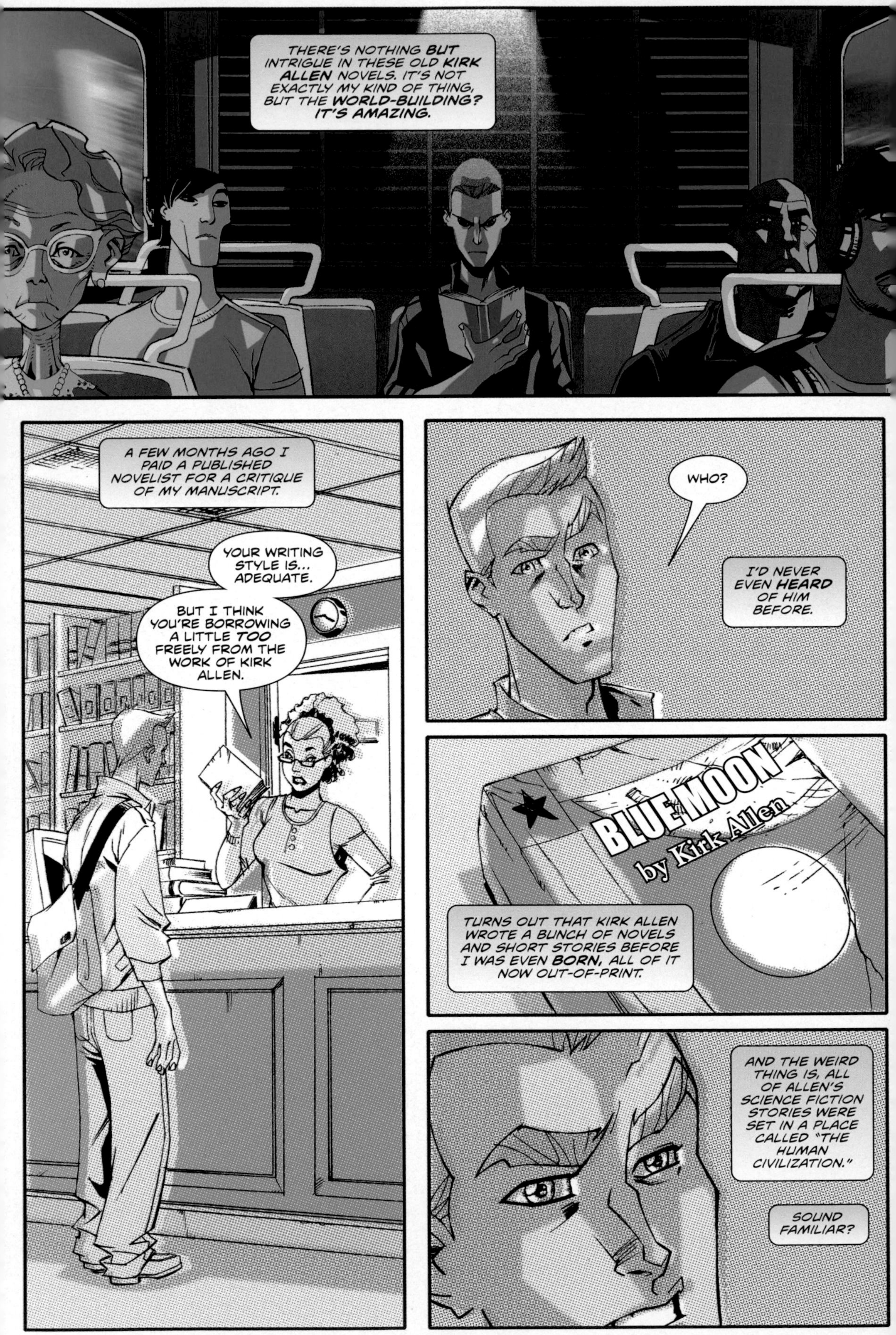
THERE'S NOTHING BUT INTRIGUE IN THESE OLD KIRK ALLEN NOVELS. IT'S NOT EXACTLY MY KIND OF THING, BUT THE WORLD-BUILDING? IT'S AMAZING.
A FEW MONTHS AGO I PAID A PUBLISHED NOVELIST FOR A CRITIQUE OF MY MANUSCRIPT.
YOUR WRITING STYLE IS... ADEQUATE.
BUT I THINK YOU'RE BORROWING A LITTLE TOO FREELY FROM THE WORK OF KIRK ALLEN.
WHO?
I'D NEVER EVEN HEARD OF HIM BEFORE.
BLUE MOON
by Kirk Allen
TURNS OUT THAT KIRK ALLEN WROTE A BUNCH OF NOVELS AND SHORT STORIES BEFORE I WAS EVEN BORN, ALL OF IT NOW OUT-OF-PRINT.
AND THE WEIRD THING IS, ALL OF ALLEN'S SCIENCE FICTION STORIES WERE SET IN A PLACE CALLED "THE HUMAN CIVILIZATION."
SOUND FAMILIAR?

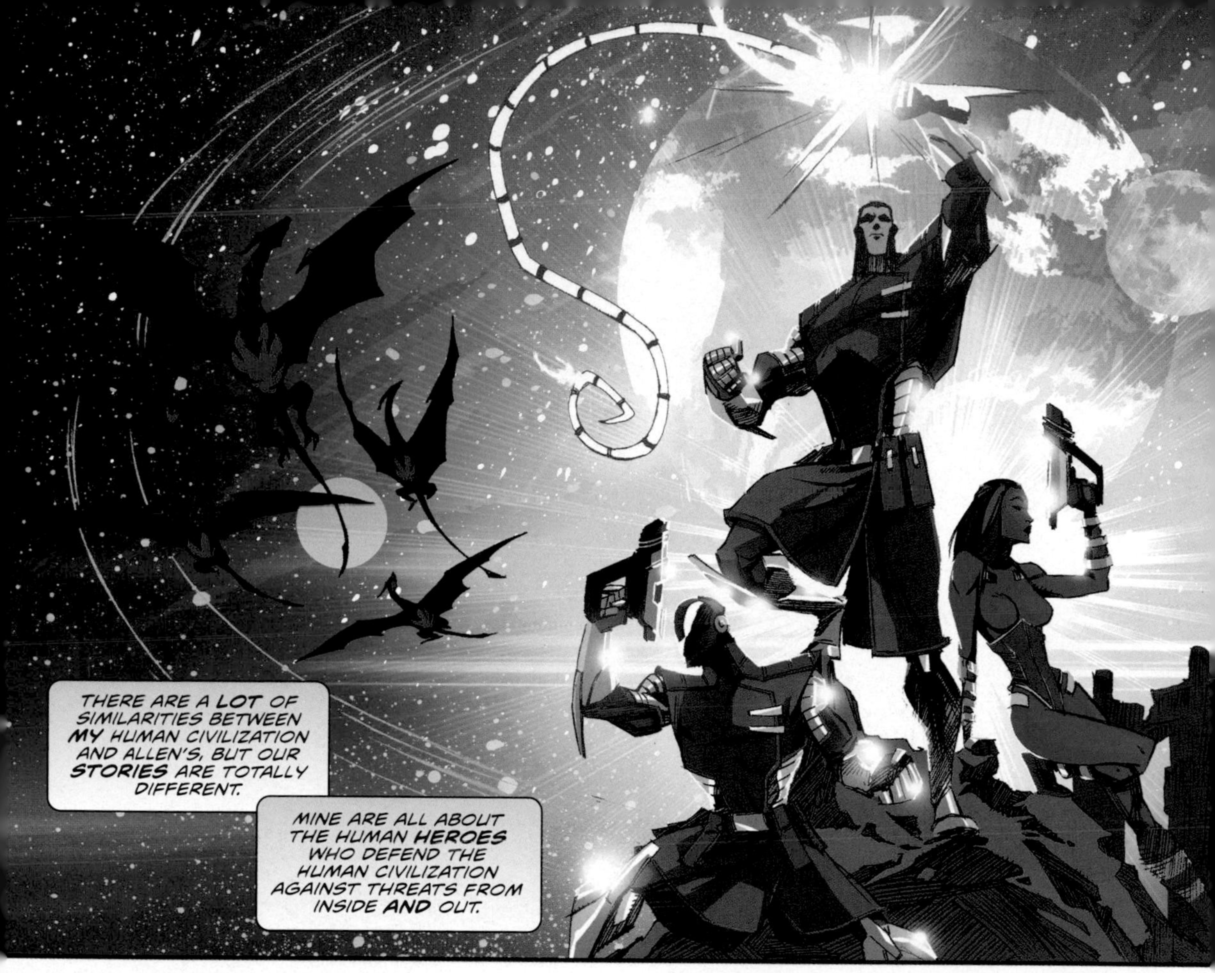
THERE ARE A LOT OF SIMILARITIES BETWEEN MY HUMAN CIVILIZATION AND ALLEN'S, BUT OUR STORIES ARE TOTALLY DIFFERENT.
MINE ARE ALL ABOUT THE HUMAN HEROES WHO DEFEND THE HUMAN CIVILIZATION AGAINST THREATS FROM INSIDE AND OUT.

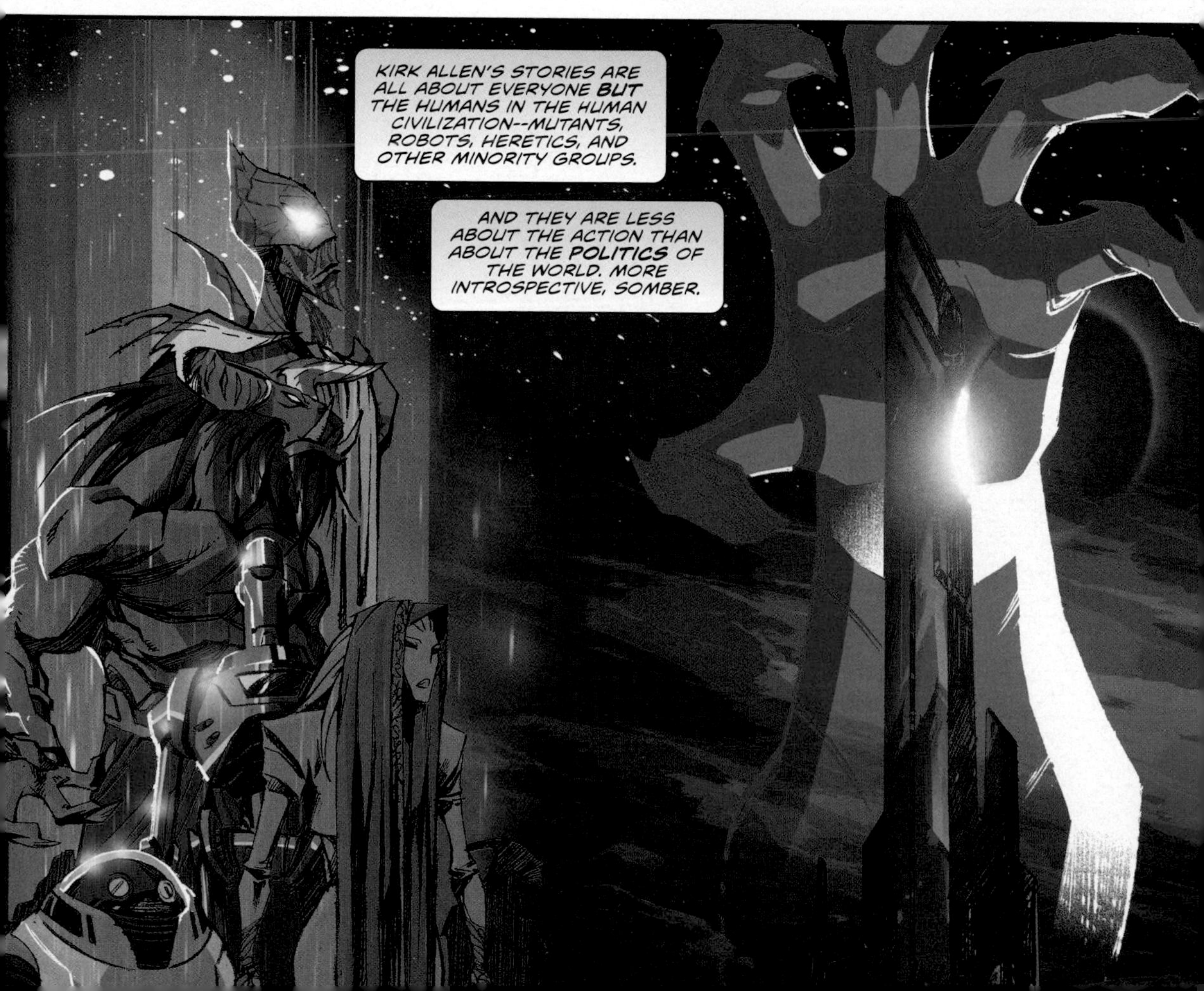
KIRK ALLEN'S STORIES ARE ALL ABOUT EVERYONE BUT THE HUMANS IN THE HUMAN CIVILIZATION--MUTANTS, ROBOTS, HERETICS, AND OTHER MINORITY GROUPS.
AND THEY ARE LESS ABOUT THE ACTION THAN ABOUT THE POLITICS OF THE WORLD. MORE INTROSPECTIVE, SOMBER.

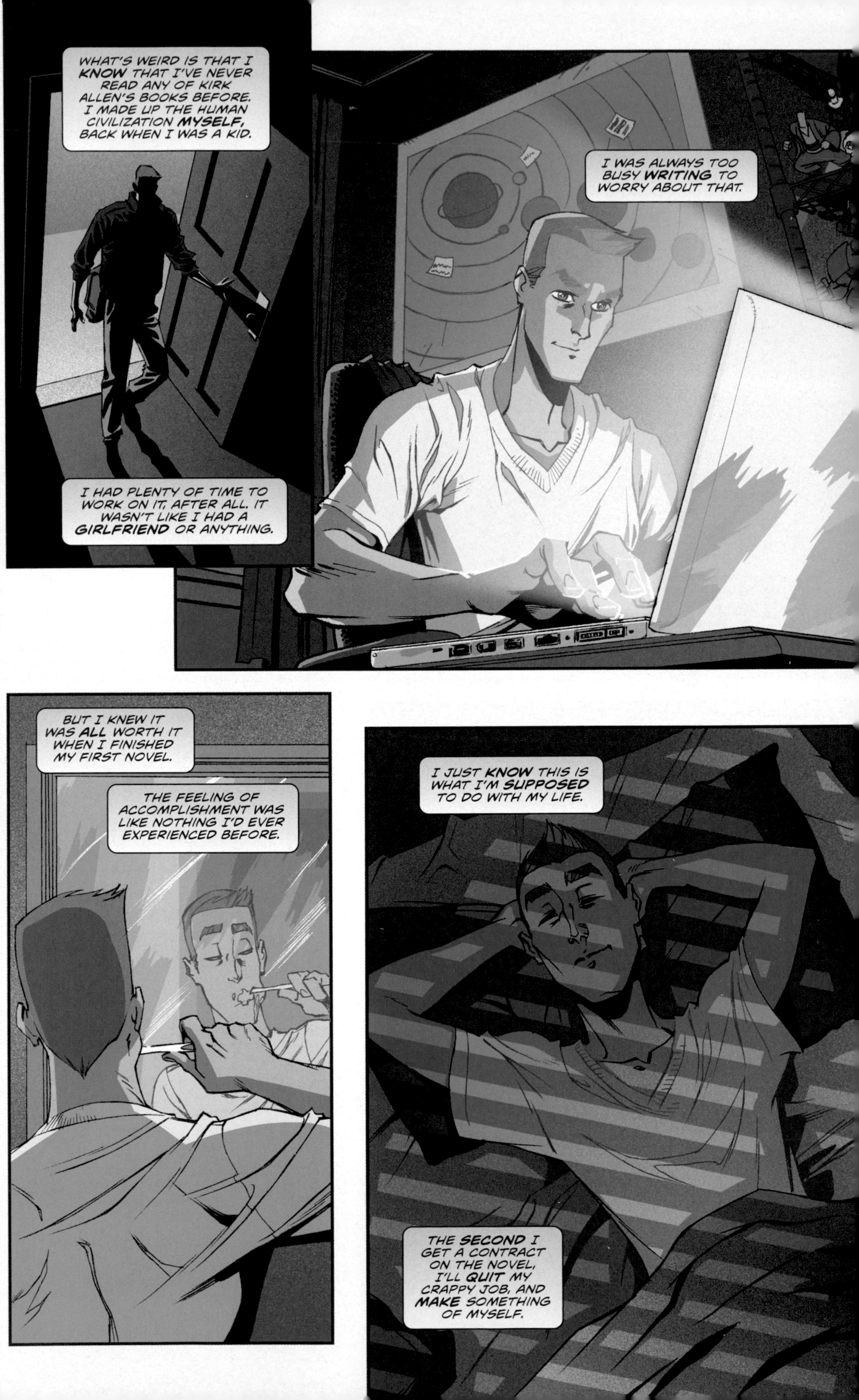
WHAT'S WEIRD IS THAT I KNOW THAT I'VE NEVER READ ANY OF KIRK ALLEN'S BOOKS BEFORE. I MADE UP THE HUMAN CIVILIZATION MYSELF, BACK WHEN I WAS A KID.
I HAD PLENTY OF TIME TO WORK ON IT, AFTER ALL. IT WASN'T LIKE I HAD A GIRLFRIEND OR ANYTHING.
I WAS ALWAYS TOO BUSY WRITING TO WORRY ABOUT THAT.
BUT I KNEW IT WAS ALL WORTH IT WHEN I FINISHED MY FIRST NOVEL.
THE FEELING OF ACCOMPLISHMENT WAS LIKE NOTHING I'D EVER EXPERIENCED BEFORE.
I JUST KNOW THIS IS WHAT I'M SUPPOSED TO DO WITH MY LIFE.
THE SECOND I GET A CONTRACT ON THE NOVEL, I'LL QUIT MY CRAPPY JOB, AND MAKE SOMETHING OF MYSELF.

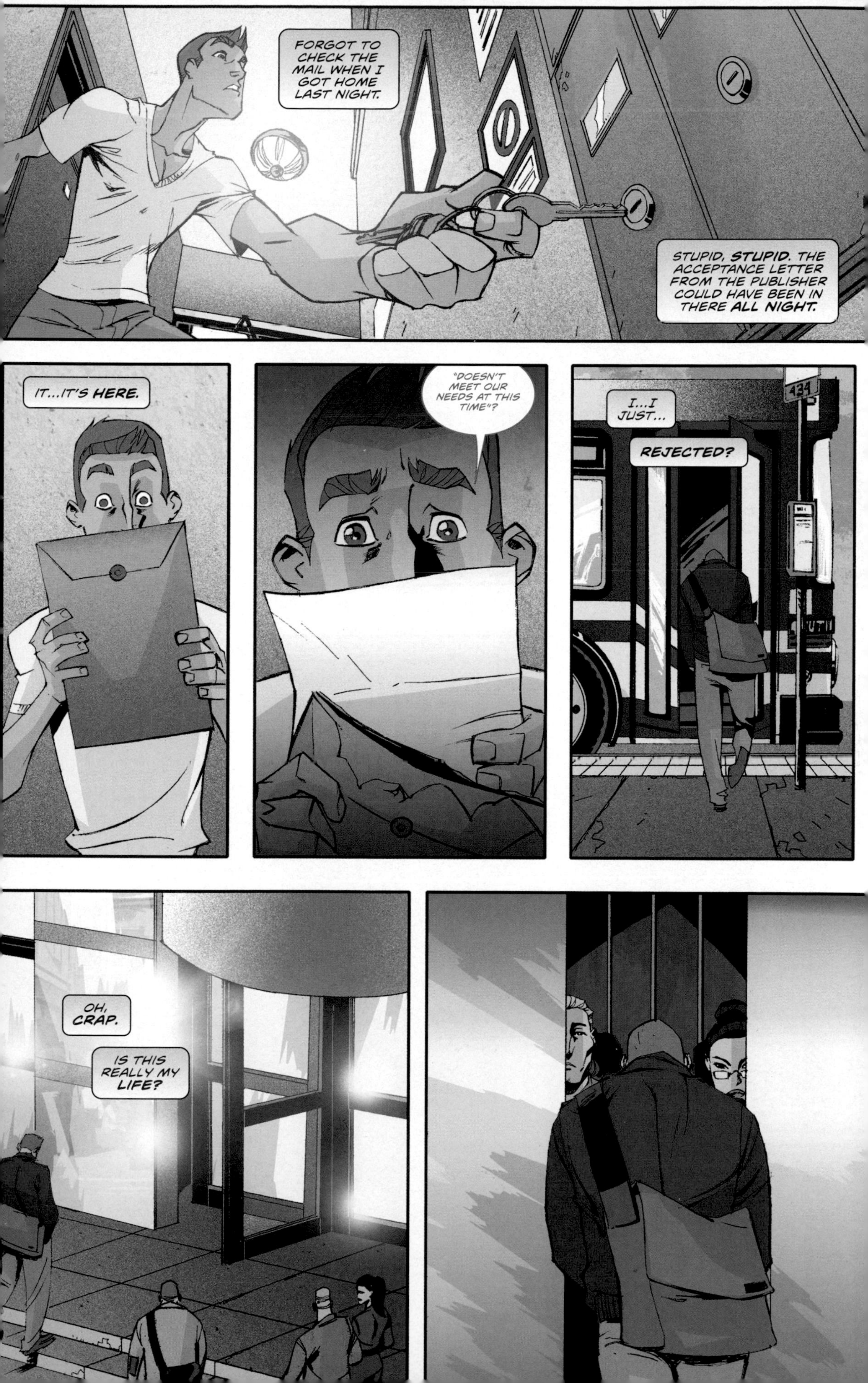
FORGOT TO CHECK THE MAIL WHEN I GOT HOME LAST NIGHT.
STUPID, STUPID. THE ACCEPTANCE LETTER FROM THE PUBLISHER COULD HAVE BEEN IN THERE ALL NIGHT.
IT...IT'S HERE.
"DOESN'T MEET OUR NEEDS AT THIS TIME"?
I...I JUST...
REJECTED?
434
OH, CRAP.
IS THIS REALLY MY LIFE?

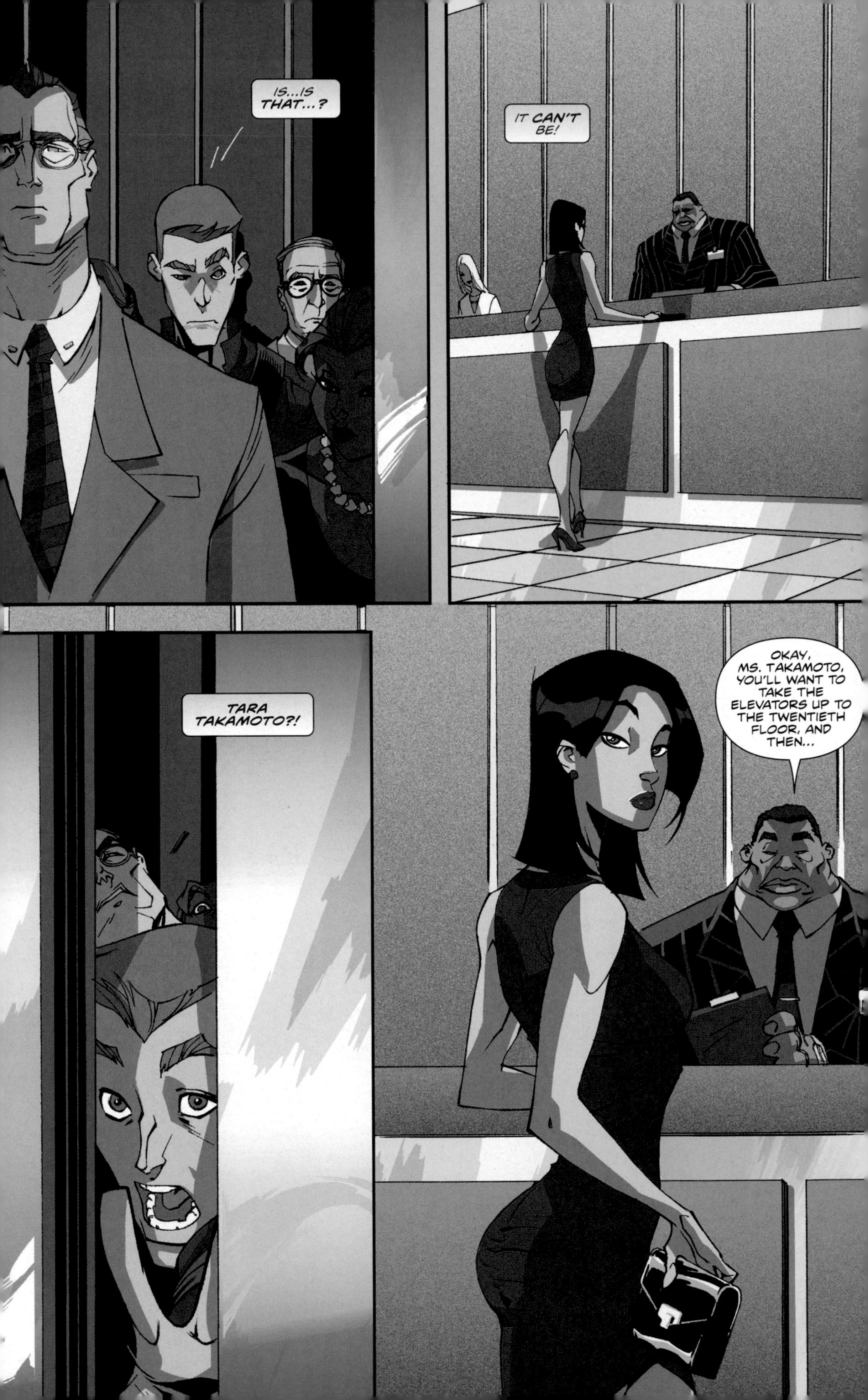
IS...IS THAT...?
IT CAN'T BE!
TARA TAKAMOTO?!
OKAY, MS. TAKAMOTO, YOU'LL WANT TO TAKE THE ELEVATORS UP TO THE TWENTIETH FLOOR, AND THEN...

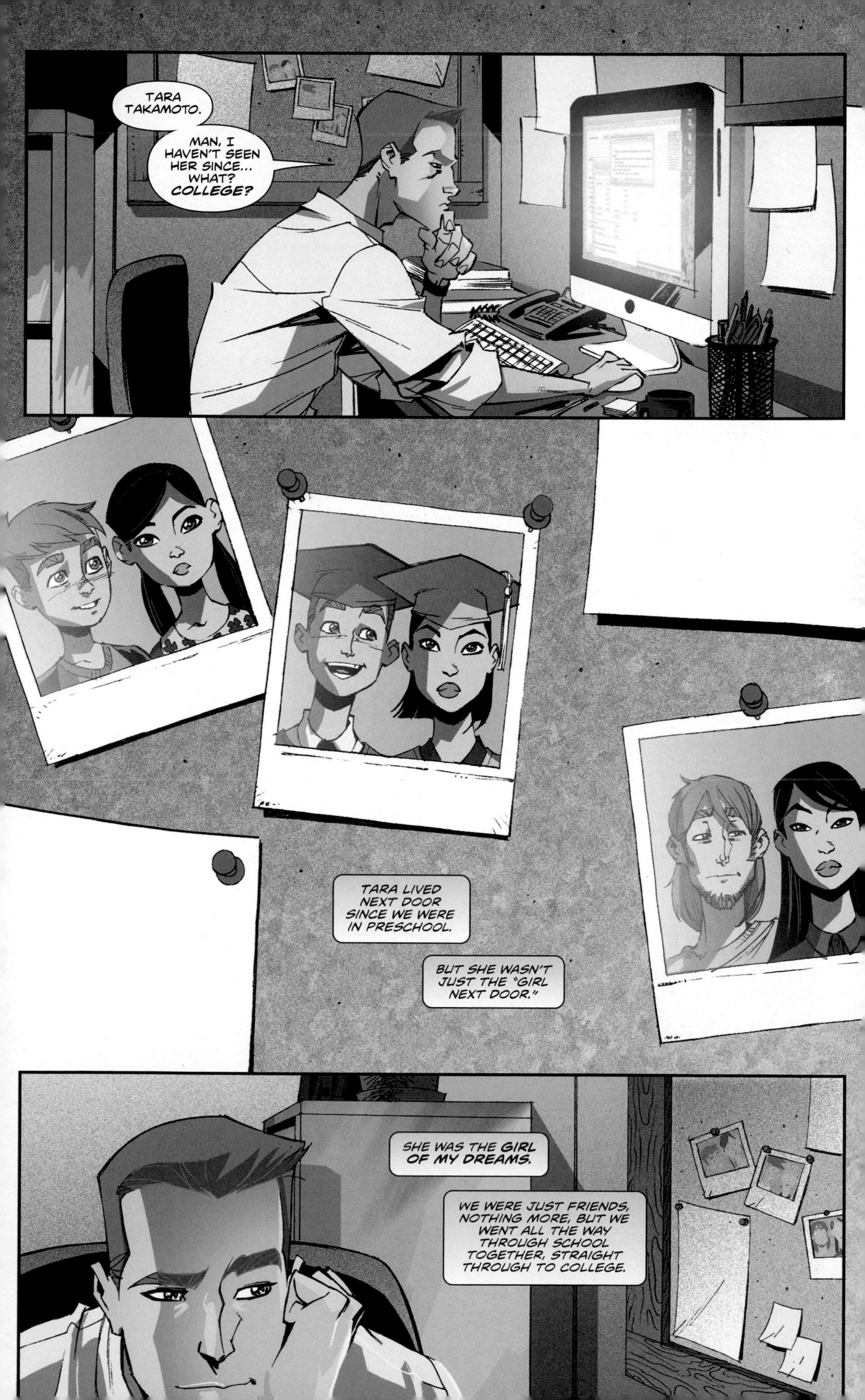
TARA TAKAMOTO.
MAN, I HAVEN'T SEEN HER SINCE... WHAT? COLLEGE?
TARA LIVED NEXT DOOR SINCE WE WERE IN PRESCHOOL.
BUT SHE WASN'T JUST THE "GIRL NEXT DOOR."
SHE WAS THE GIRL OF MY DREAMS.
WE WERE JUST FRIENDS, NOTHING MORE, BUT WE WENT ALL THE WAY THROUGH SCHOOL TOGETHER, STRAIGHT THROUGH TO COLLEGE.

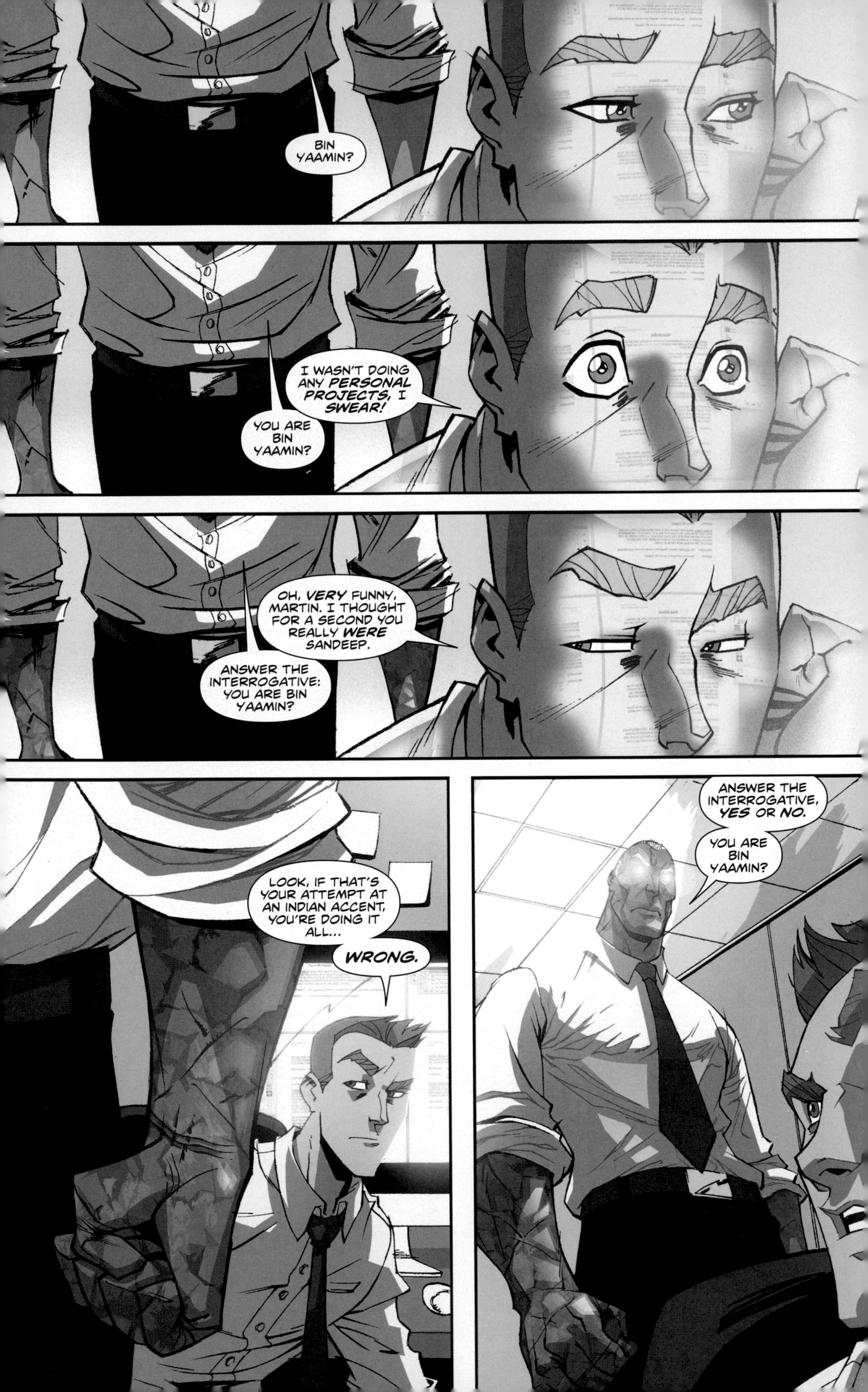
BIN YAAMIN?
I WASN'T DOING ANY PERSONAL PROJECTS, I SWEAR!
YOU ARE BIN YAAMIN?
OH, VERY FUNNY, MARTIN. I THOUGHT FOR A SECOND YOU REALLY WERE SANDEEP.
ANSWER THE INTERROGATIVE: YOU ARE BIN YAAMIN?
LOOK, IF THAT'S YOUR ATTEMPT AT AN INDIAN ACCENT, YOU'RE DOING IT ALL...
WRONG.
ANSWER THE INTERROGATIVE, YES OR NO.
YOU ARE BIN YAAMIN?

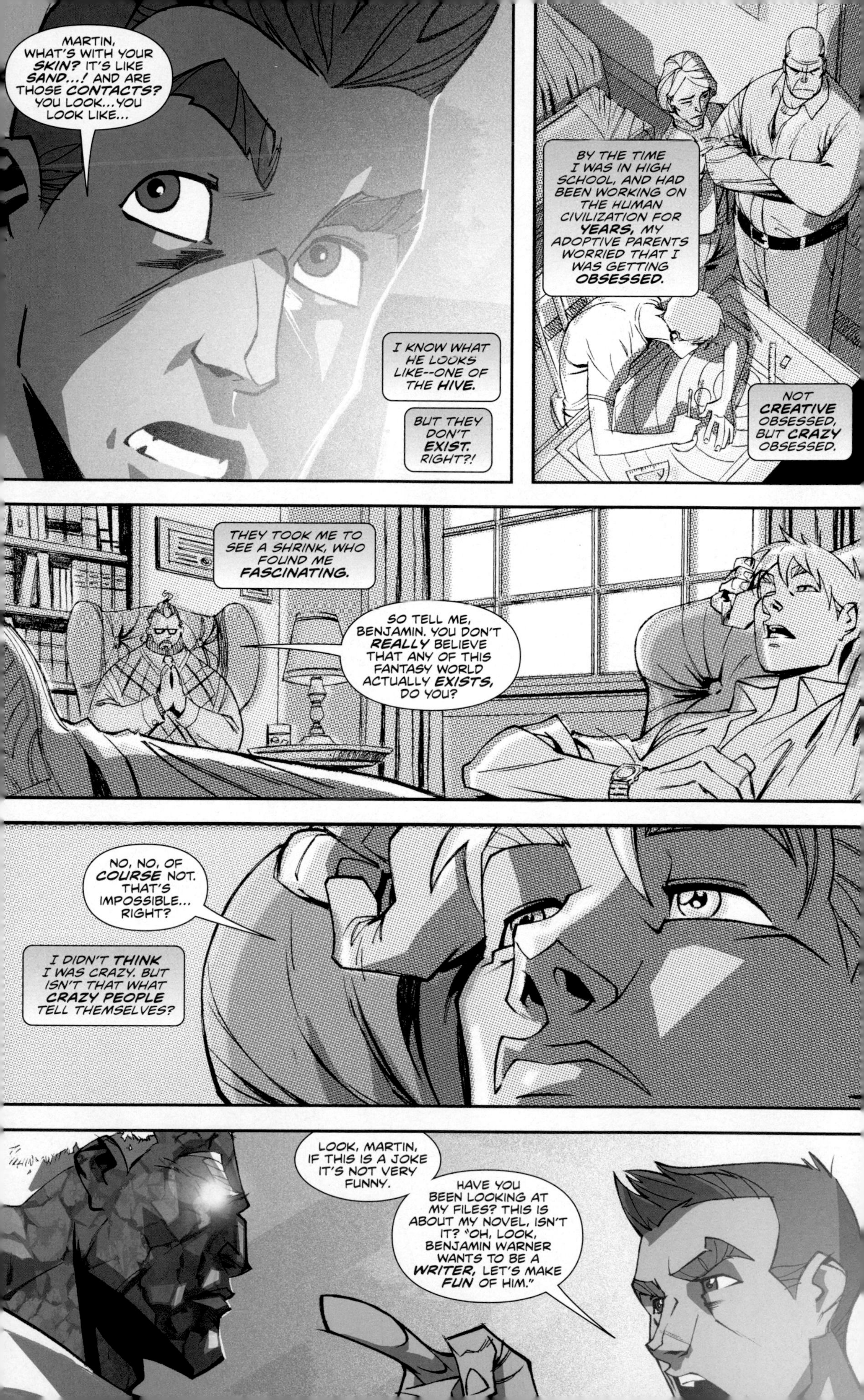
MARTIN, WHAT'S WITH YOUR SKIN? IT'S LIKE SAND...! AND ARE THOSE CONTACTS? YOU LOOK... YOU LOOK LIKE...
I KNOW WHAT HE LOOKS LIKE--ONE OF THE HIVE.
BUT THEY DON'T EXIST. RIGHT?!
BY THE TIME I WAS IN HIGH SCHOOL, AND HAD BEEN WORKING ON THE HUMAN CIVILIZATION FOR YEARS, MY ADOPTIVE PARENTS WORRIED THAT I WAS GETTING OBSESSED.
NOT CREATIVE OBSESSED, BUT CRAZY OBSESSED.
THEY TOOK ME TO SEE A SHRINK, WHO FOUND ME FASCINATING.
SO TELL ME, BENJAMIN. YOU DON'T REALLY BELIEVE THAT ANY OF THIS FANTASY WORLD ACTUALLY EXISTS, DO YOU?
NO, NO, OF COURSE NOT. THAT'S IMPOSSIBLE... RIGHT?
I DIDN'T THINK I WAS CRAZY. BUT ISN'T THAT WHAT CRAZY PEOPLE TELL THEMSELVES?
LOOK, MARTIN, IF THIS IS A JOKE IT'S NOT VERY FUNNY.
HAVE YOU BEEN LOOKING AT MY FILES? THIS IS ABOUT MY NOVEL, ISN'T IT? "OH, LOOK, BENJAMIN WARNER WANTS TO BE A WRITER, LET'S MAKE FUN OF HIM."

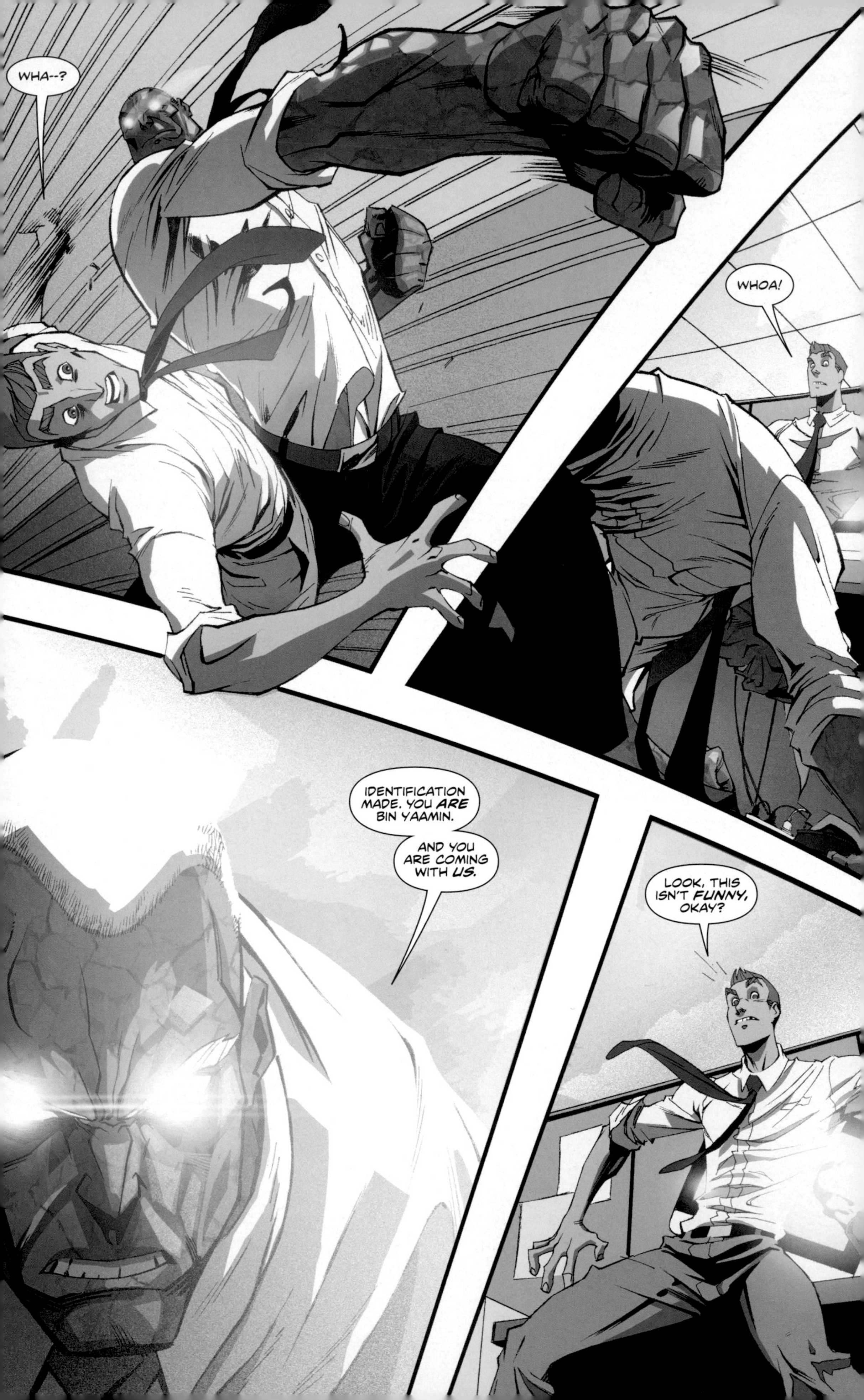
WHA--?
WHOA!
IDENTIFICATION MADE. YOU *ARE* BIN YAAMIN.
AND YOU ARE COMING WITH *US*.
LOOK, THIS ISN'T *FUNNY*, OKAY?

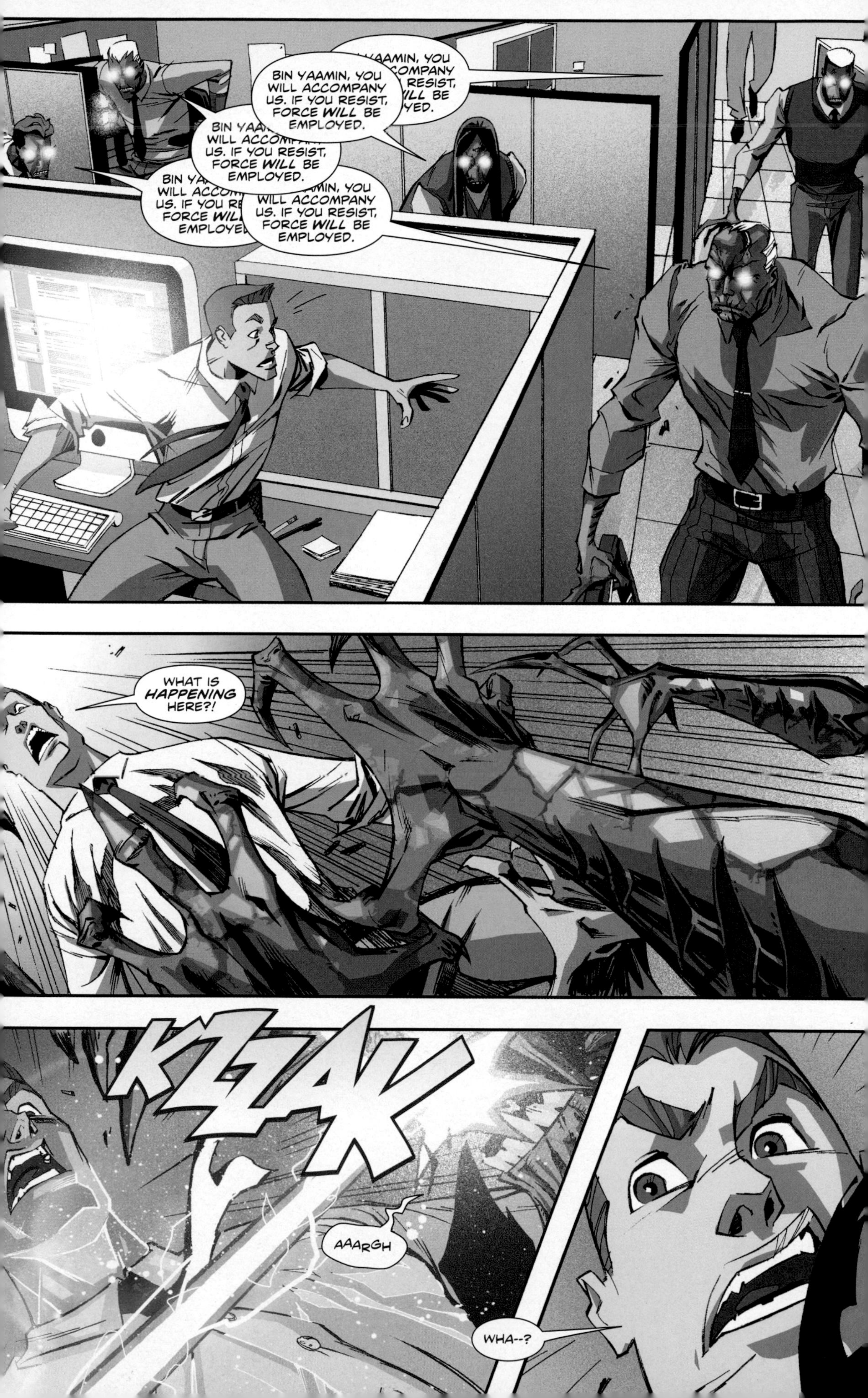

BIN YAAMIN, YOU WILL ACCOMPANY US. IF YOU RESIST, FORCE WILL BE EMPLOYED.
YAAMIN, YOU WILL ACCOMPANY US. IF YOU RESIST, FORCE WILL BE EMPLOYED.
WHAT IS HAPPENING HERE?!
KZZAK
AAARGH
WHA--?

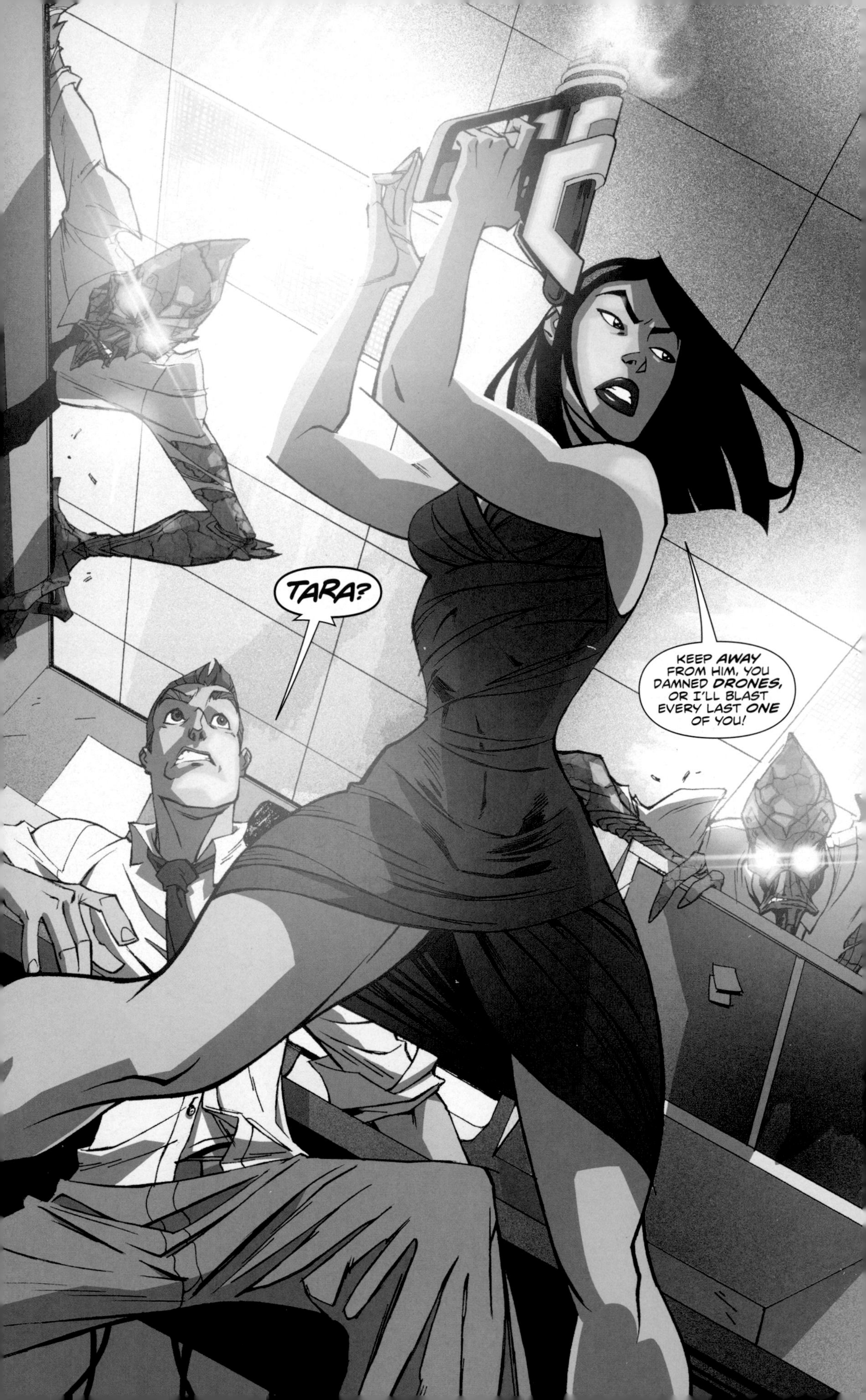
TARA?
KEEP AWAY FROM HIM, YOU DAMNED DRONES, OR I'LL BLAST EVERY LAST ONE OF YOU!

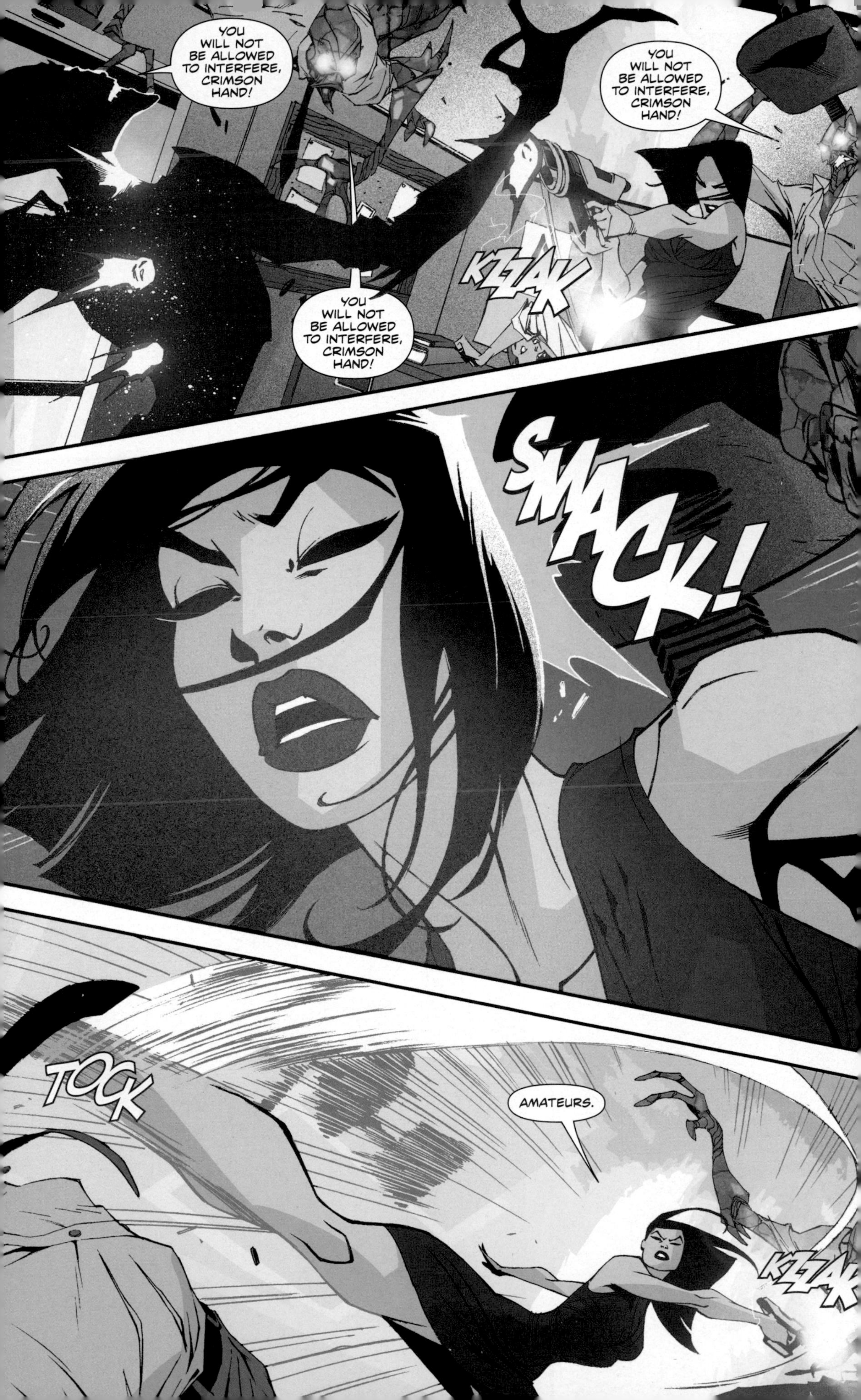
YOU WILL NOT BE ALLOWED TO INTERFERE, CRIMSON HAND!
YOU WILL NOT BE ALLOWED TO INTERFERE, CRIMSON HAND!
KZZAK
YOU WILL NOT BE ALLOWED TO INTERFERE, CRIMSON HAND!
SMACK!
TOCK
AMATEURS.
KZZAK

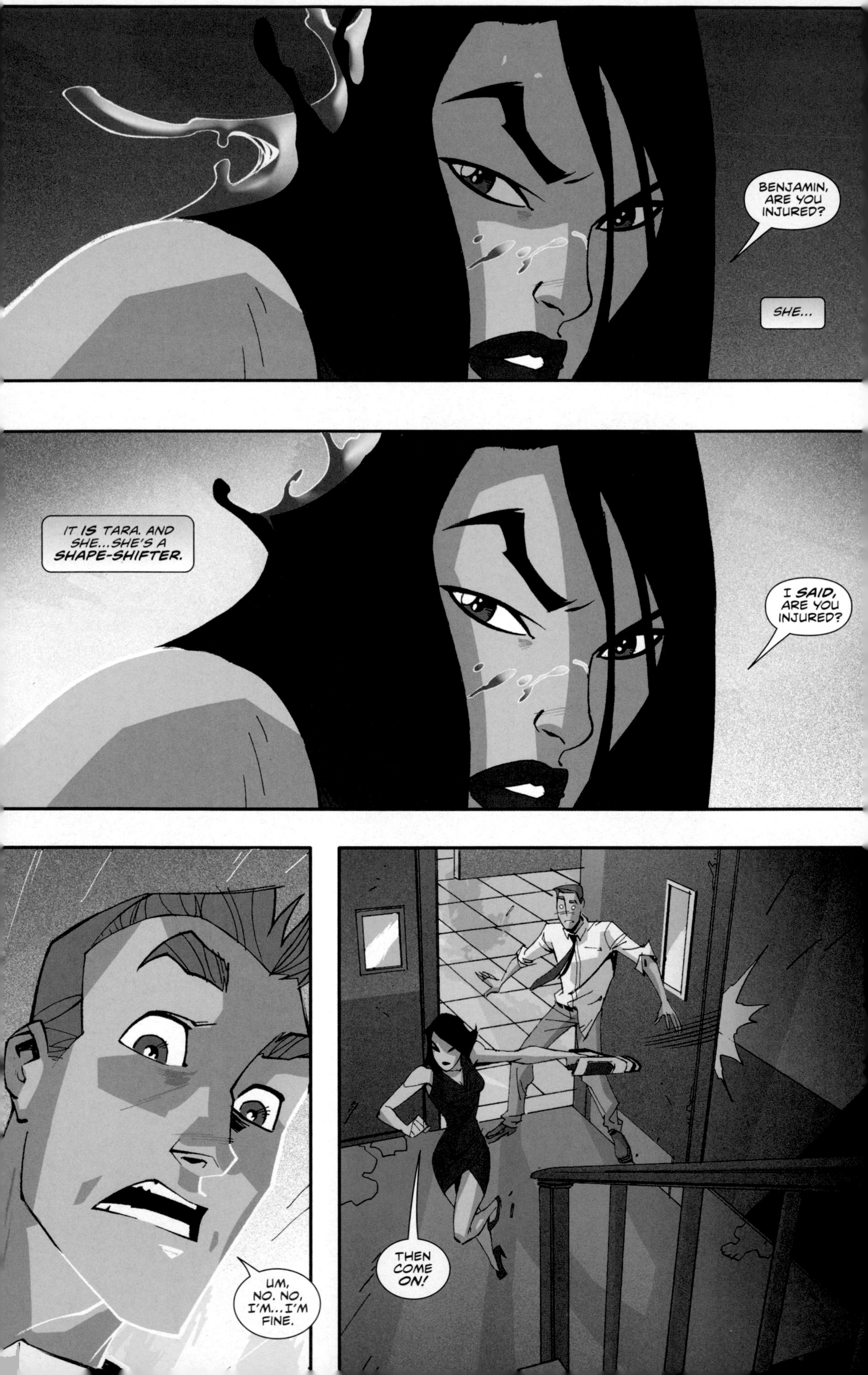
BENJAMIN, ARE YOU INJURED?
SHE...
IT IS TARA. AND SHE...SHE'S A SHAPE-SHIFTER.
I SAID, ARE YOU INJURED?
UM, NO. NO, I'M...I'M FINE.
THEN COME ON!

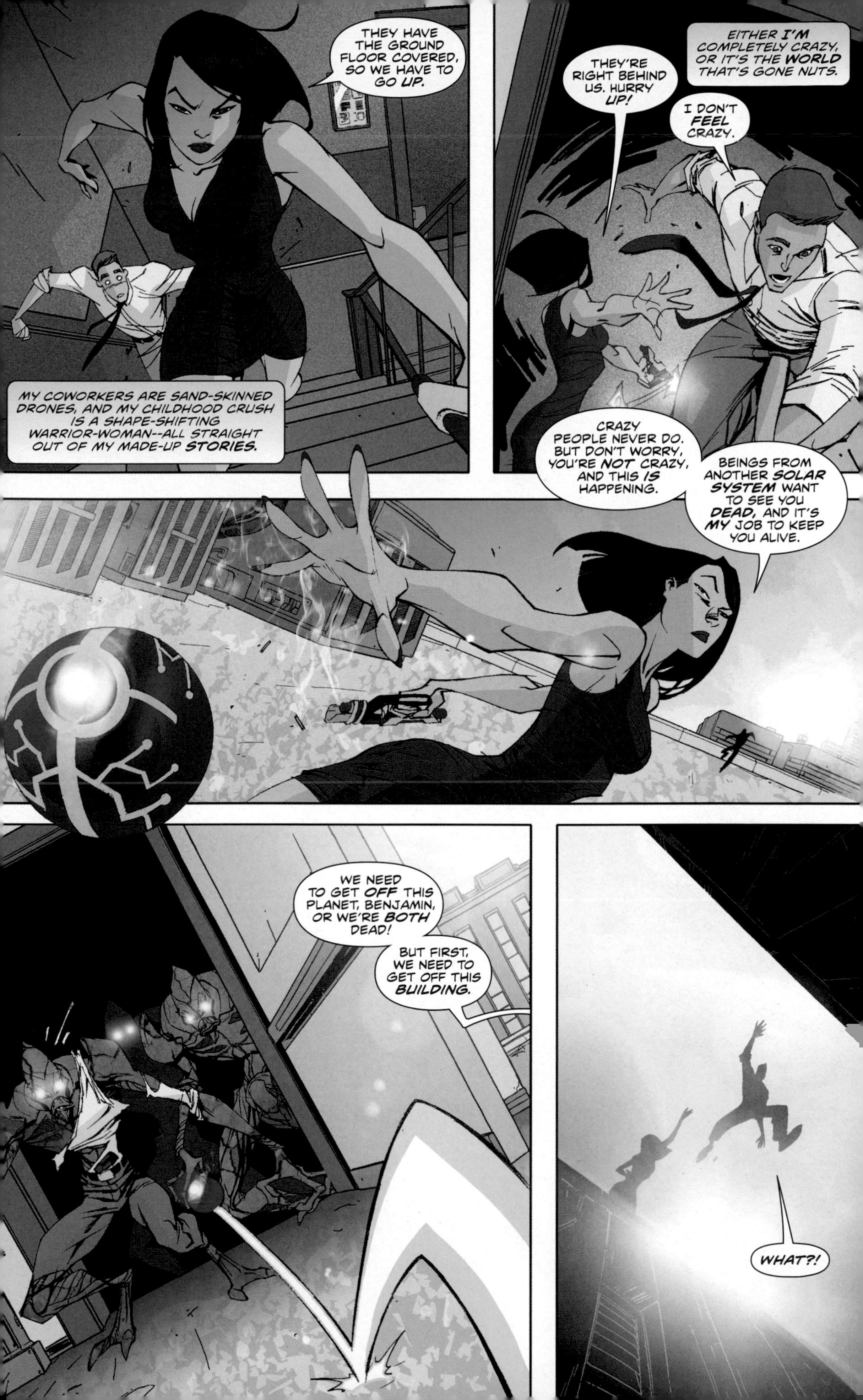
THEY HAVE THE GROUND FLOOR COVERED, SO WE HAVE TO GO UP.
MY COWORKERS ARE SAND-SKINNED DRONES, AND MY CHILDHOOD CRUSH IS A SHAPE-SHIFTING WARRIOR-WOMAN--ALL STRAIGHT OUT OF MY MADE-UP STORIES.
EITHER I'M COMPLETELY CRAZY, OR IT'S THE WORLD THAT'S GONE NUTS.
THEY'RE RIGHT BEHIND US. HURRY UP!
I DON'T FEEL CRAZY.
CRAZY PEOPLE NEVER DO. BUT DON'T WORRY, YOU'RE NOT CRAZY, AND THIS IS HAPPENING.
BEINGS FROM ANOTHER SOLAR SYSTEM WANT TO SEE YOU DEAD, AND IT'S MY JOB TO KEEP YOU ALIVE.
WE NEED TO GET OFF THIS PLANET, BENJAMIN, OR WE'RE BOTH DEAD!
BUT FIRST, WE NEED TO GET OFF THIS BUILDING.
WHAT?!

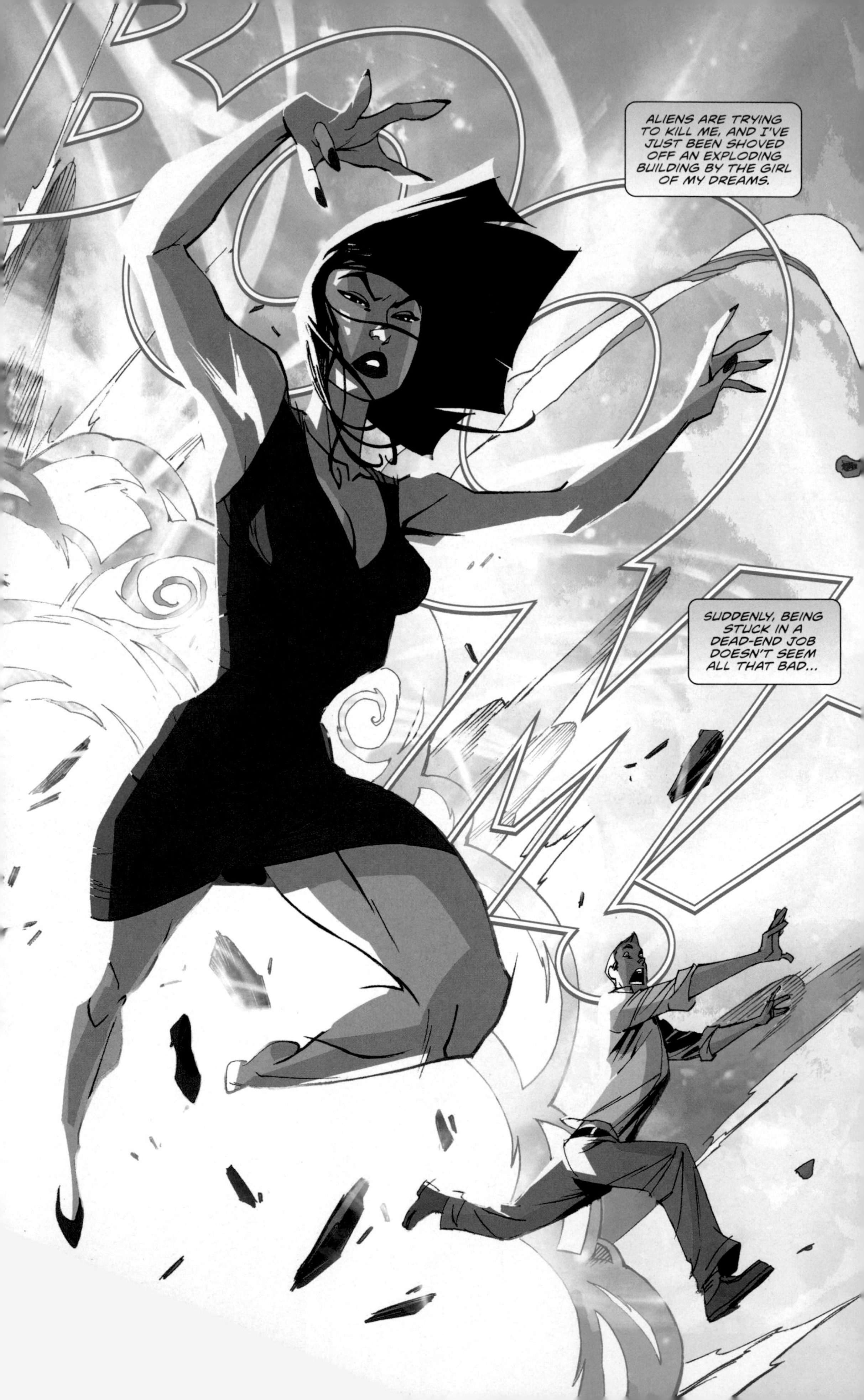
ALIENS ARE TRYING TO KILL ME, AND I'VE JUST BEEN SHOVED OFF AN EXPLODING BUILDING BY THE GIRL OF MY DREAMS.
SUDDENLY, BEING STUCK IN A DEAD-END JOB DOESN'T SEEM ALL THAT BAD...

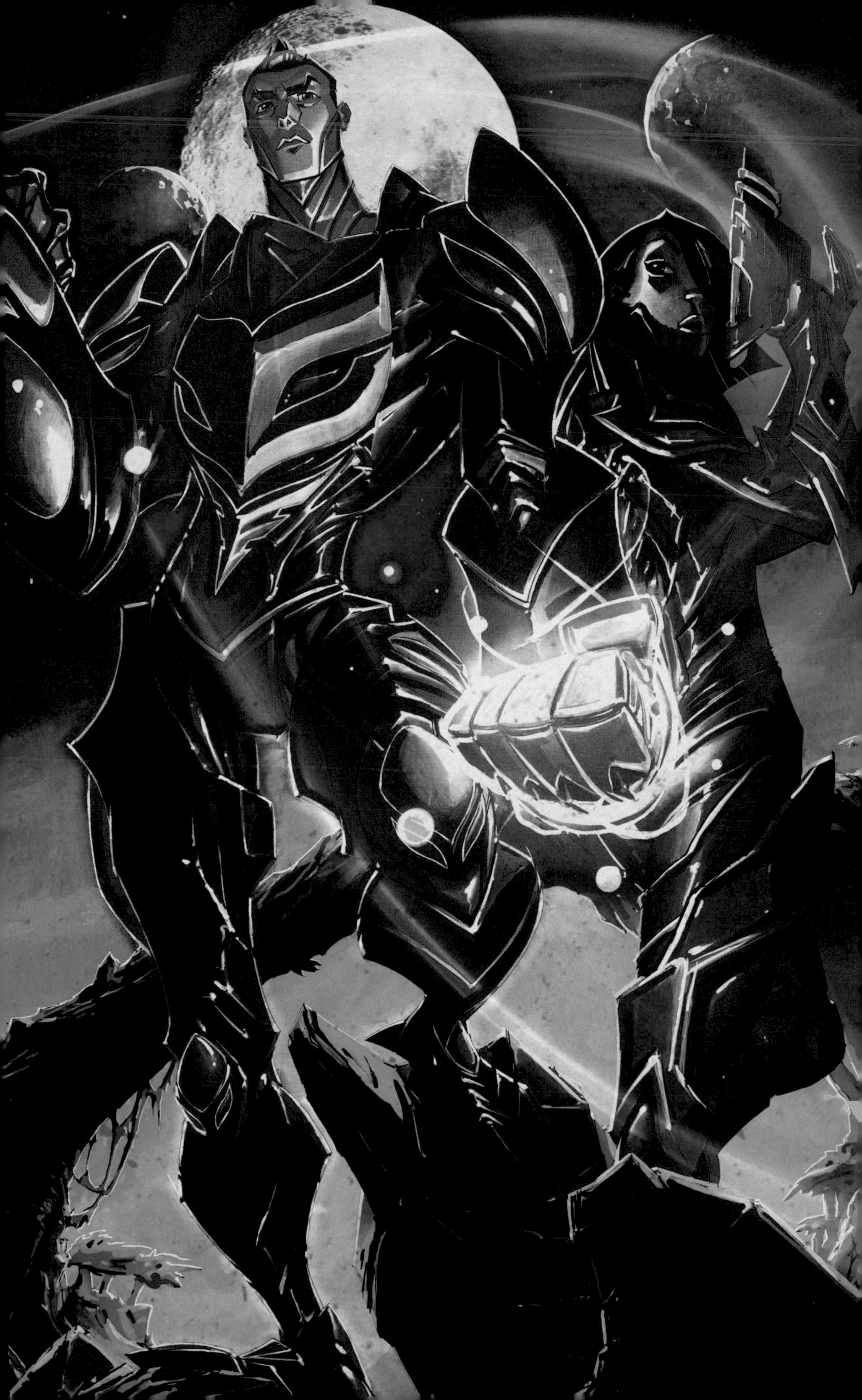

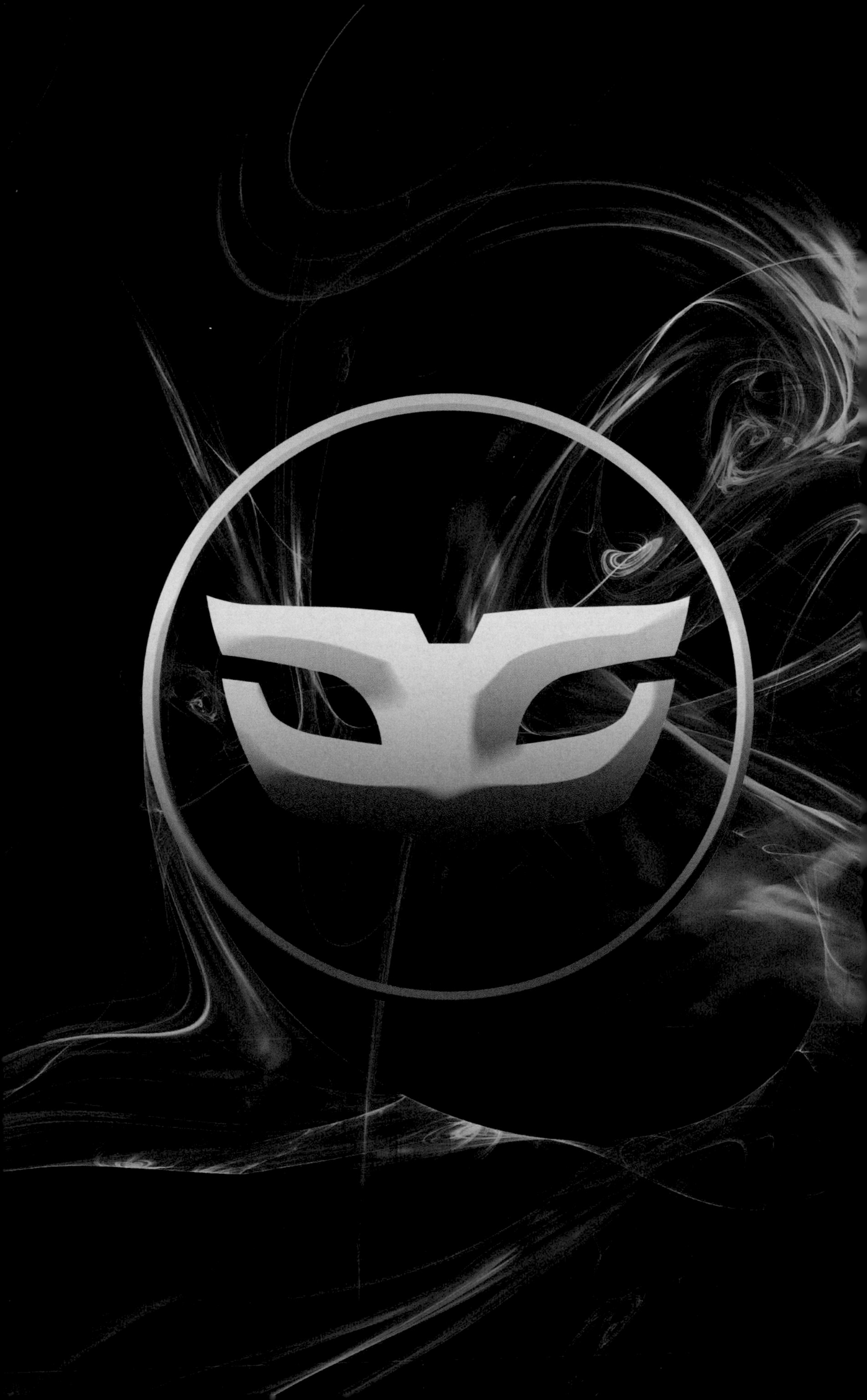

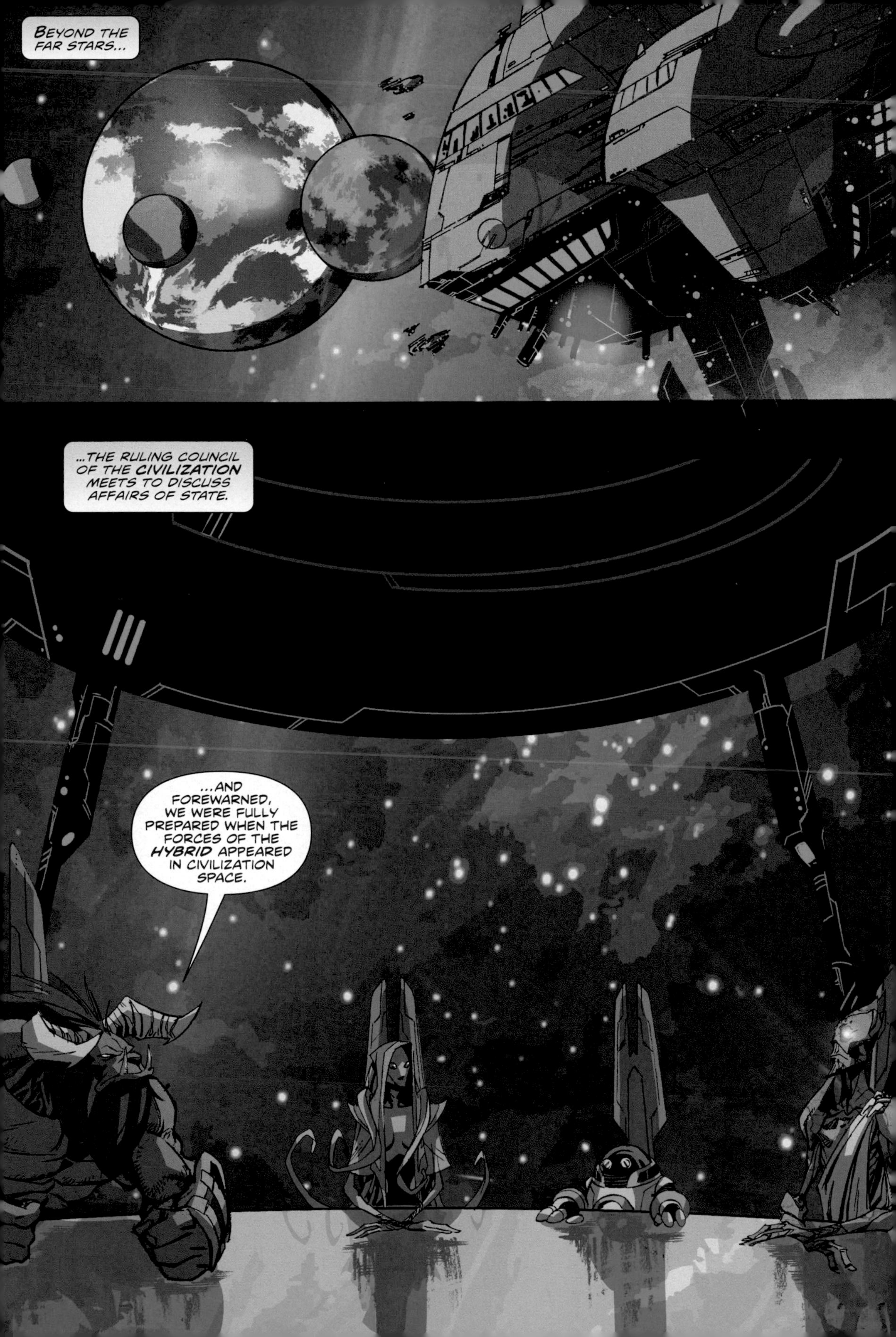
BEYOND THE FAR STARS...
...THE RULING COUNCIL OF THE CIVILIZATION MEETS TO DISCUSS AFFAIRS OF STATE.
...AND FOREWARNED, WE WERE FULLY PREPARED WHEN THE FORCES OF THE HYBRID APPEARED IN CIVILIZATION SPACE.

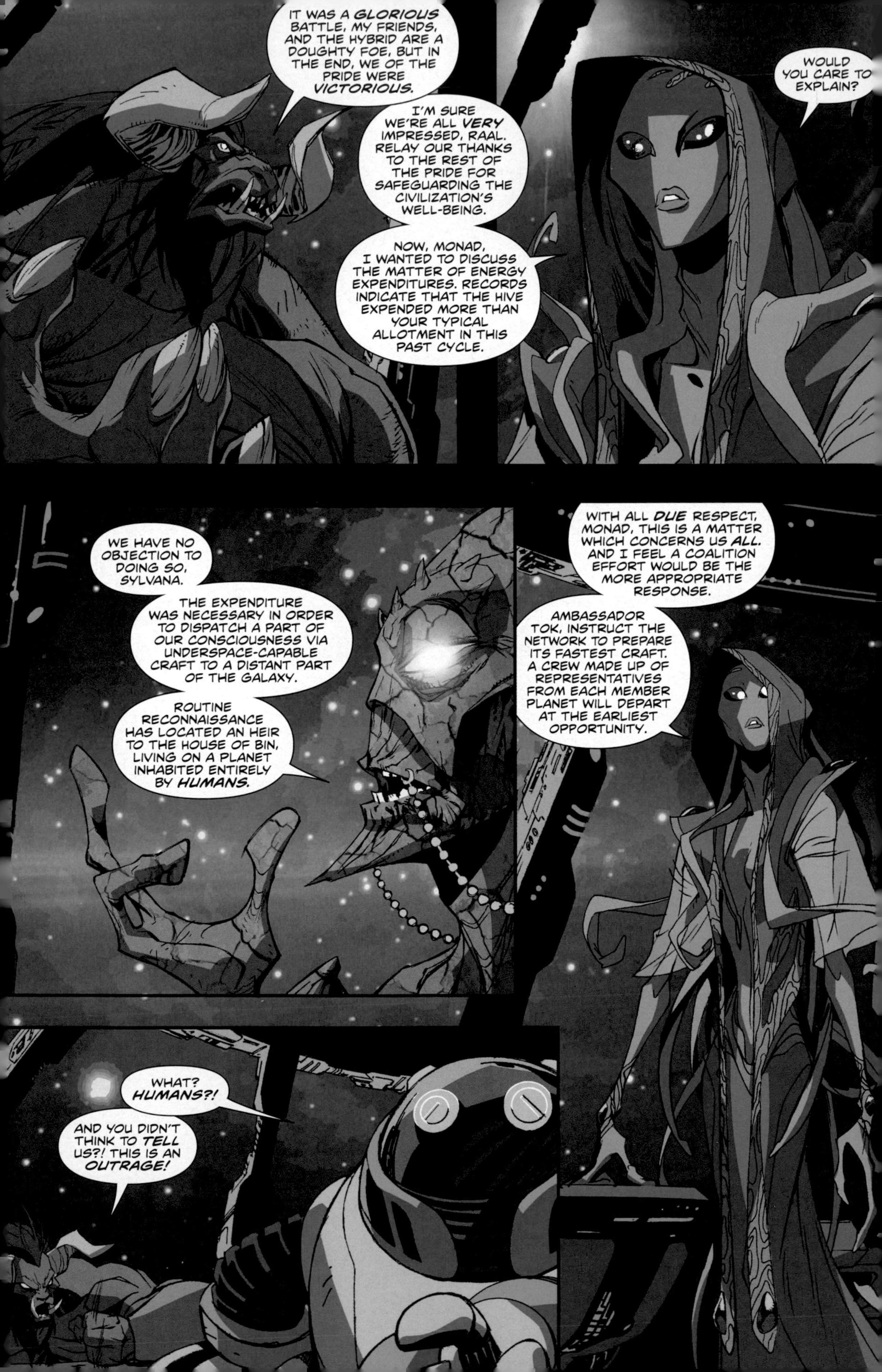
IT WAS A GLORIOUS BATTLE, MY FRIENDS, AND THE HYBRID ARE A DOUGHTY FOE, BUT IN THE END, WE OF THE PRIDE WERE VICTORIOUS.
I'M SURE WE'RE ALL VERY IMPRESSED, RAAL. RELAY OUR THANKS TO THE REST OF THE PRIDE FOR SAFEGUARDING THE CIVILIZATION'S WELL-BEING.
NOW, MONAD, I WANTED TO DISCUSS THE MATTER OF ENERGY EXPENDITURES. RECORDS INDICATE THAT THE HIVE EXPENDED MORE THAN YOUR TYPICAL ALLOTMENT IN THIS PAST CYCLE.
WOULD YOU CARE TO EXPLAIN?
WE HAVE NO OBJECTION TO DOING SO, SYLVANA.
THE EXPENDITURE WAS NECESSARY IN ORDER TO DISPATCH A PART OF OUR CONSCIOUSNESS VIA UNDERSPACE-CAPABLE CRAFT TO A DISTANT PART OF THE GALAXY.
ROUTINE RECONNAISSANCE HAS LOCATED AN HEIR TO THE HOUSE OF BIN, LIVING ON A PLANET INHABITED ENTIRELY BY HUMANS.
WHAT? HUMANS?!
AND YOU DIDN'T THINK TO TELL US?! THIS IS AN OUTRAGE!
WITH ALL DUE RESPECT, MONAD, THIS IS A MATTER WHICH CONCERNS US ALL. AND I FEEL A COALITION EFFORT WOULD BE THE MORE APPROPRIATE RESPONSE.
AMBASSADOR TOK, INSTRUCT THE NETWORK TO PREPARE ITS FASTEST CRAFT. A CREW MADE UP OF REPRESENTATIVES FROM EACH MEMBER PLANET WILL DEPART AT THE EARLIEST OPPORTUNITY.

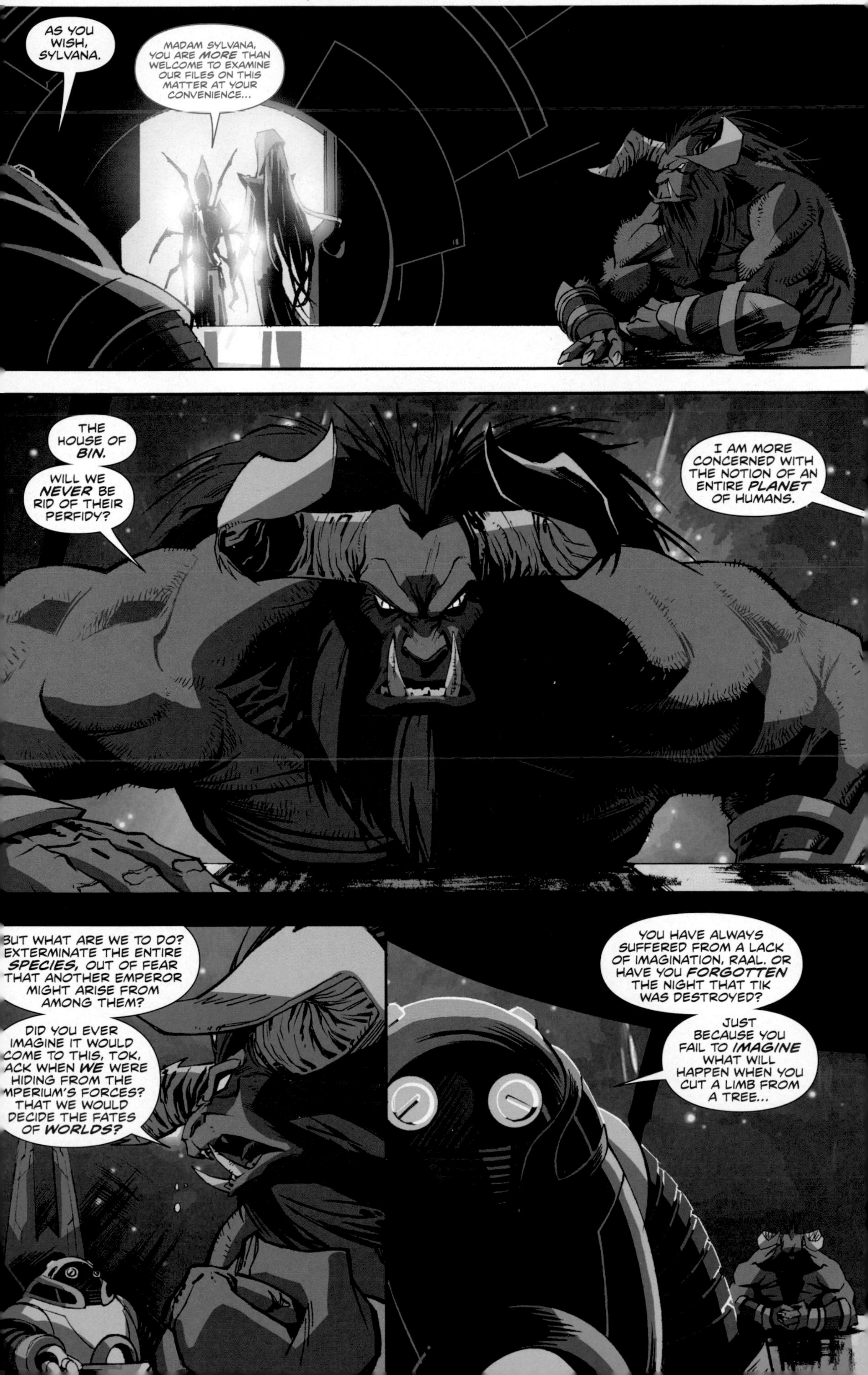

AS YOU WISH, SYLVANA.
MADAM SYLVANA, YOU ARE MORE THAN WELCOME TO EXAMINE OUR FILES ON THIS MATTER AT YOUR CONVENIENCE...
THE HOUSE OF BIN.
WILL WE NEVER BE RID OF THEIR PERFIDY?
I AM MORE CONCERNED WITH THE NOTION OF AN ENTIRE PLANET OF HUMANS.
BUT WHAT ARE WE TO DO? EXTERMINATE THE ENTIRE SPECIES, OUT OF FEAR THAT ANOTHER EMPEROR MIGHT ARISE FROM AMONG THEM?
DID YOU EVER IMAGINE IT WOULD COME TO THIS, TOK, BACK WHEN WE WERE HIDING FROM THE IMPERIUM'S FORCES? THAT WE WOULD DECIDE THE FATES OF WORLDS?
YOU HAVE ALWAYS SUFFERED FROM A LACK OF IMAGINATION, RAAL. OR HAVE YOU FORGOTTEN THE NIGHT THAT TIK WAS DESTROYED?
JUST BECAUSE YOU FAIL TO IMAGINE WHAT WILL HAPPEN WHEN YOU CUT A LIMB FROM A TREE...

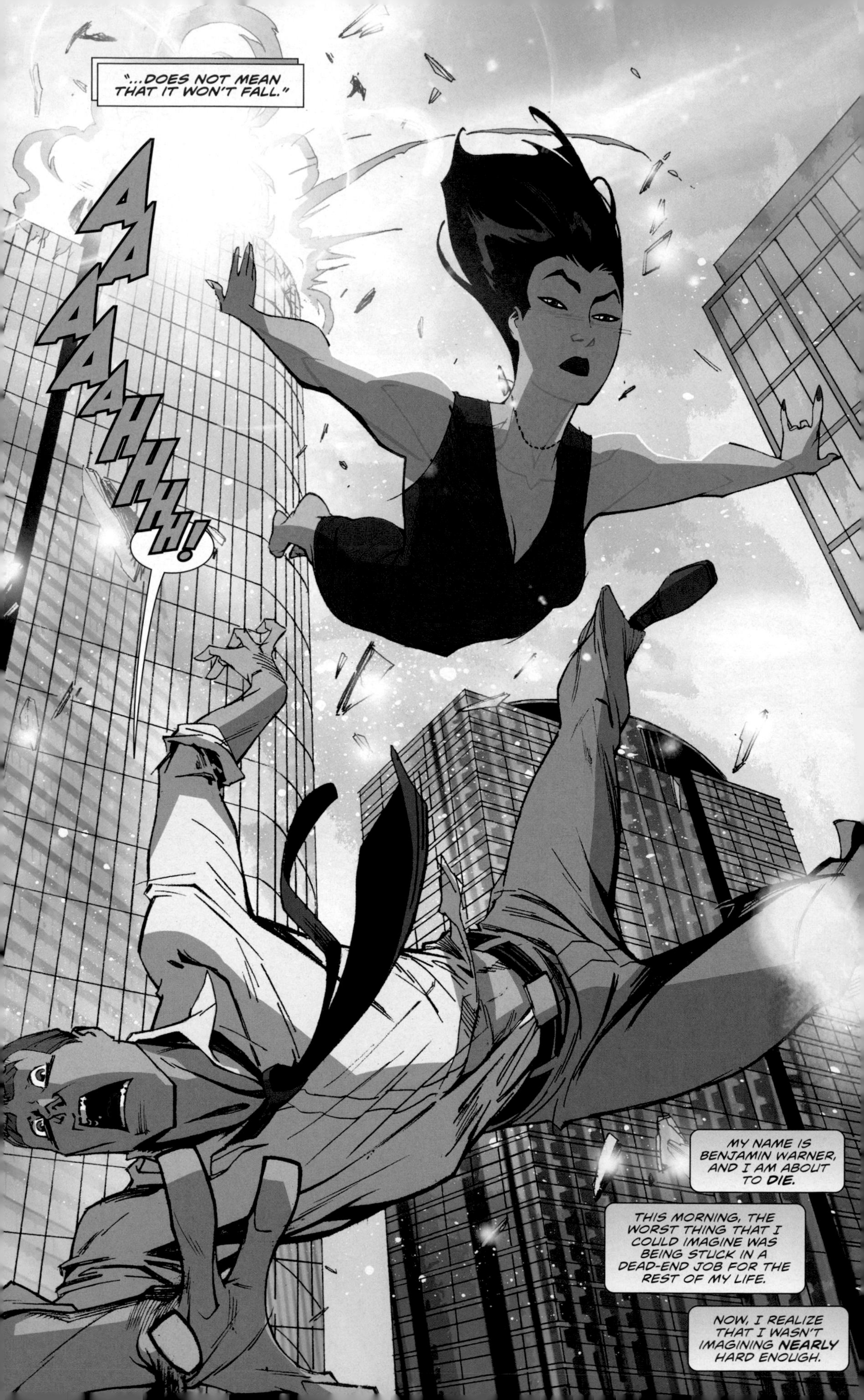
"...DOES NOT MEAN THAT IT WON'T FALL."
AAAAAHHHH!
MY NAME IS BENJAMIN WARNER, AND I AM ABOUT TO DIE.
THIS MORNING, THE WORST THING THAT I COULD IMAGINE WAS BEING STUCK IN A DEAD-END JOB FOR THE REST OF MY LIFE.
NOW, I REALIZE THAT I WASN'T IMAGINING NEARLY HARD ENOUGH.

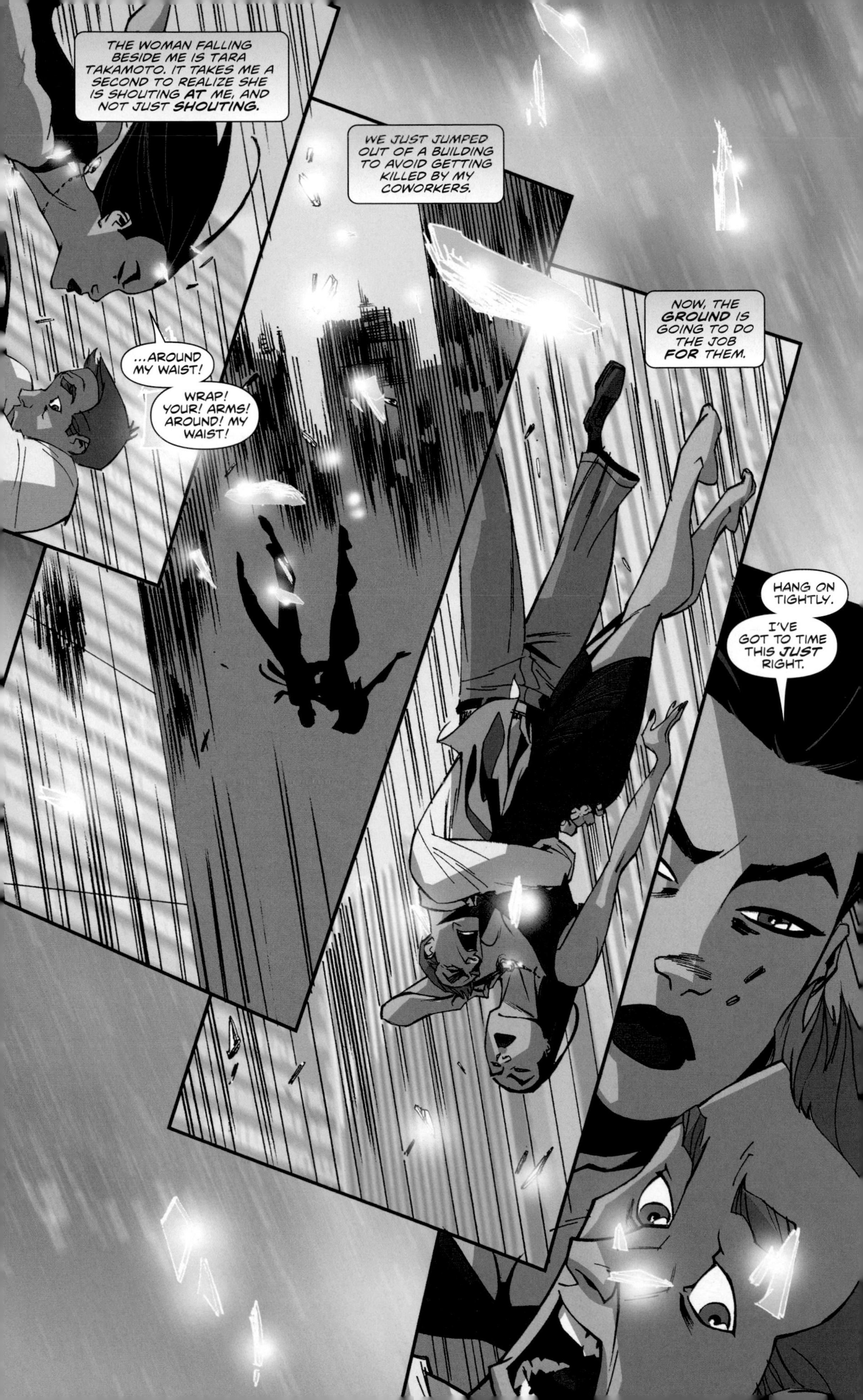
THE WOMAN FALLING BESIDE ME IS TARA TAKAMOTO. IT TAKES ME A SECOND TO REALIZE SHE IS SHOUTING **AT ME**, AND NOT JUST **SHOUTING.**
...AROUND MY WAIST!
WRAP! YOUR! ARMS! AROUND! MY WAIST!
WE JUST JUMPED OUT OF A BUILDING TO AVOID GETTING KILLED BY MY COWORKERS.
NOW, THE **GROUND** IS GOING TO DO THE JOB **FOR** THEM.
HANG ON TIGHTLY.
I'VE GOT TO TIME THIS **JUST** RIGHT.

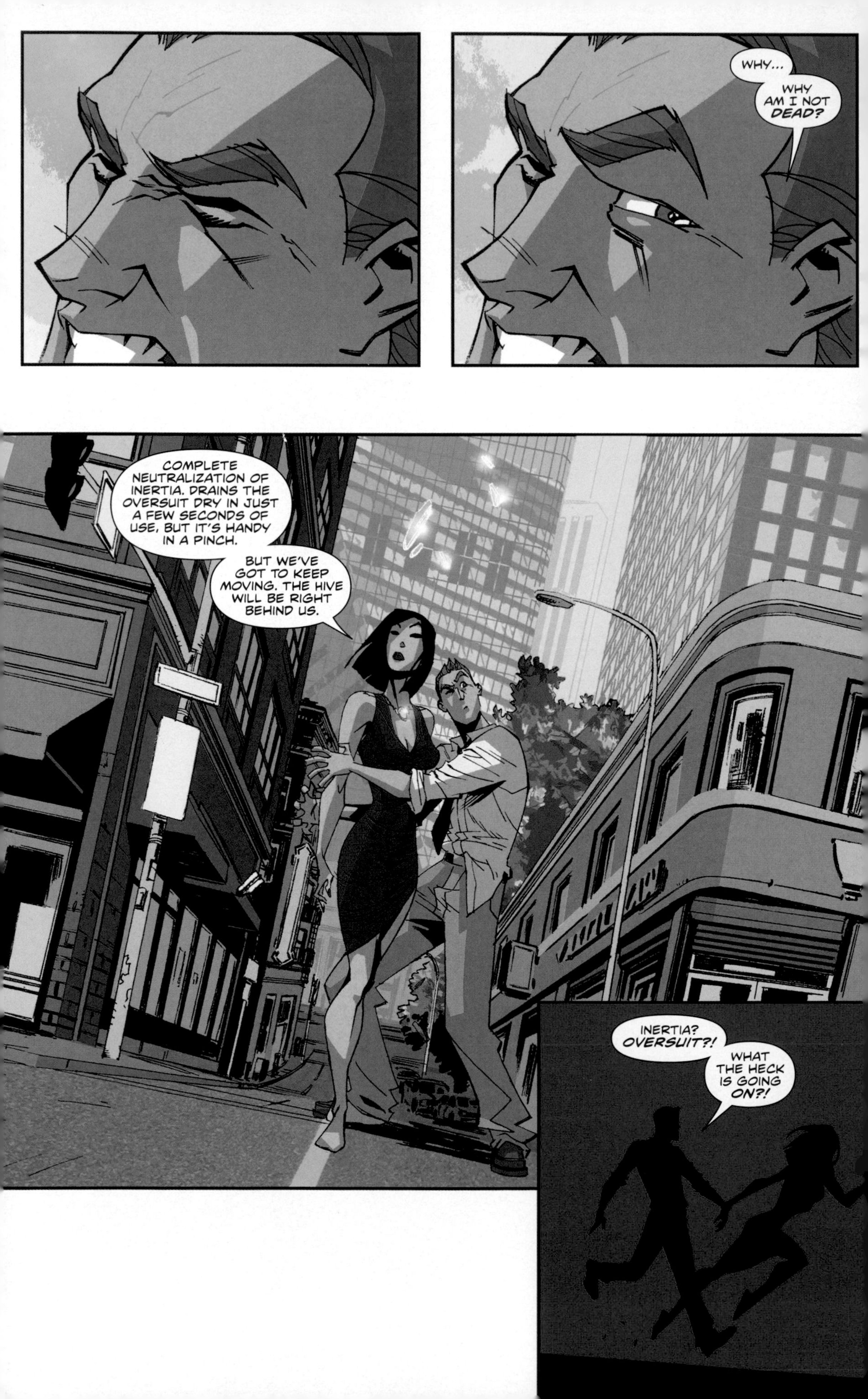
WHY...
WHY AM I NOT DEAD?
COMPLETE NEUTRALIZATION OF INERTIA. DRAINS THE OVERSUIT DRY IN JUST A FEW SECONDS OF USE, BUT IT'S HANDY IN A PINCH.
BUT WE'VE GOT TO KEEP MOVING. THE HIVE WILL BE RIGHT BEHIND US.
INERTIA? OVERSUIT?!
WHAT THE HECK IS GOING ON?!

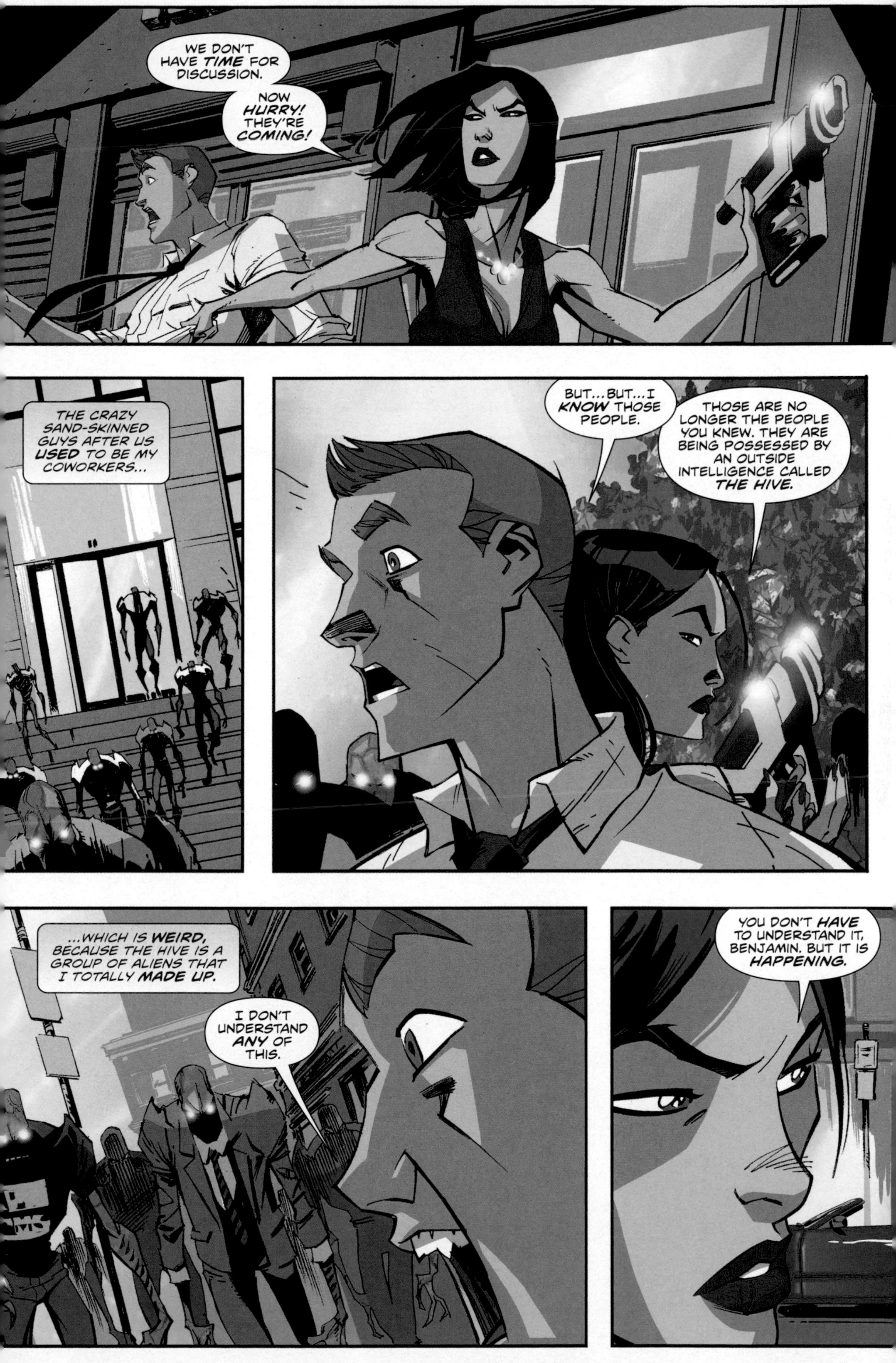
WE DON'T HAVE TIME FOR DISCUSSION.
NOW HURRY! THEY'RE COMING!
THE CRAZY SAND-SKINNED GUYS AFTER US USED TO BE MY COWORKERS...
BUT...BUT...I KNOW THOSE PEOPLE.
THOSE ARE NO LONGER THE PEOPLE YOU KNEW. THEY ARE BEING POSSESSED BY AN OUTSIDE INTELLIGENCE CALLED THE HIVE.
...WHICH IS WEIRD, BECAUSE THE HIVE IS A GROUP OF ALIENS THAT I TOTALLY MADE UP.
I DON'T UNDERSTAND ANY OF THIS.
YOU DON'T HAVE TO UNDERSTAND IT, BENJAMIN. BUT IT IS HAPPENING.

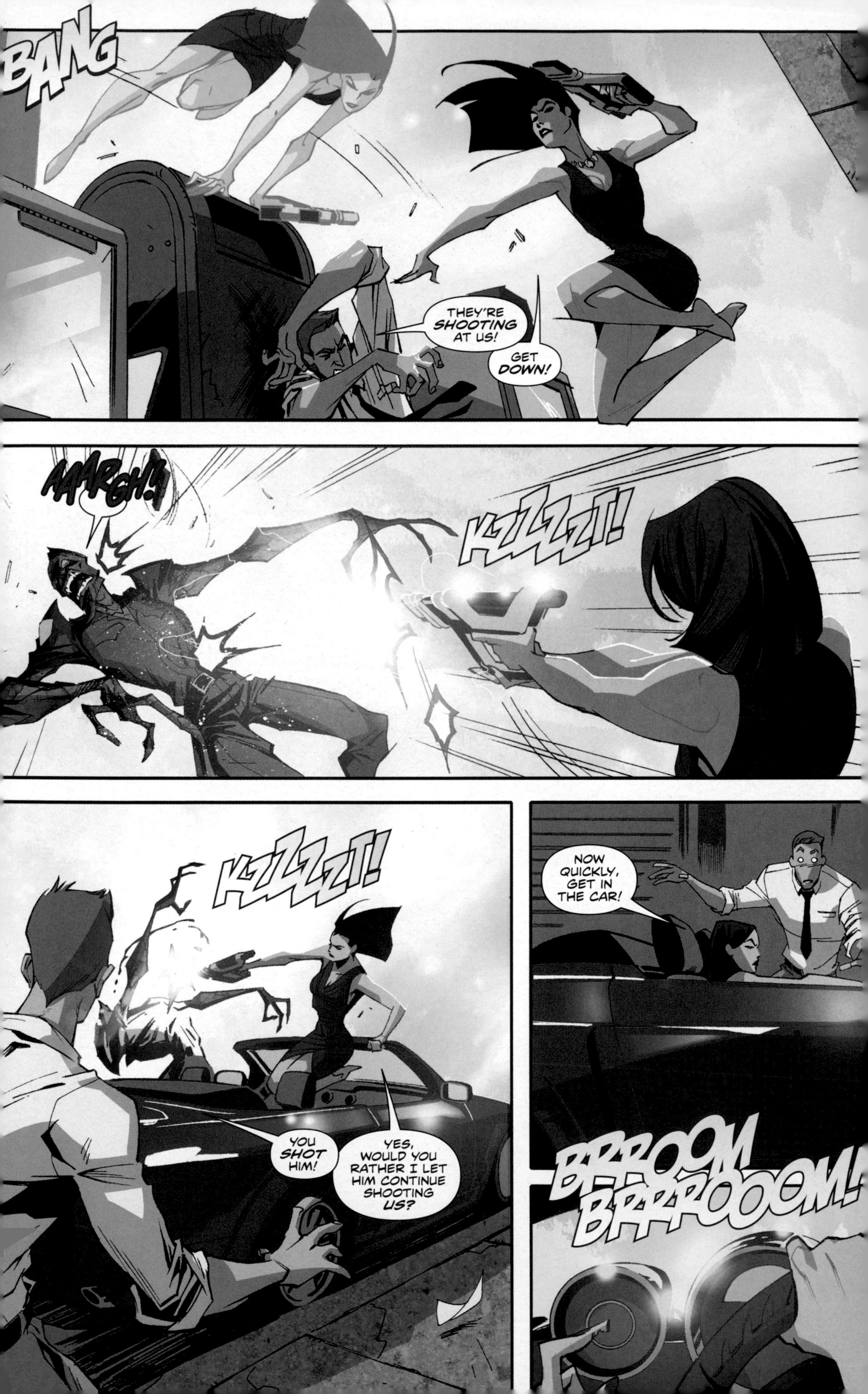
BANG
THEY'RE SHOOTING AT US!
GET DOWN!
AAARGH!!
KZZZZT!
KZZZZT!
YOU SHOT HIM!
YES, WOULD YOU RATHER I LET HIM CONTINUE SHOOTING US?
NOW QUICKLY, GET IN THE CAR!
BRRROOM-BRRROOOM!

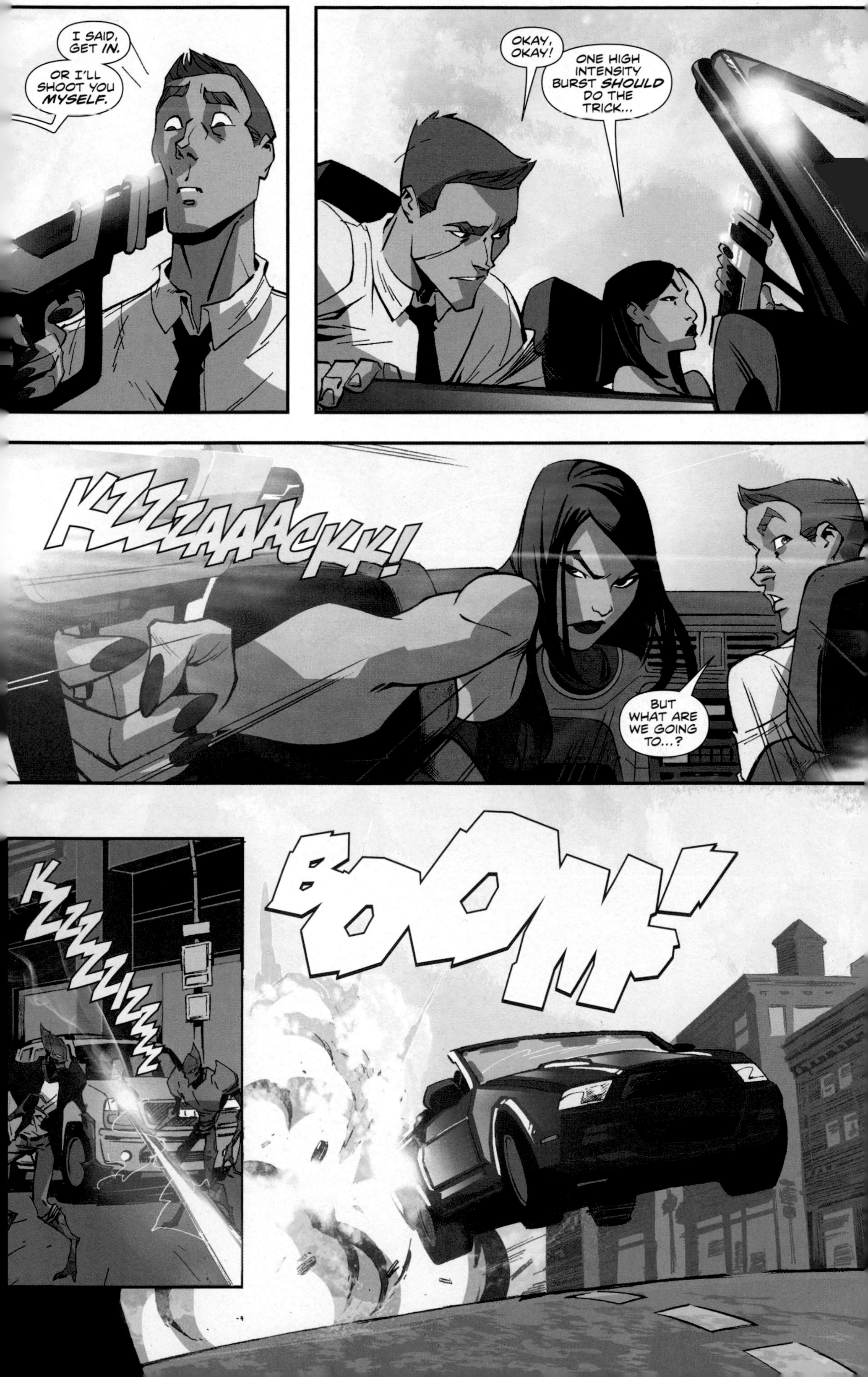
I SAID, GET IN.
OR I'LL SHOOT YOU MYSELF.
OKAY, OKAY!
ONE HIGH INTENSITY BURST SHOULD DO THE TRICK...
KZZZAAACKK!
BUT WHAT ARE WE GOING TO...?
KZZZZZZZZZ
BOOM!

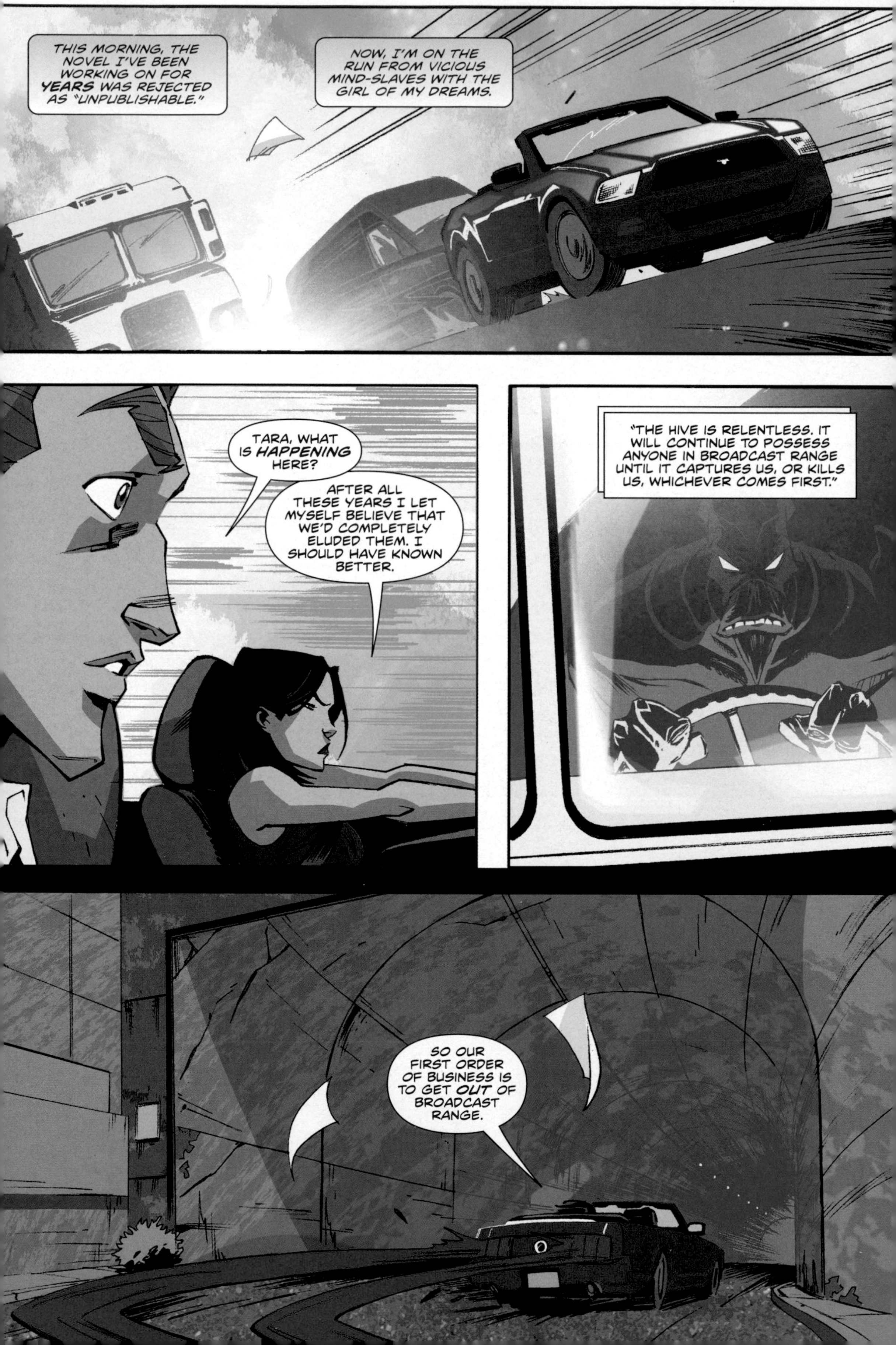

THIS MORNING, THE NOVEL I'VE BEEN WORKING ON FOR YEARS WAS REJECTED AS "UNPUBLISHABLE."
NOW, I'M ON THE RUN FROM VICIOUS MIND-SLAVES WITH THE GIRL OF MY DREAMS.
TARA, WHAT IS HAPPENING HERE?
AFTER ALL THESE YEARS I LET MYSELF BELIEVE THAT WE'D COMPLETELY ELUDED THEM. I SHOULD HAVE KNOWN BETTER.
"THE HIVE IS RELENTLESS. IT WILL CONTINUE TO POSSESS ANYONE IN BROADCAST RANGE UNTIL IT CAPTURES US, OR KILLS US, WHICHEVER COMES FIRST."
SO OUR FIRST ORDER OF BUSINESS IS TO GET OUT OF BROADCAST RANGE.

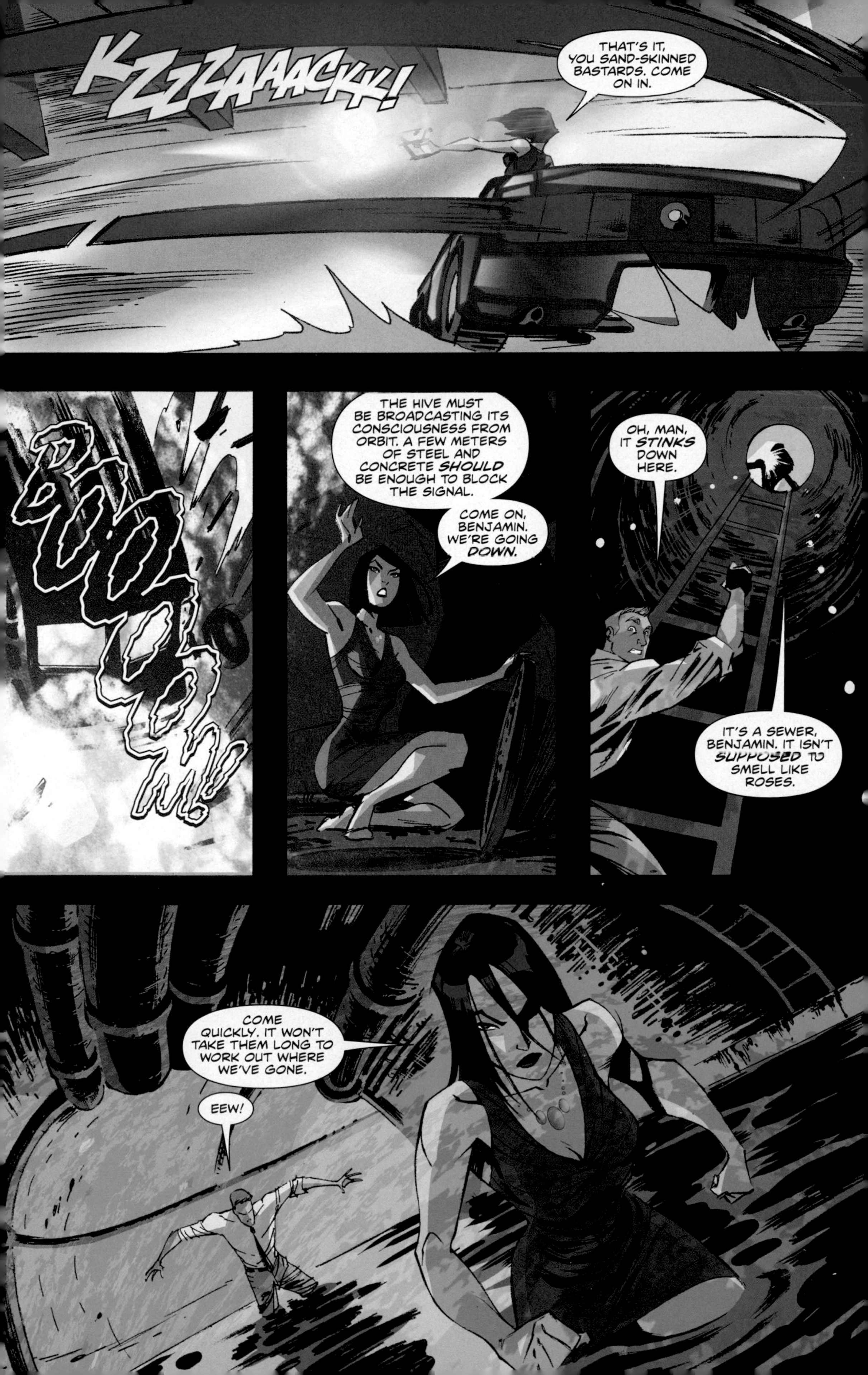
KZZZAAACKK!
THAT'S IT, YOU SAND-SKINNED BASTARDS. COME ON IN.
THE HIVE MUST BE BROADCASTING ITS CONSCIOUSNESS FROM ORBIT. A FEW METERS OF STEEL AND CONCRETE SHOULD BE ENOUGH TO BLOCK THE SIGNAL.
COME ON, BENJAMIN. WE'RE GOING DOWN.
OH, MAN, IT STINKS DOWN HERE.
IT'S A SEWER, BENJAMIN. IT ISN'T SUPPOSED TO SMELL LIKE ROSES.
COME QUICKLY. IT WON'T TAKE THEM LONG TO WORK OUT WHERE WE'VE GONE.
EEW!

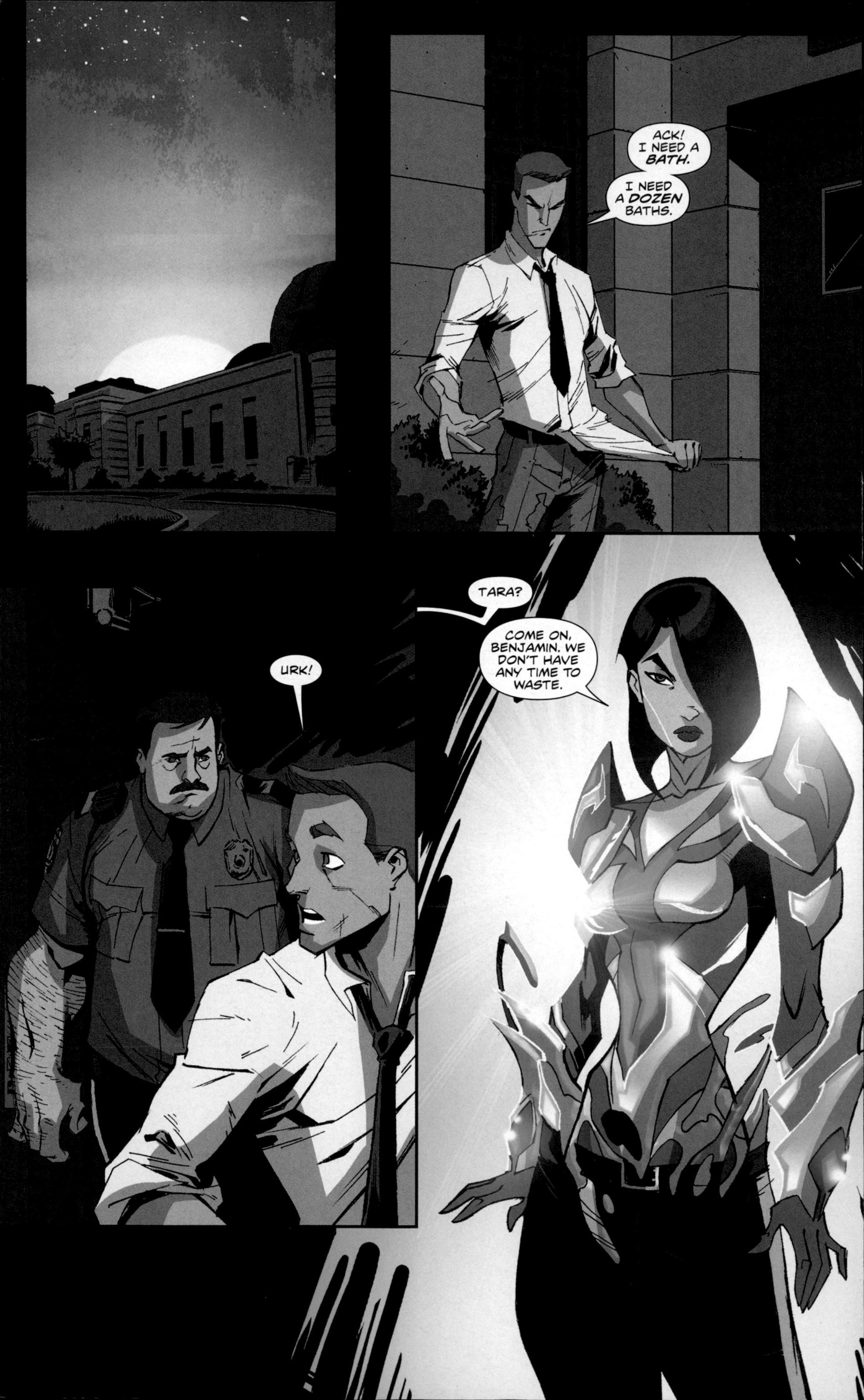
ACK! I NEED A BATH.
I NEED A DOZEN BATHS.
URK!
TARA?
COME ON, BENJAMIN. WE DON'T HAVE ANY TIME TO WASTE.

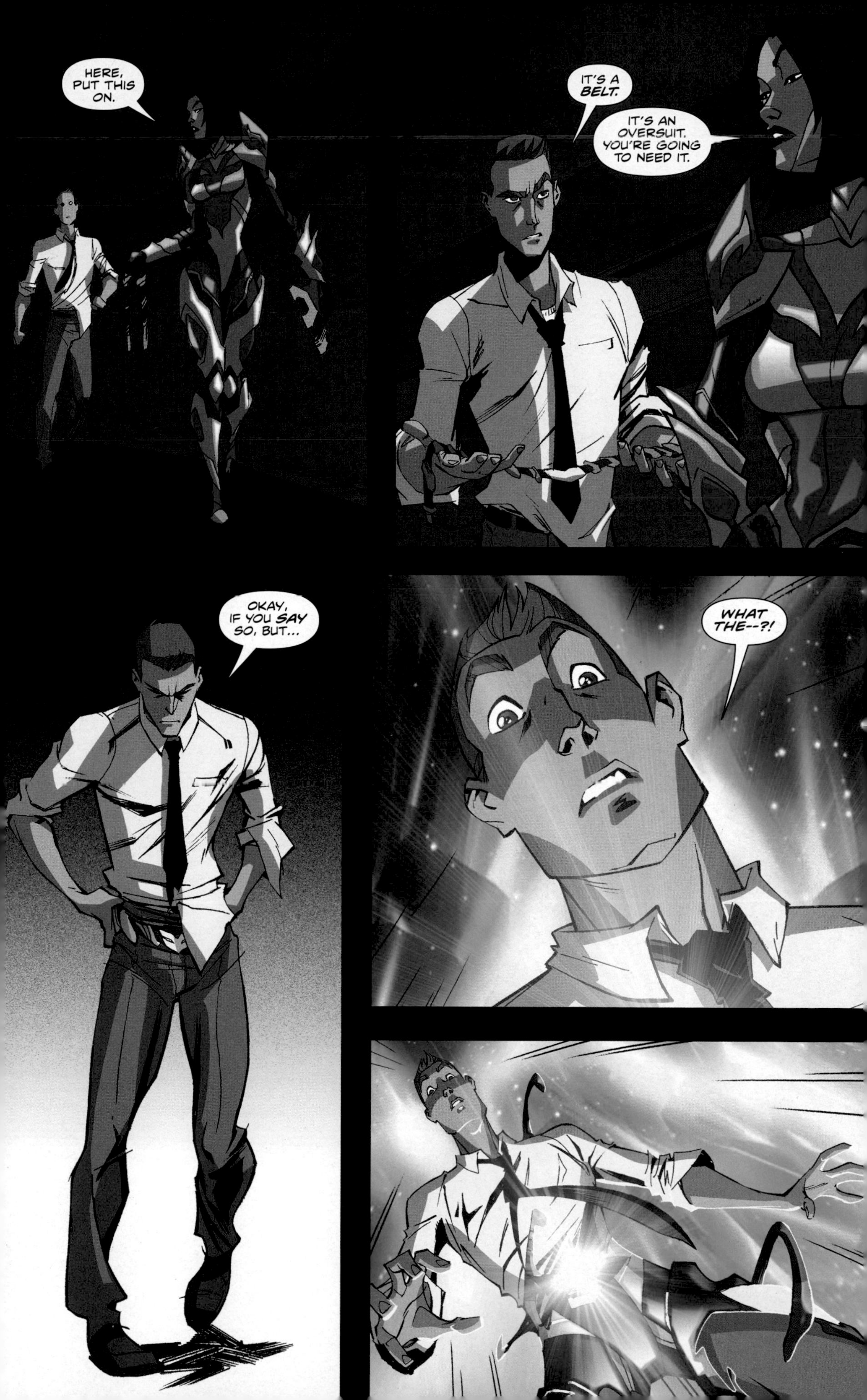
HERE, PUT THIS ON.
IT'S A BELT.
IT'S AN OVERSUIT. YOU'RE GOING TO NEED IT.
OKAY, IF YOU SAY SO, BUT...
WHAT THE--?!

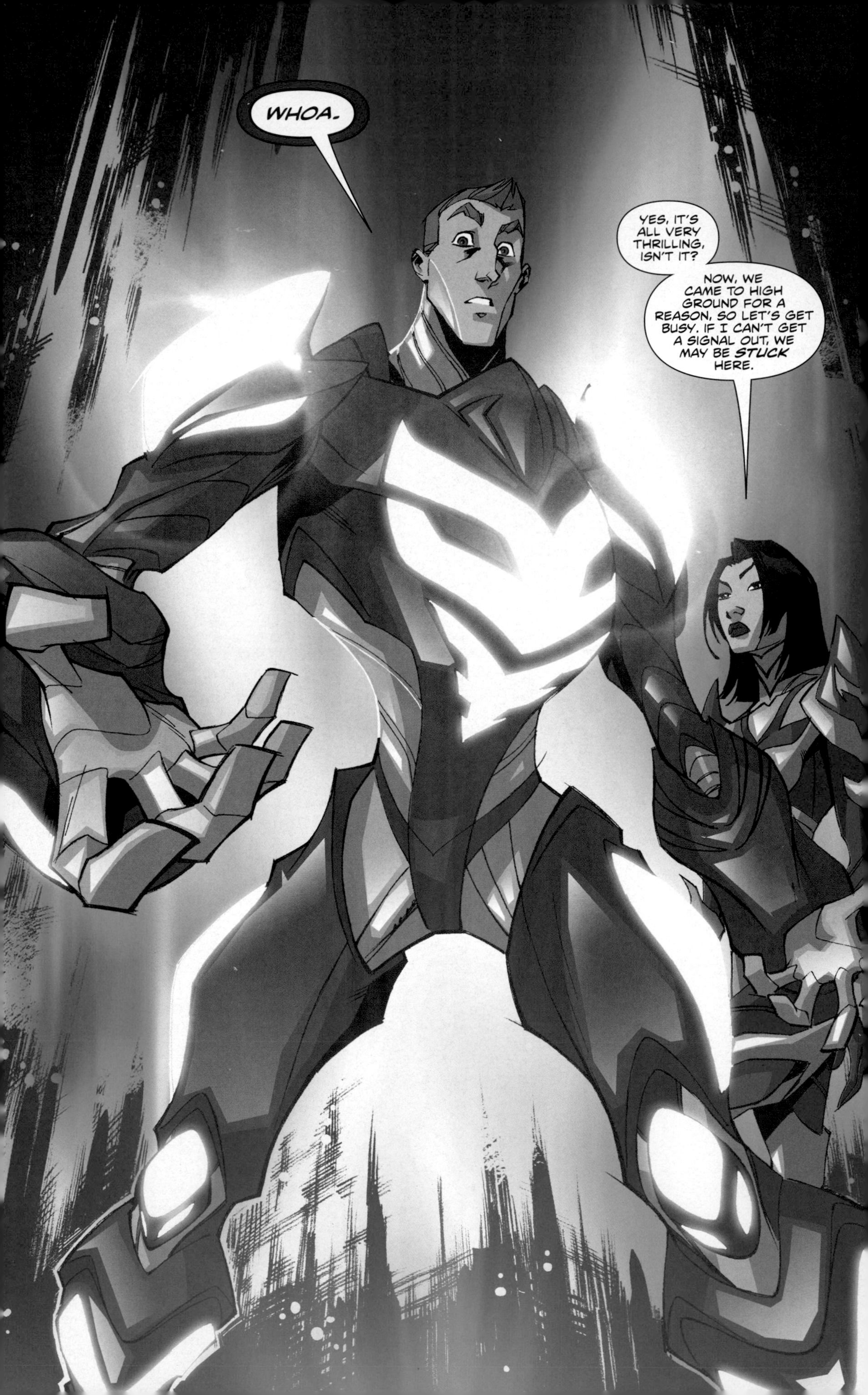
WHOA.
YES, IT'S ALL VERY THRILLING, ISN'T IT?
NOW, WE CAME TO HIGH GROUND FOR A REASON, SO LET'S GET BUSY. IF I CAN'T GET A SIGNAL OUT, WE MAY BE STUCK HERE.

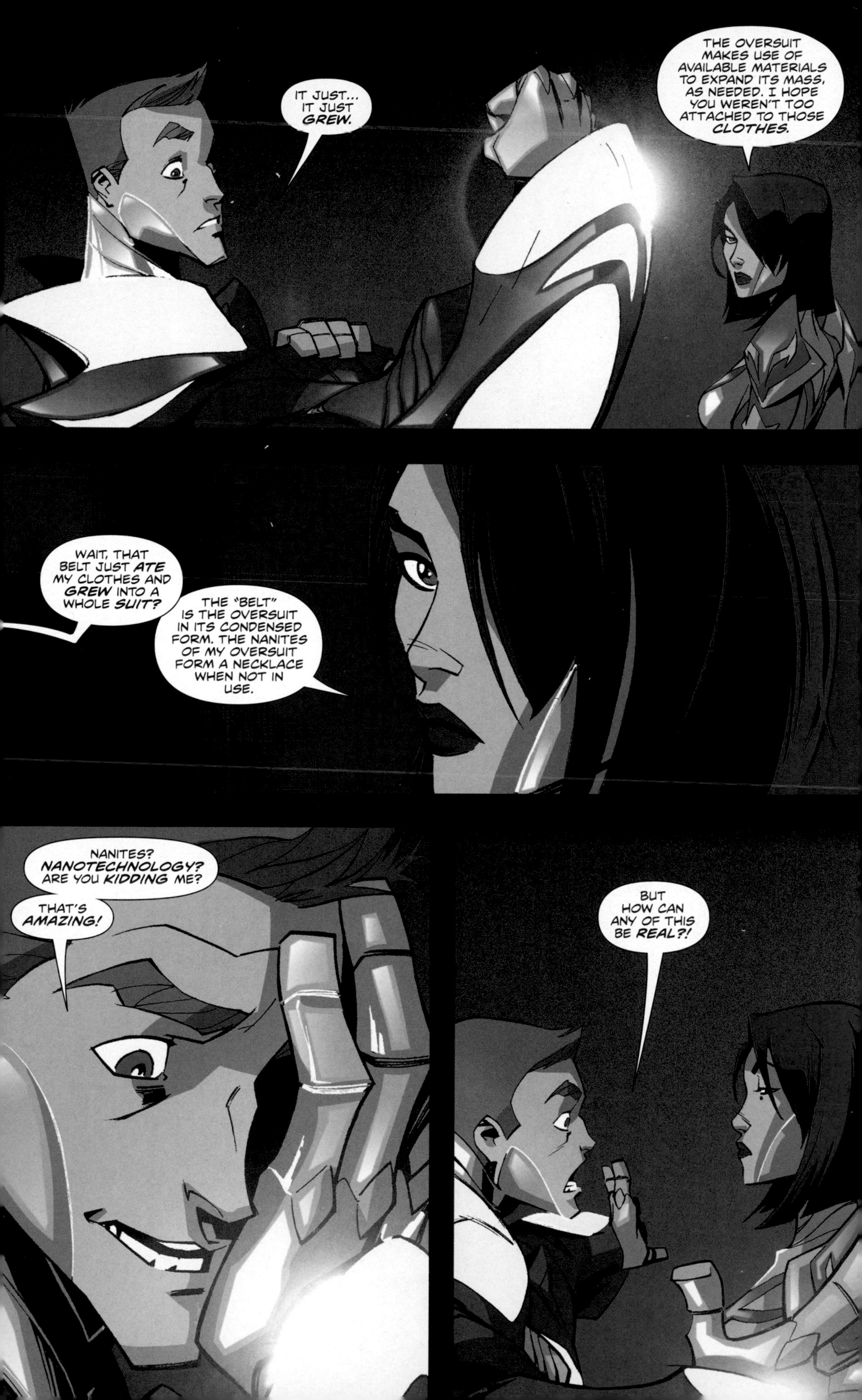
IT JUST... IT JUST GREW.
THE OVERSUIT MAKES USE OF AVAILABLE MATERIALS TO EXPAND ITS MASS, AS NEEDED. I HOPE YOU WEREN'T TOO ATTACHED TO THOSE CLOTHES.
WAIT, THAT BELT JUST ATE MY CLOTHES AND GREW INTO A WHOLE SUIT?
THE "BELT" IS THE OVERSUIT IN ITS CONDENSED FORM. THE NANITES OF MY OVERSUIT FORM A NECKLACE WHEN NOT IN USE.
NANITES? NANOTECHNOLOGY? ARE YOU KIDDING ME?
THAT'S AMAZING!
BUT HOW CAN ANY OF THIS BE REAL?!

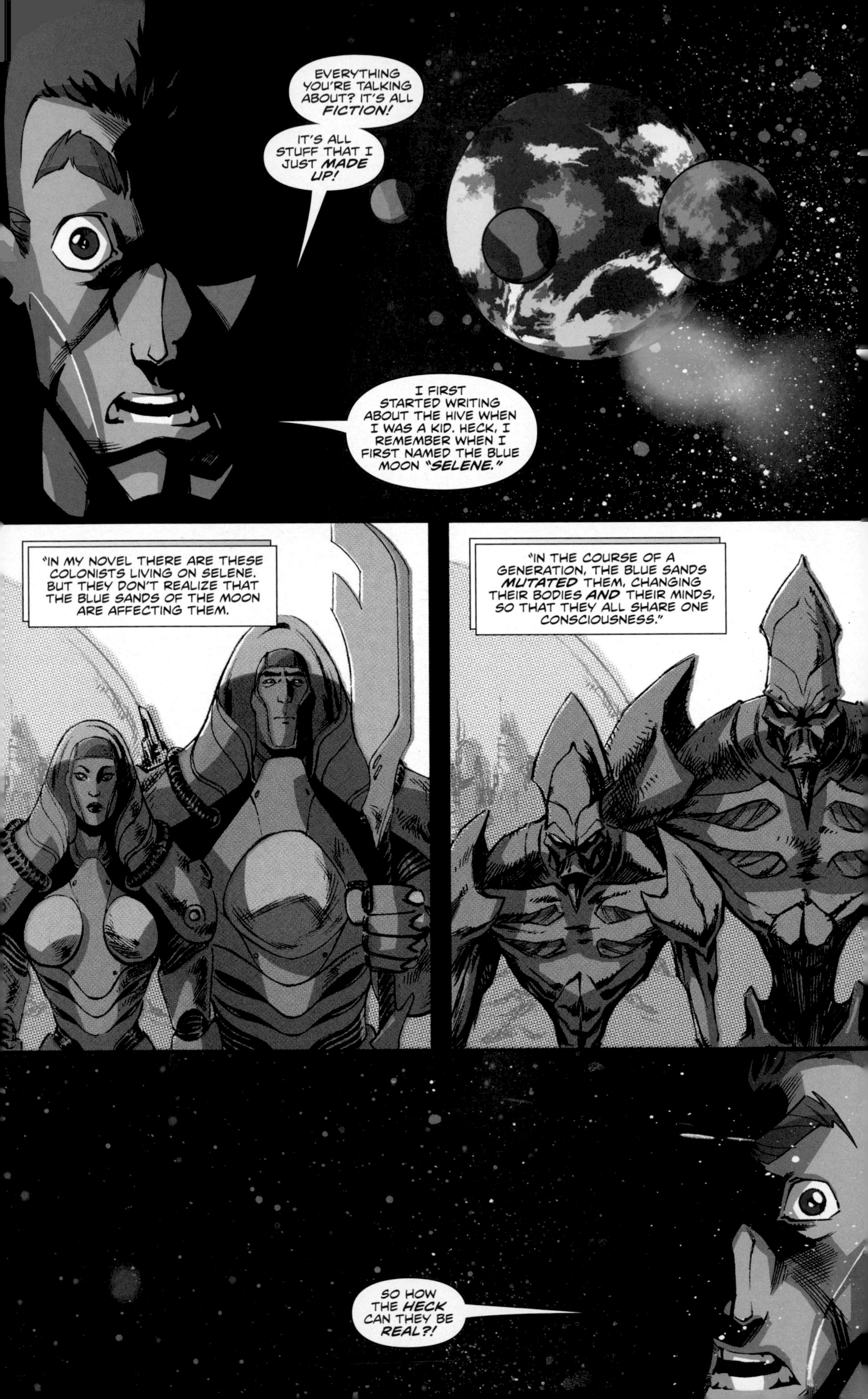
EVERYTHING YOU'RE TALKING ABOUT? IT'S ALL FICTION!
IT'S ALL STUFF THAT I JUST MADE UP!
I FIRST STARTED WRITING ABOUT THE HIVE WHEN I WAS A KID. HECK, I REMEMBER WHEN I FIRST NAMED THE BLUE MOON "SELENE."
"IN MY NOVEL THERE ARE THESE COLONISTS LIVING ON SELENE. BUT THEY DON'T REALIZE THAT THE BLUE SANDS OF THE MOON ARE AFFECTING THEM.
"IN THE COURSE OF A GENERATION, THE BLUE SANDS MUTATED THEM, CHANGING THEIR BODIES AND THEIR MINDS, SO THAT THEY ALL SHARE ONE CONSCIOUSNESS."
SO HOW THE HECK CAN THEY BE REAL?!

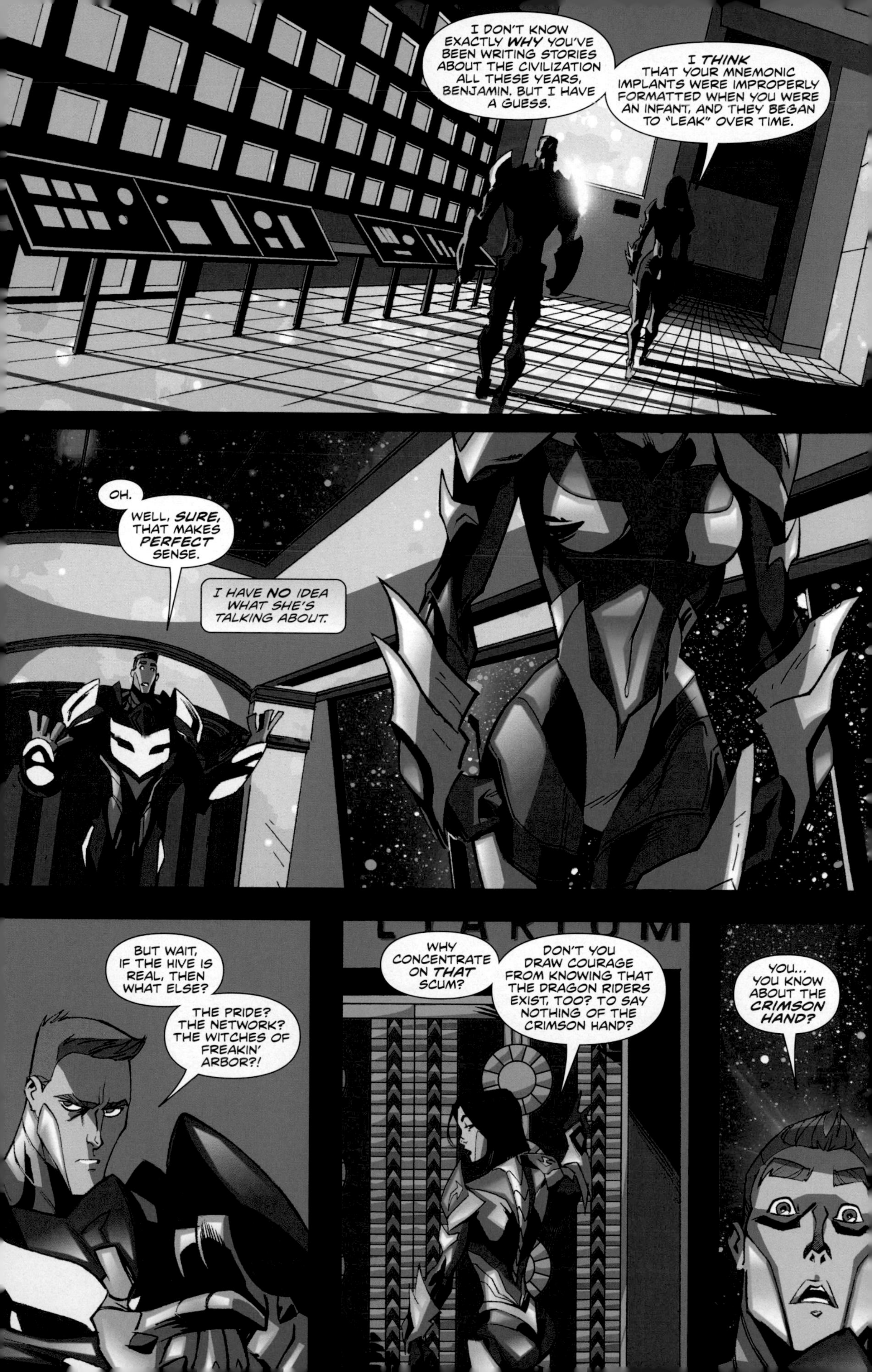
I DON'T KNOW EXACTLY WHY YOU'VE BEEN WRITING STORIES ABOUT THE CIVILIZATION ALL THESE YEARS, BENJAMIN. BUT I HAVE A GUESS.
I THINK THAT YOUR MNEMONIC IMPLANTS WERE IMPROPERLY FORMATTED WHEN YOU WERE AN INFANT, AND THEY BEGAN TO "LEAK" OVER TIME.
OH.
WELL, SURE, THAT MAKES PERFECT SENSE.
I HAVE NO IDEA WHAT SHE'S TALKING ABOUT.
BUT WAIT, IF THE HIVE IS REAL, THEN WHAT ELSE?
THE PRIDE? THE NETWORK? THE WITCHES OF FREAKIN' ARBOR?!
WHY CONCENTRATE ON THAT SCUM?
DON'T YOU DRAW COURAGE FROM KNOWING THAT THE DRAGON RIDERS EXIST, TOO? TO SAY NOTHING OF THE CRIMSON HAND?
YOU... YOU KNOW ABOUT THE CRIMSON HAND?

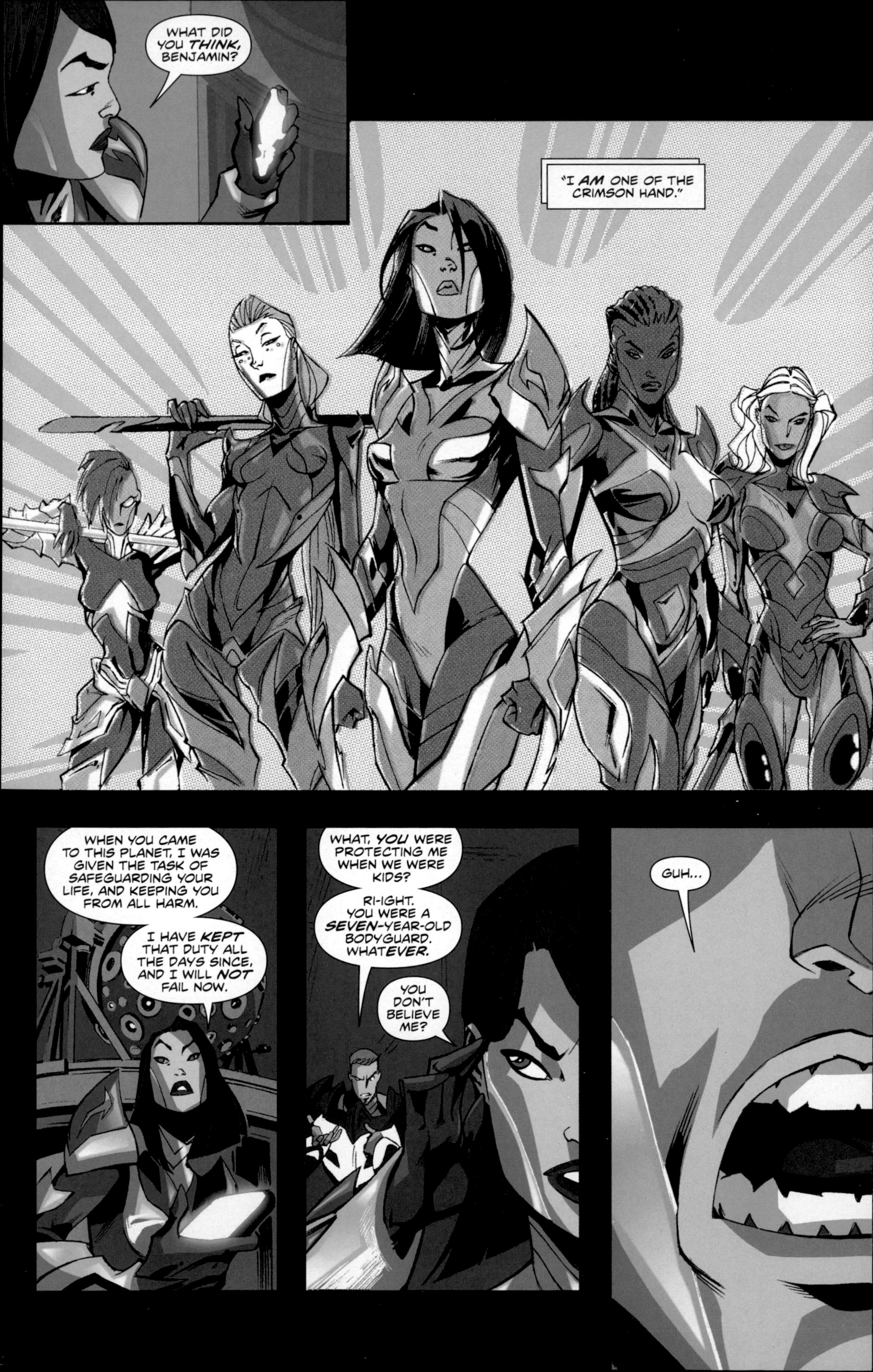
WHAT DID YOU *THINK,* BENJAMIN?
"I *AM* ONE OF THE CRIMSON HAND."
WHEN YOU CAME TO THIS PLANET, I WAS GIVEN THE TASK OF SAFEGUARDING YOUR LIFE, AND KEEPING YOU FROM ALL HARM.
I HAVE *KEPT* THAT DUTY ALL THE DAYS SINCE, AND I WILL *NOT* FAIL NOW.
WHAT, *YOU* WERE PROTECTING ME WHEN WE WERE KIDS?
RI-IGHT. YOU WERE A *SEVEN*-YEAR-OLD BODYGUARD. WHAT*EVER.*
YOU DON'T BELIEVE ME?
GUH...

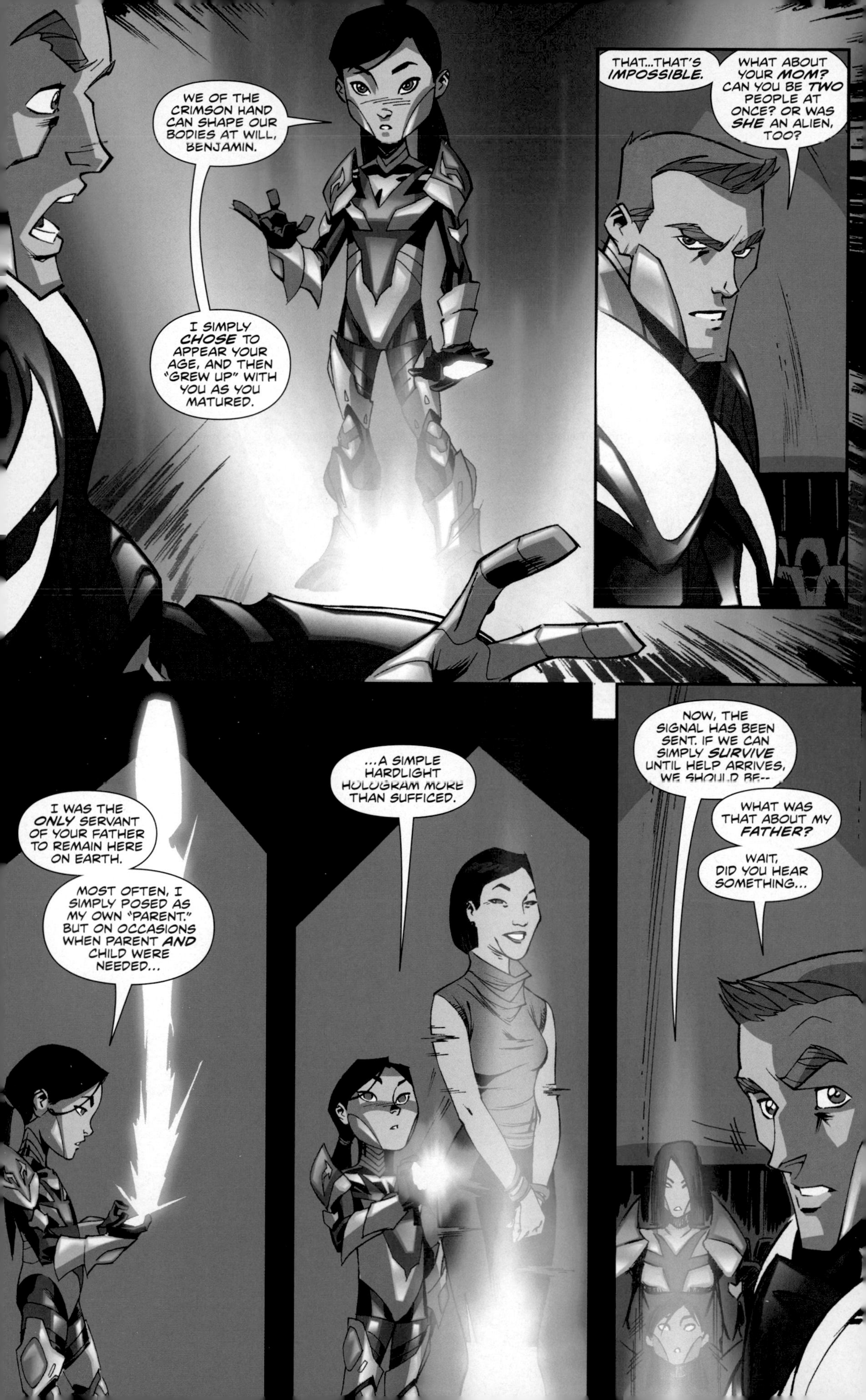
WE OF THE CRIMSON HAND CAN SHAPE OUR BODIES AT WILL, BENJAMIN.
I SIMPLY CHOSE TO APPEAR YOUR AGE, AND THEN "GREW UP" WITH YOU AS YOU MATURED.
THAT...THAT'S IMPOSSIBLE.
WHAT ABOUT YOUR MOM? CAN YOU BE TWO PEOPLE AT ONCE? OR WAS SHE AN ALIEN, TOO?
I WAS THE ONLY SERVANT OF YOUR FATHER TO REMAIN HERE ON EARTH.
MOST OFTEN, I SIMPLY POSED AS MY OWN "PARENT." BUT ON OCCASIONS WHEN PARENT AND CHILD WERE NEEDED...
...A SIMPLE HARDLIGHT HOLOGRAM MORE THAN SUFFICED.
NOW, THE SIGNAL HAS BEEN SENT. IF WE CAN SIMPLY SURVIVE UNTIL HELP ARRIVES, WE SHOULD BE--
WHAT WAS THAT ABOUT MY FATHER?
WAIT, DID YOU HEAR SOMETHING...

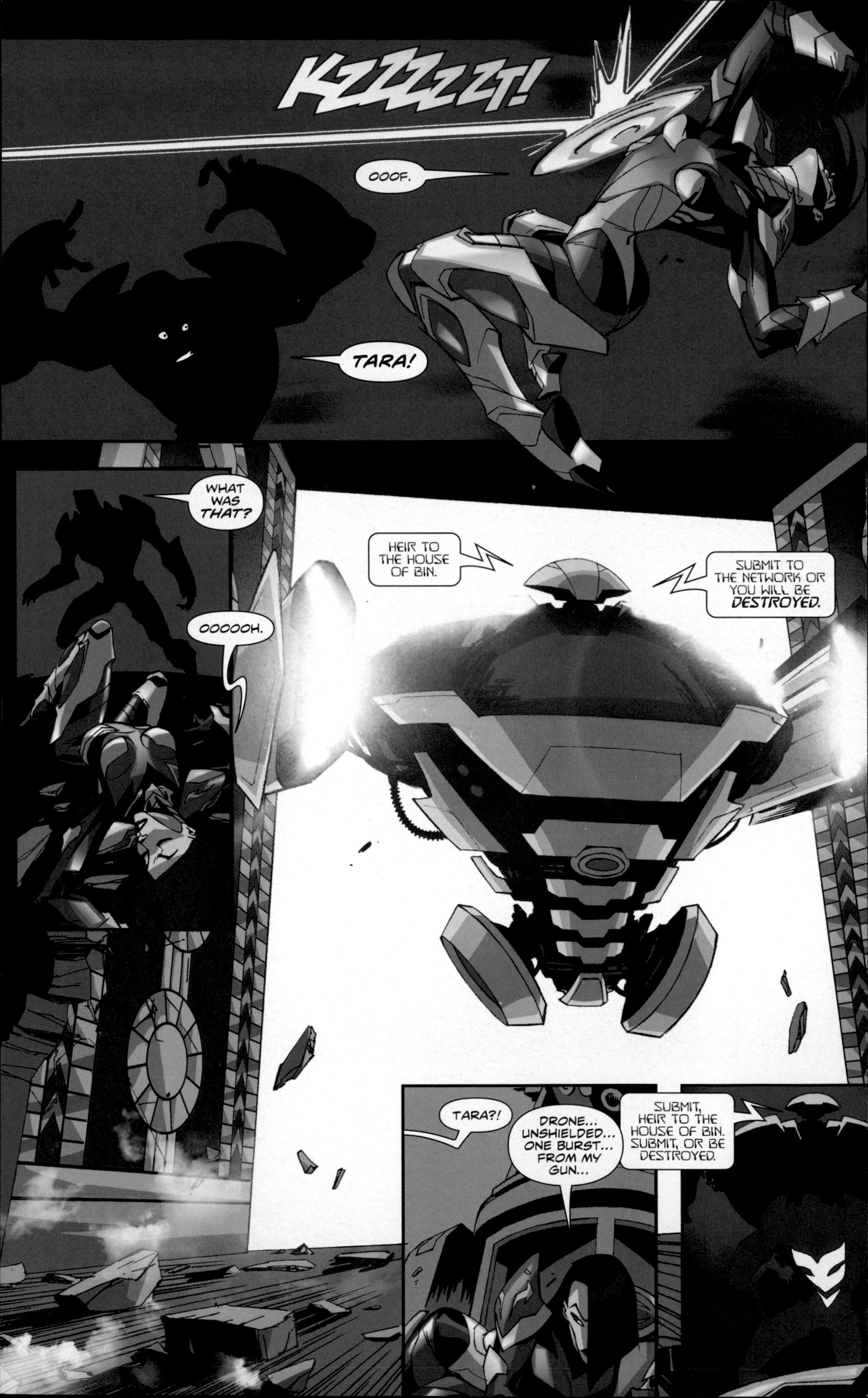
KZZZZZZT!
OOOF.
TARA!
WHAT WAS THAT?
OOOOOH.
HEIR TO THE HOUSE OF BIN.
SUBMIT TO THE NETWORK OR YOU WILL BE DESTROYED.
TARA?!
DRONE... UNSHIELDED... ONE BURST... FROM MY GUN...
SUBMIT, HEIR TO THE HOUSE OF BIN. SUBMIT, OR BE DESTROYED.

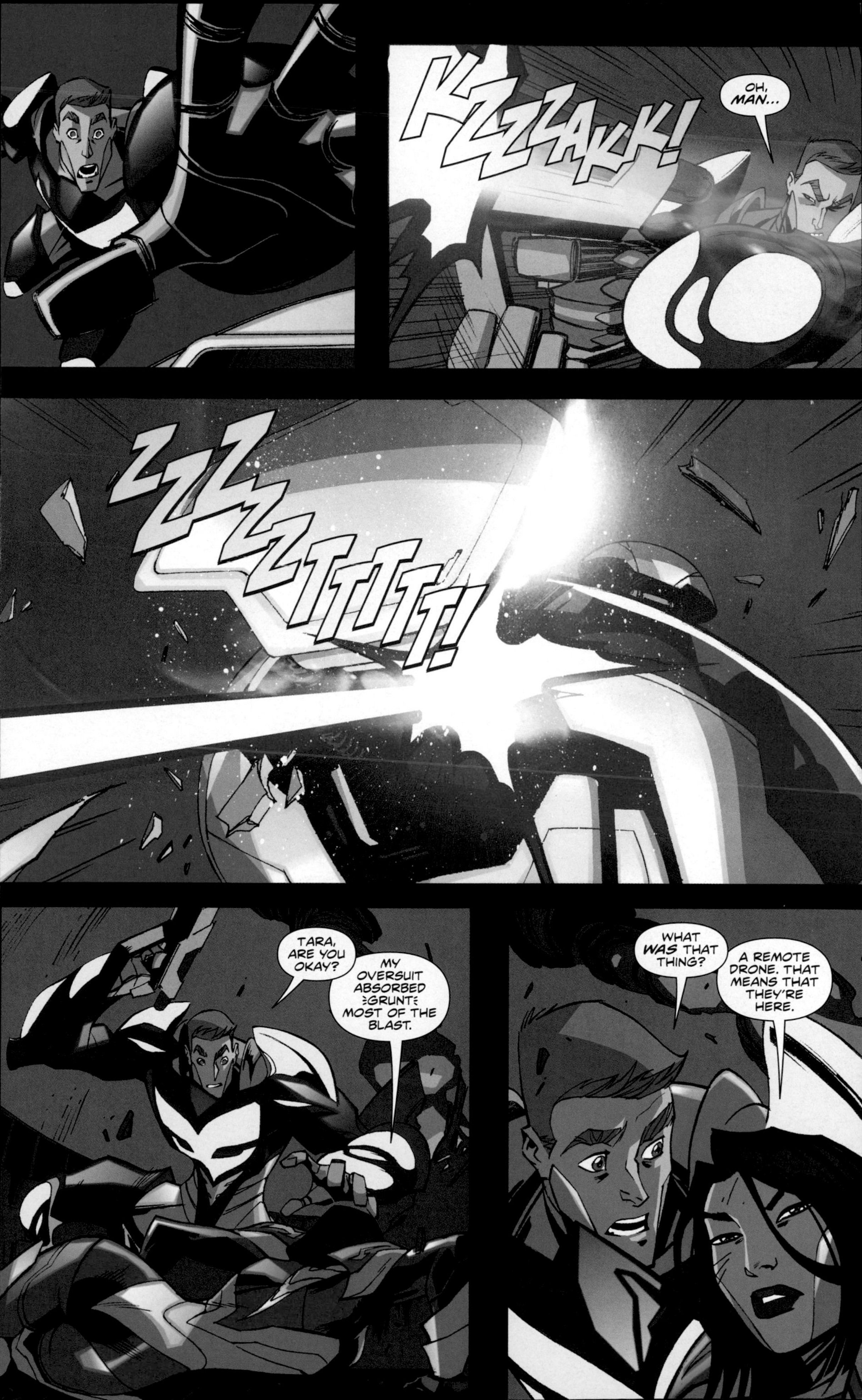
KZZZAKK!
OH, MAN...
ZZZZTTTTT!
TARA, ARE YOU OKAY?
MY OVERSUIT ABSORBED *GRUNT* MOST OF THE BLAST.
WHAT WAS THAT THING?
A REMOTE DRONE. THAT MEANS THAT THEY'RE HERE.

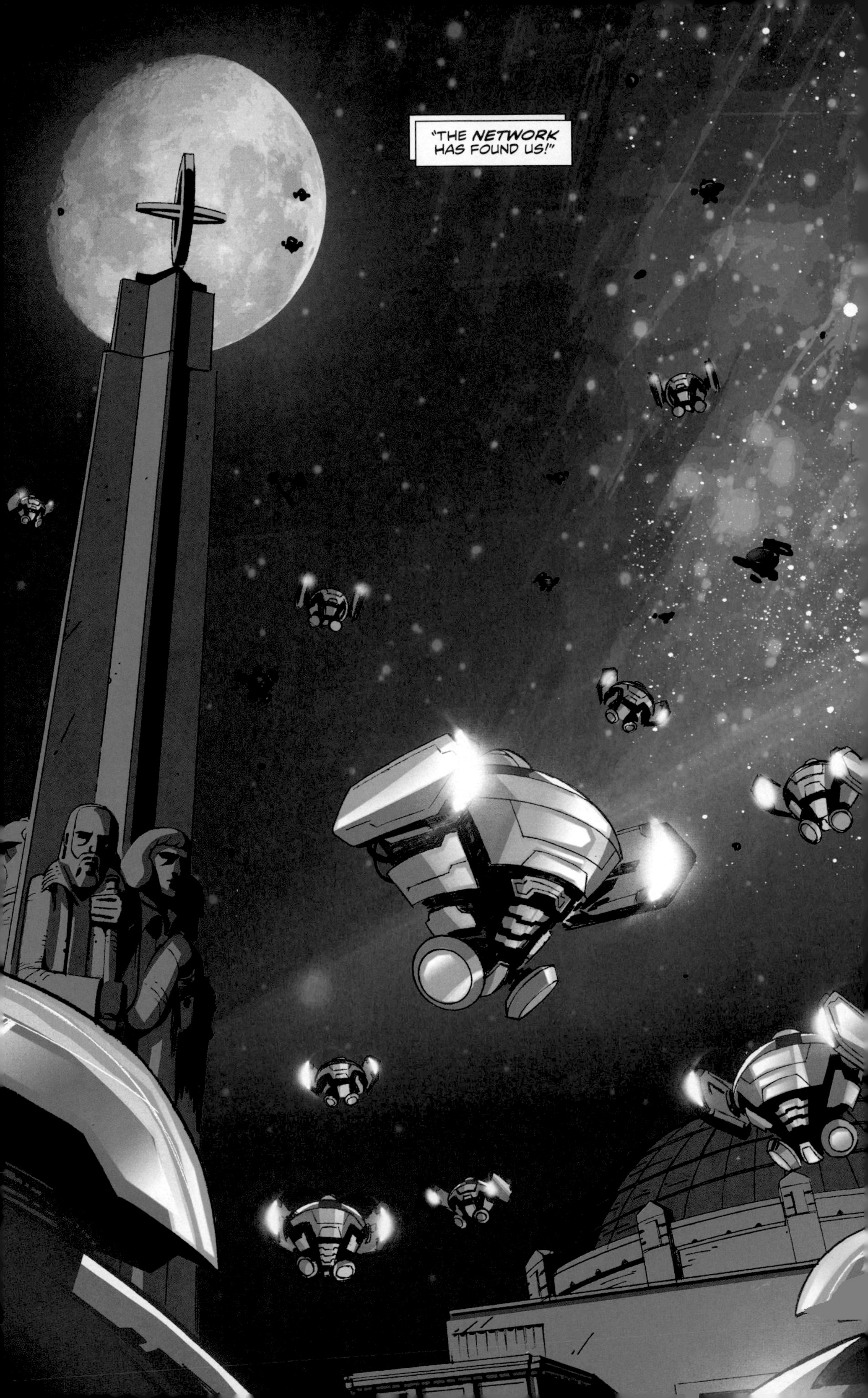
"THE NETWORK HAS FOUND US!"

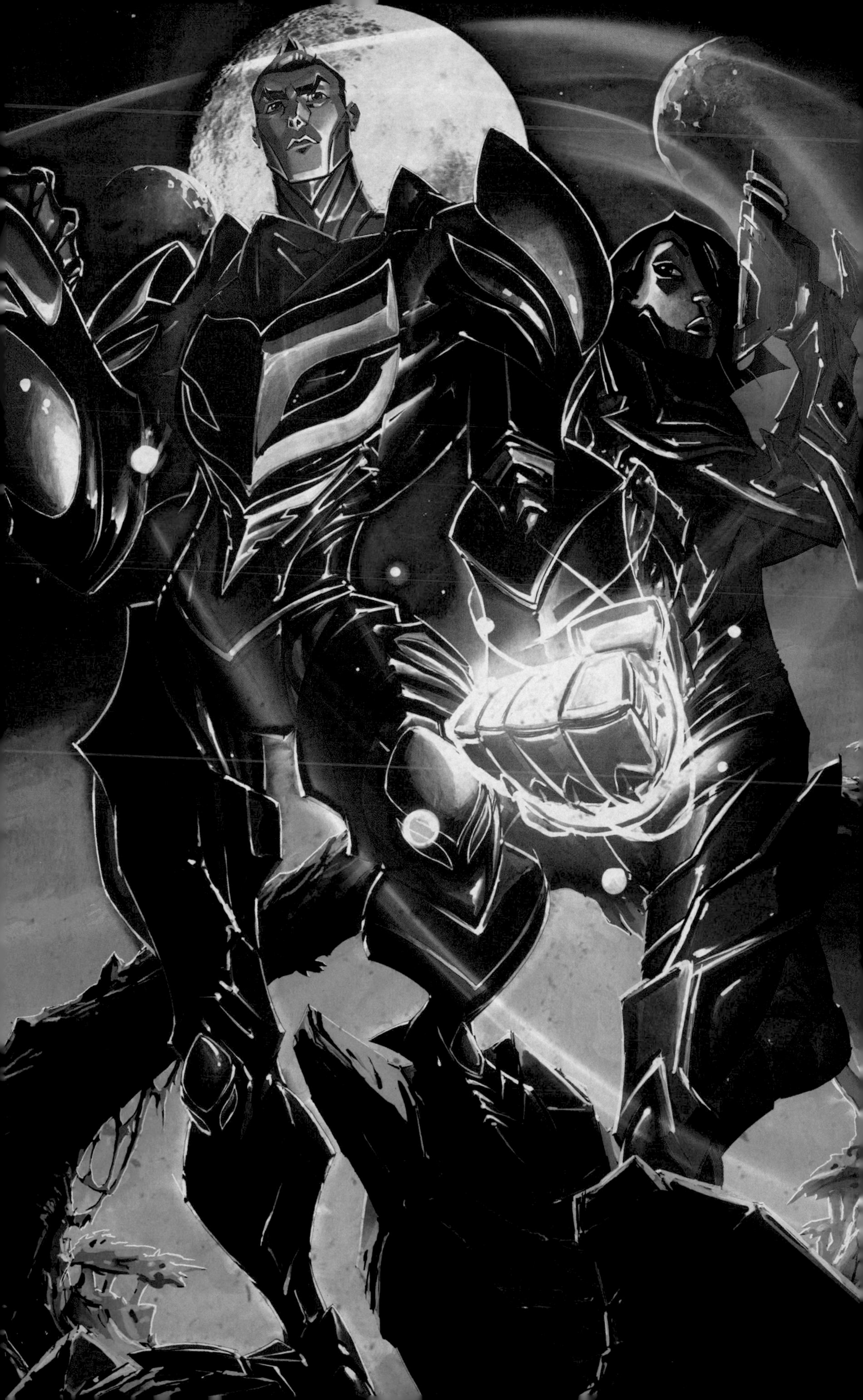

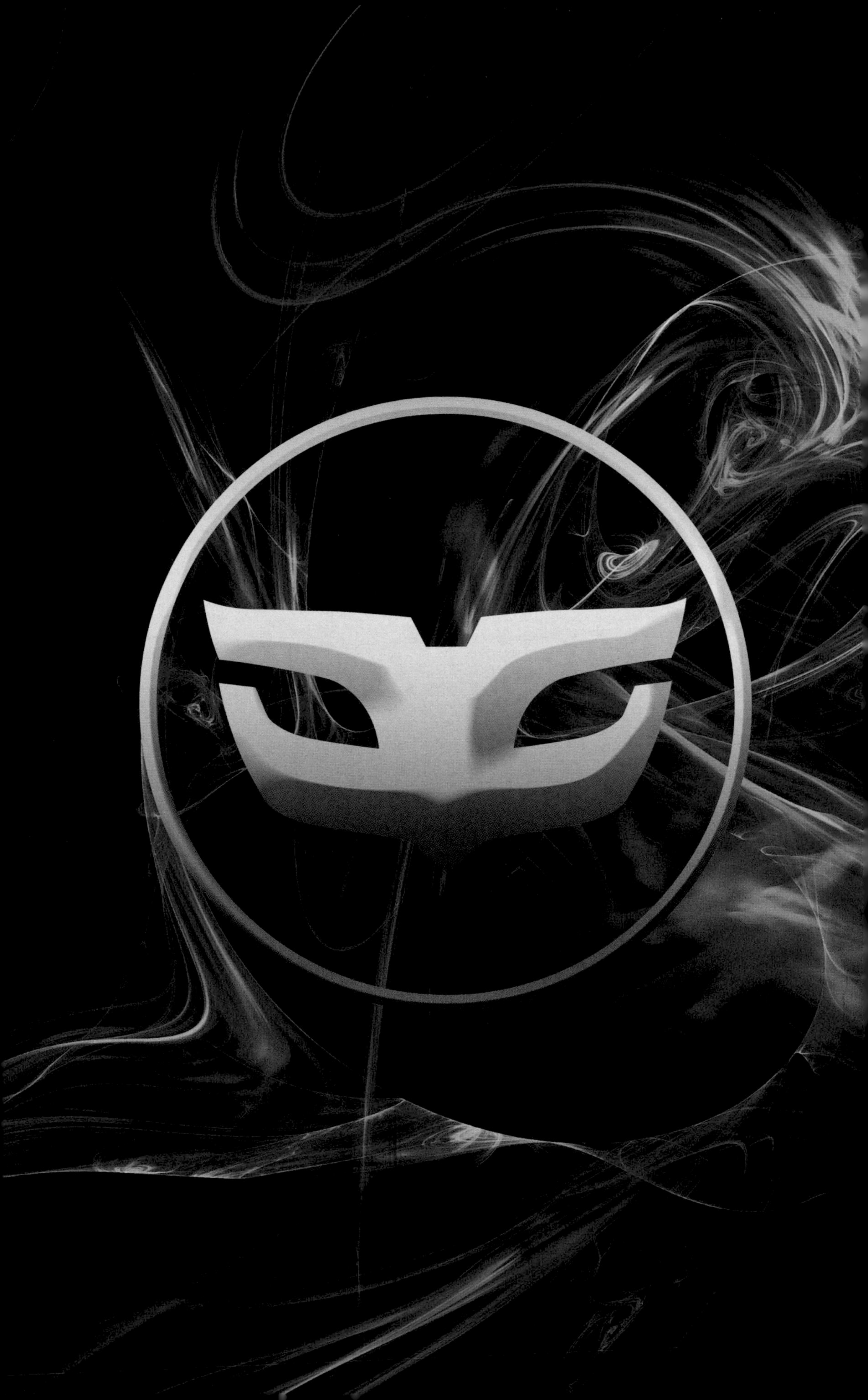

FAR, FAR AWAY...

ᔕᒥᑎᘮᐳ

ᒋᒪᒥᒥᕬᔕ ᕫᕬ ᕼᒥᑎᔕᑎᐳ :
ᒥᕼᔕᕫᕫᕬᒥᒥᑎ ᐸᑎᕬᒥᕫᕫᑎ

BREEDEEP
BREEDEEP

A CRIMSON HAND DISTRESS CALL?

AFTER ALL THESE YEARS? COULD IT BE...?

ᔕᒥᑎᘮᐳ
ᒋᒪᒥᒥᕬᔕ ᕫᕬ ᕼᒥᑎᔕᑎᐳ :
ᒥᕼᔕᕫᕫᕬᒥᒥᑎ ᐸᑎᕬᒥᕫᕫᑎ

MMMM. INTERESTING.

MEANWHILE, BACK ON EARTH...

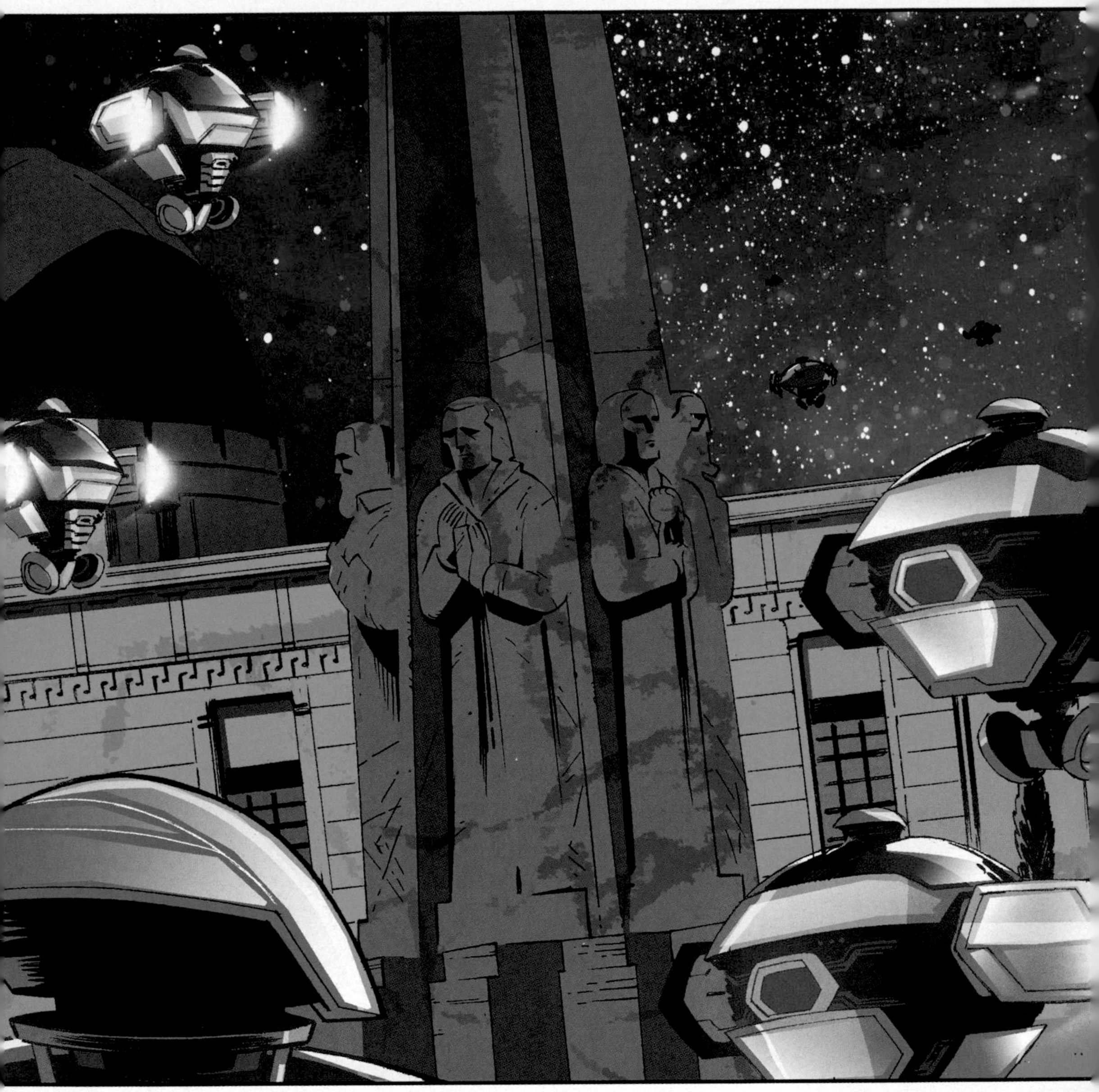

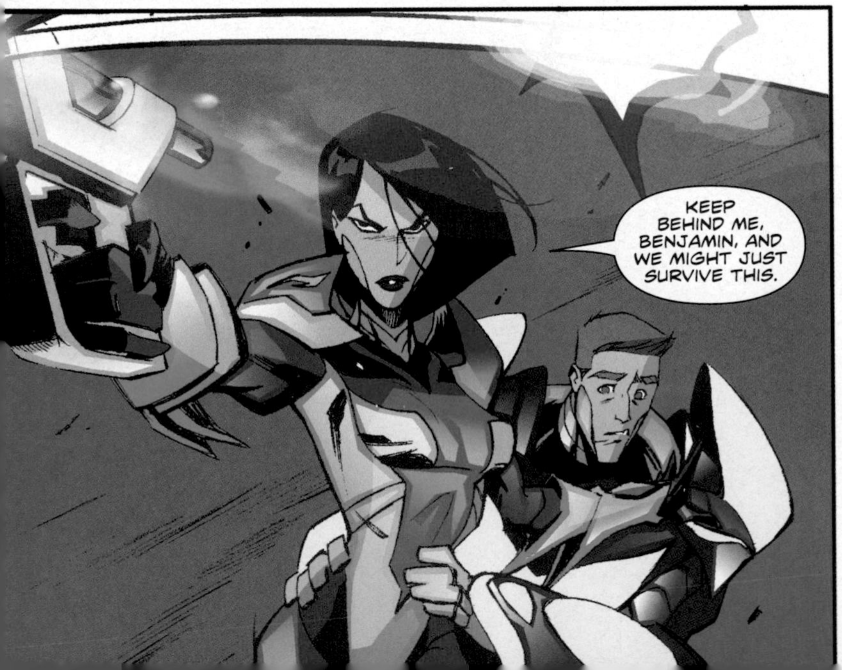
KEEP BEHIND ME, BENJAMIN, AND WE MIGHT JUST SURVIVE THIS.

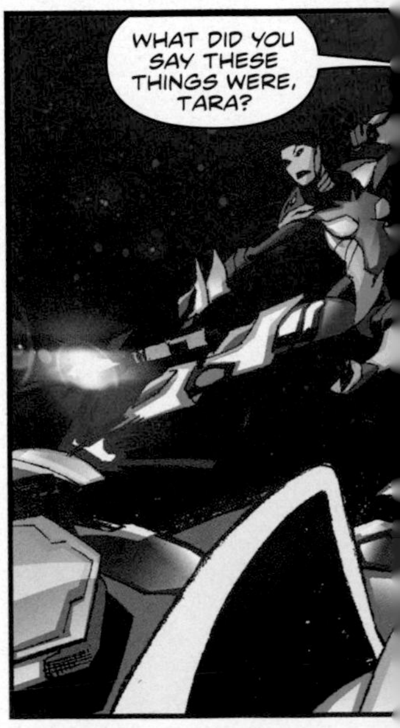
WHAT DID YOU SAY THESE THINGS WERE, TARA?

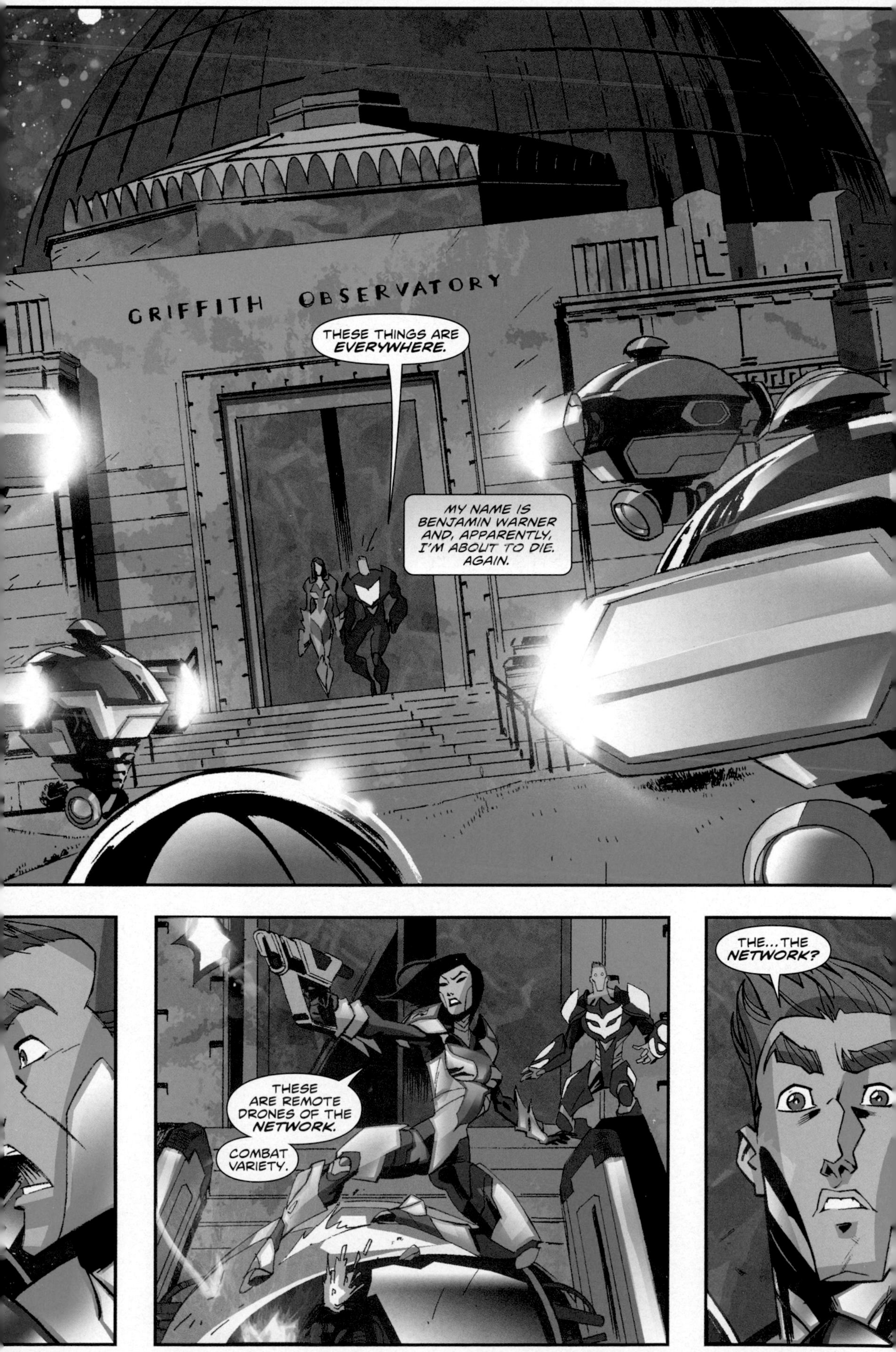
GRIFFITH OBSERVATORY
THESE THINGS ARE EVERYWHERE.
MY NAME IS BENJAMIN WARNER AND, APPARENTLY, I'M ABOUT TO DIE. AGAIN.
THESE ARE REMOTE DRONES OF THE NETWORK.
COMBAT VARIETY.
THE... THE NETWORK?

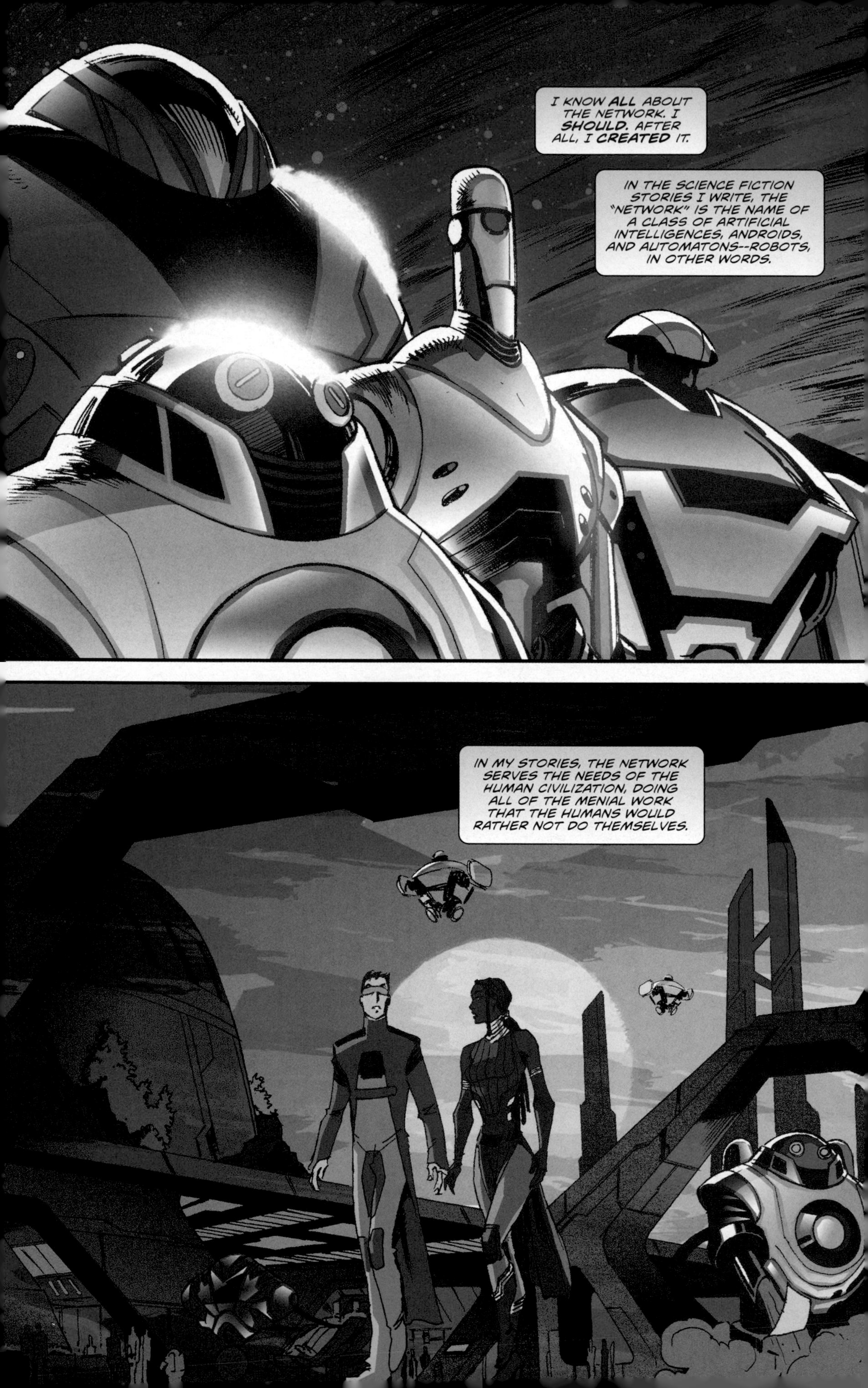
I KNOW **ALL** ABOUT THE NETWORK. I **SHOULD.** AFTER ALL, I **CREATED** IT.
IN THE SCIENCE FICTION STORIES I WRITE, THE "NETWORK" IS THE NAME OF A CLASS OF ARTIFICIAL INTELLIGENCES, ANDROIDS, AND AUTOMATONS--ROBOTS, IN OTHER WORDS.
IN MY STORIES, THE NETWORK SERVES THE NEEDS OF THE HUMAN CIVILIZATION, DOING ALL OF THE MENIAL WORK THAT THE HUMANS WOULD RATHER NOT DO THEMSELVES.

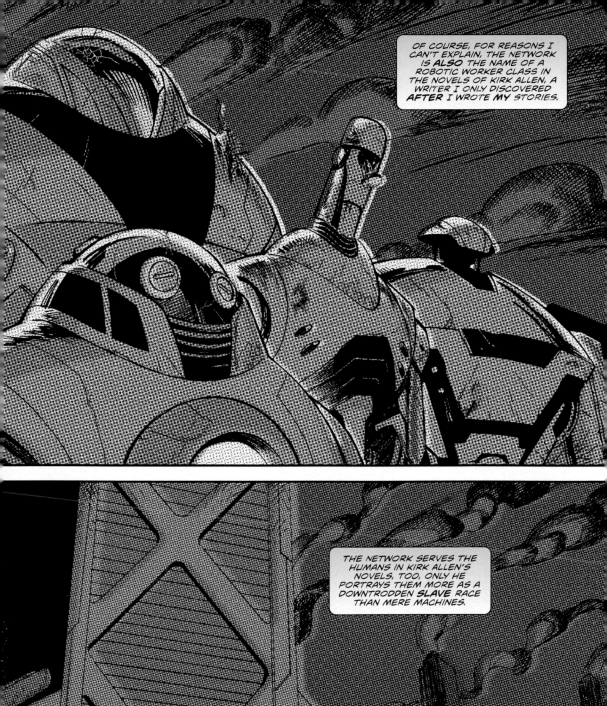

OF COURSE, FOR REASONS I CAN'T EXPLAIN, THE NETWORK IS **ALSO** THE NAME OF A ROBOTIC WORKER CLASS IN THE NOVELS OF KIRK ALLEN, A WRITER I ONLY DISCOVERED **AFTER** I WROTE **MY** STORIES.

THE NETWORK SERVES THE HUMANS IN KIRK ALLEN'S NOVELS, TOO, ONLY HE PORTRAYS THEM MORE AS A DOWNTRODDEN **SLAVE** RACE THAN MERE MACHINES.

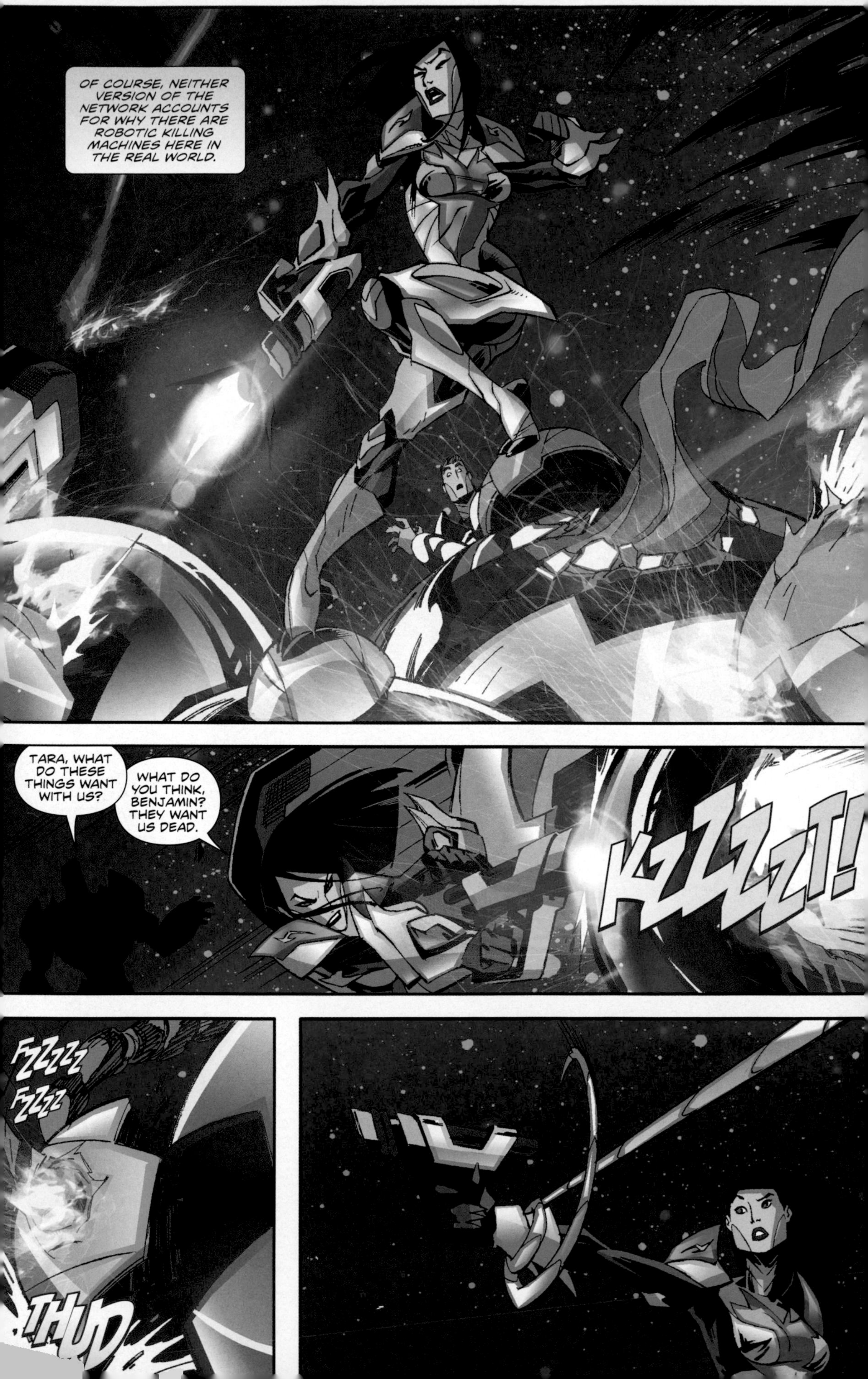
OF COURSE, NEITHER VERSION OF THE NETWORK ACCOUNTS FOR WHY THERE ARE ROBOTIC KILLING MACHINES HERE IN THE REAL WORLD.
TARA, WHAT DO THESE THINGS WANT WITH US?
WHAT DO YOU THINK, BENJAMIN? THEY WANT US DEAD.
KZZZZT!
FZZZZZ
FZZZZ
THUD

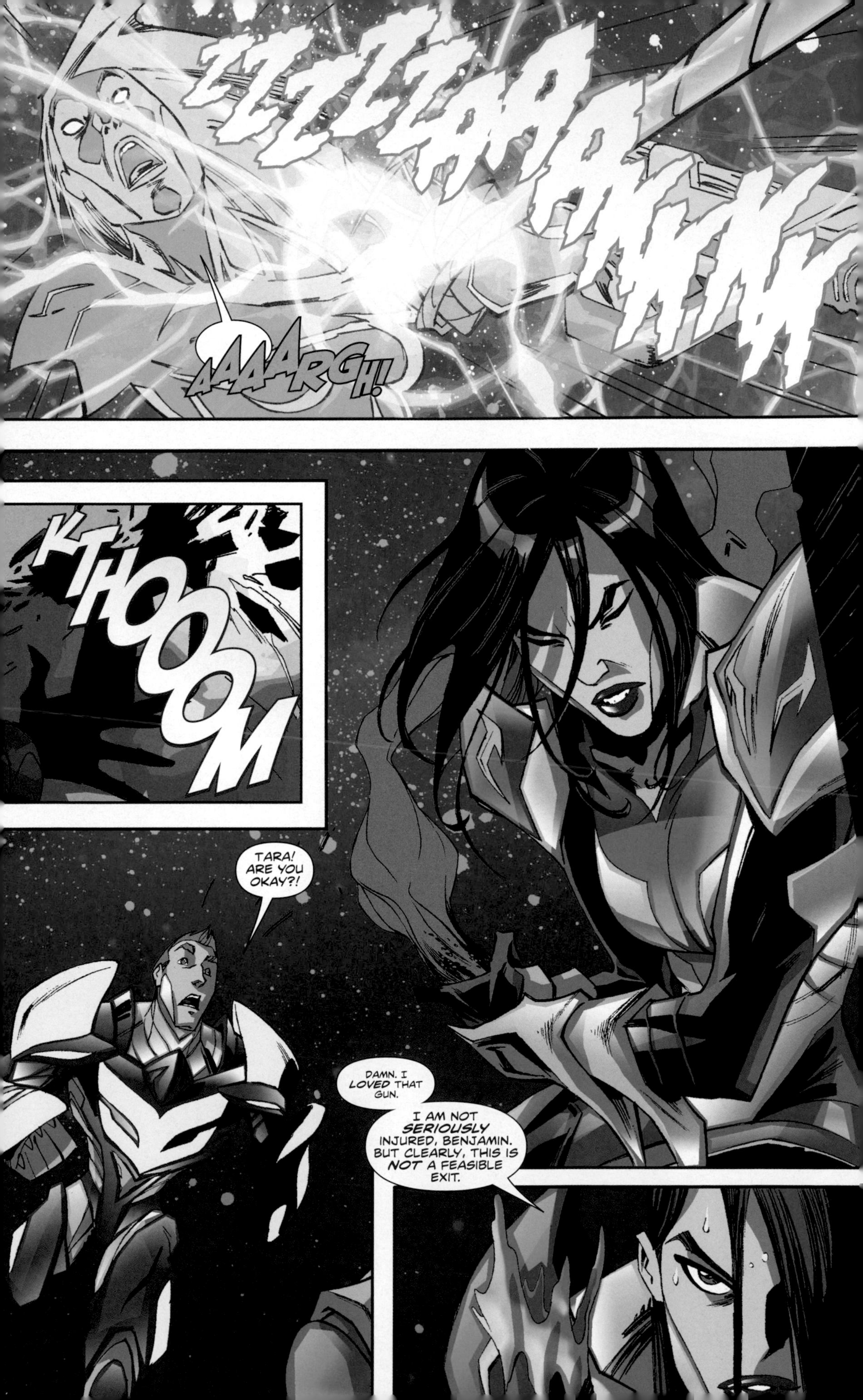
ZZZZAPAMMM
AAAARGH!
KTHOOOM
TARA! ARE YOU OKAY?!
DAMN. I LOVED THAT GUN.
I AM NOT SERIOUSLY INJURED, BENJAMIN. BUT CLEARLY, THIS IS NOT A FEASIBLE EXIT.

COME ON! BACK INSIDE!

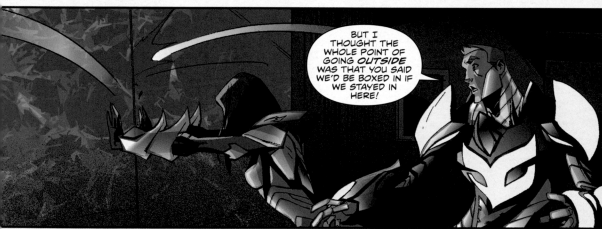

BUT I THOUGHT THE WHOLE POINT OF GOING *OUTSIDE* WAS THAT YOU SAID WE'D BE BOXED IN IF WE STAYED IN HERE!

I DON'T INTEND FOR US TO RETRENCH OUR POSITION. I JUST NEED A CLEAR MOMENT TO DO THIS.

HUMMM

I'M SORRY ABOUT THIS, BENJAMIN, I TRULY AM. I HAD HOPED TO KEEP THIS BURDEN FROM YOU A WHILE LONGER, IF I COULD.

WHAT THE...?

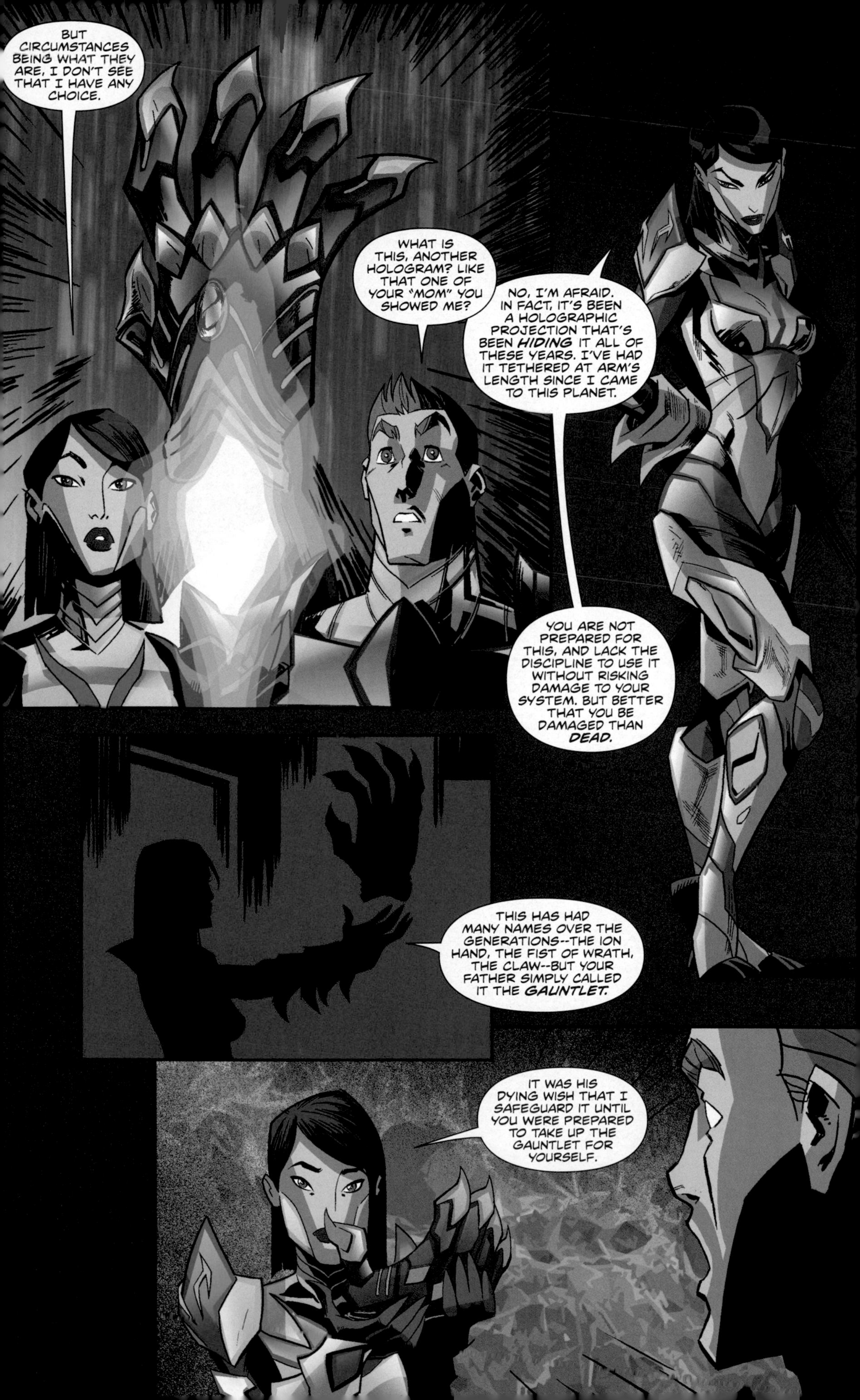
BUT CIRCUMSTANCES BEING WHAT THEY ARE, I DON'T SEE THAT I HAVE ANY CHOICE.
WHAT IS THIS, ANOTHER HOLOGRAM? LIKE THAT ONE OF YOUR "MOM" YOU SHOWED ME?
NO, I'M AFRAID. IN FACT, IT'S BEEN A HOLOGRAPHIC PROJECTION THAT'S BEEN HIDING IT ALL OF THESE YEARS. I'VE HAD IT TETHERED AT ARM'S LENGTH SINCE I CAME TO THIS PLANET.
YOU ARE NOT PREPARED FOR THIS, AND LACK THE DISCIPLINE TO USE IT WITHOUT RISKING DAMAGE TO YOUR SYSTEM. BUT BETTER THAT YOU BE DAMAGED THAN DEAD.
THIS HAS HAD MANY NAMES OVER THE GENERATIONS--THE ION HAND, THE FIST OF WRATH, THE CLAW--BUT YOUR FATHER SIMPLY CALLED IT THE GAUNTLET.
IT WAS HIS DYING WISH THAT I SAFEGUARD IT UNTIL YOU WERE PREPARED TO TAKE UP THE GAUNTLET FOR YOURSELF.

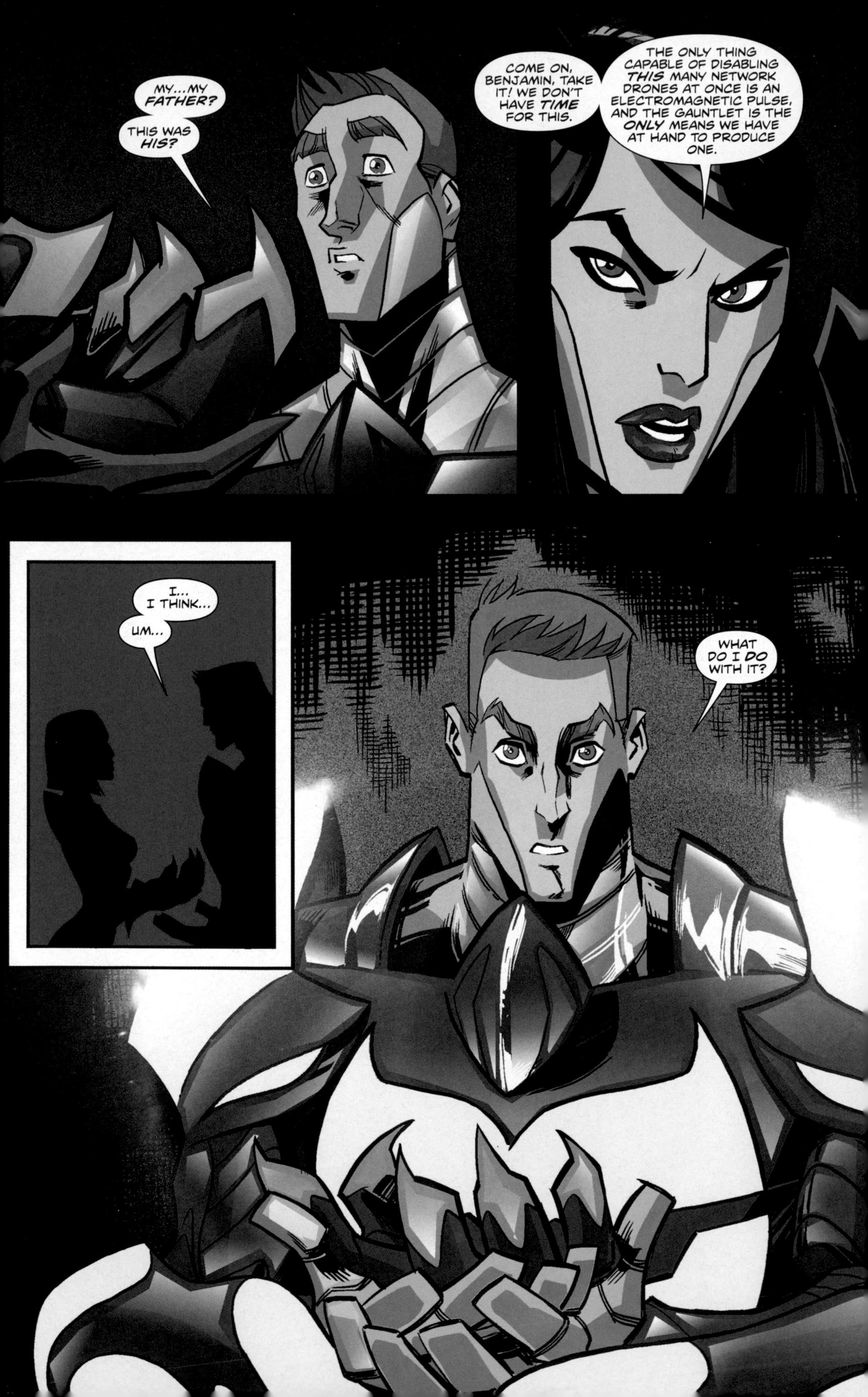
MY...MY FATHER?
THIS WAS HIS?
COME ON, BENJAMIN, TAKE IT! WE DON'T HAVE TIME FOR THIS.
THE ONLY THING CAPABLE OF DISABLING THIS MANY NETWORK DRONES AT ONCE IS AN ELECTROMAGNETIC PULSE, AND THE GAUNTLET IS THE ONLY MEANS WE HAVE AT HAND TO PRODUCE ONE.
I... I THINK...
UM...
WHAT DO I DO WITH IT?

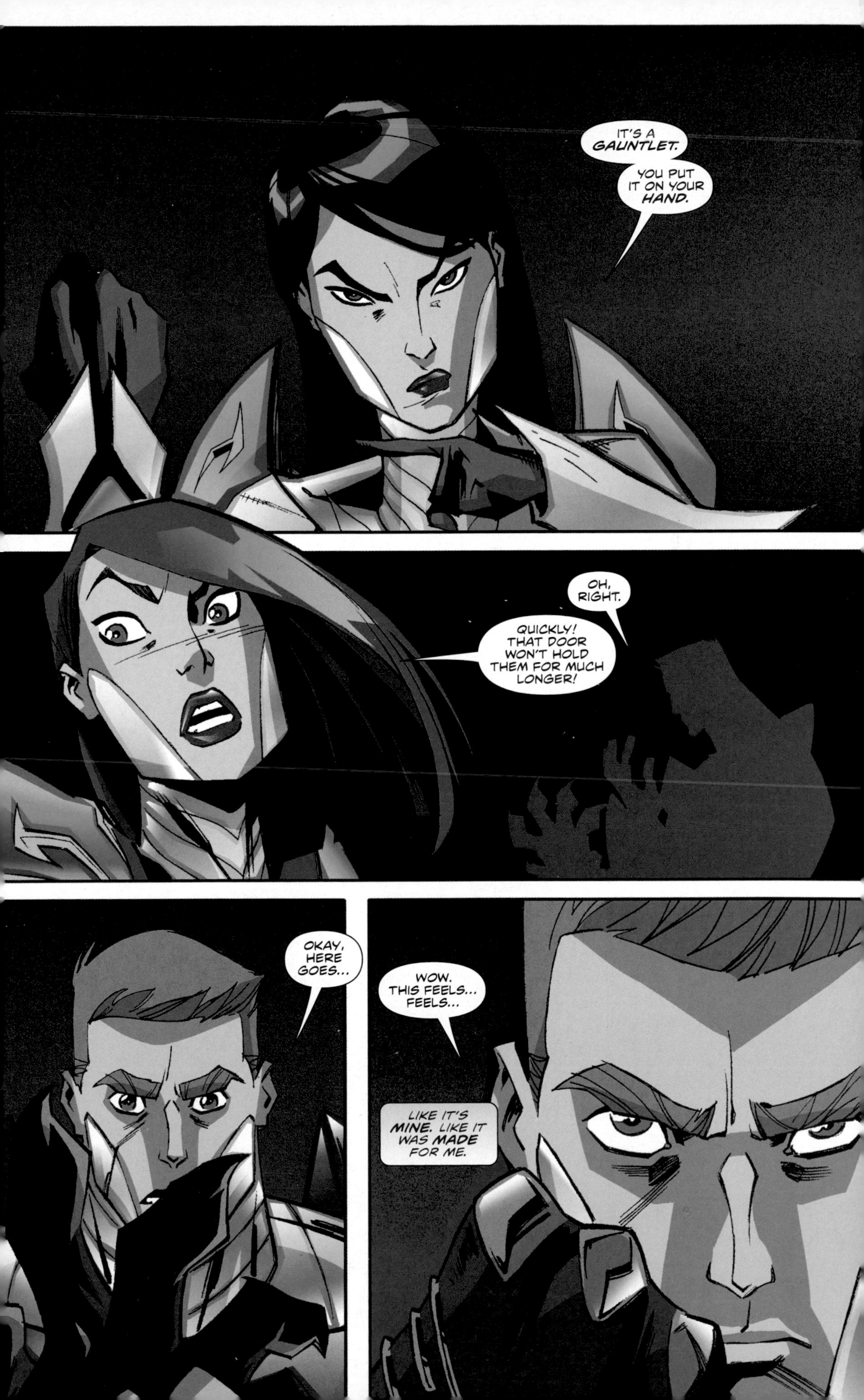
IT'S A GAUNTLET.
YOU PUT IT ON YOUR HAND.
OH, RIGHT.
QUICKLY! THAT DOOR WON'T HOLD THEM FOR MUCH LONGER!
OKAY, HERE GOES...
WOW. THIS FEELS... FEELS...
LIKE IT'S MINE. LIKE IT WAS MADE FOR ME.

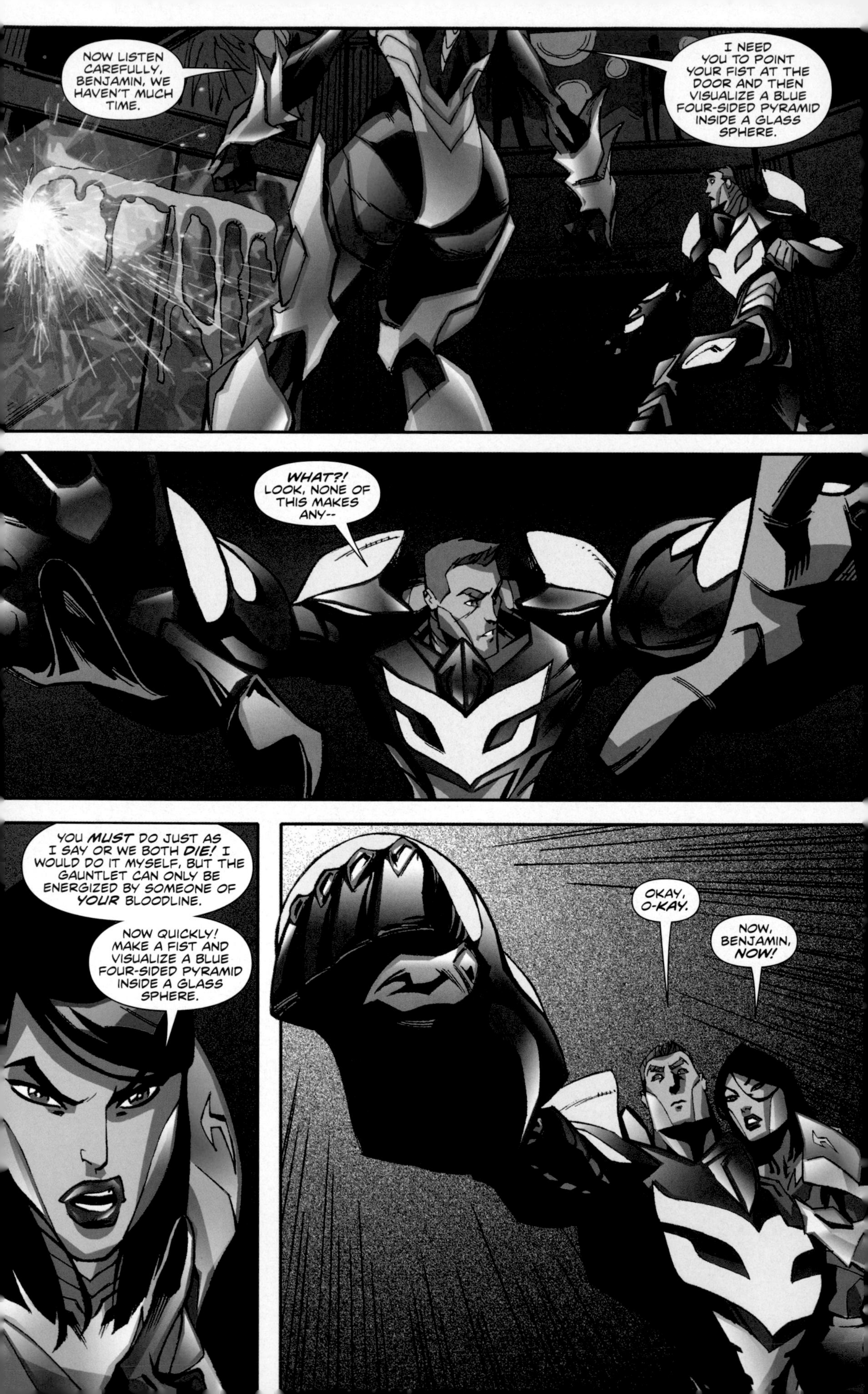
NOW LISTEN CAREFULLY, BENJAMIN, WE HAVEN'T MUCH TIME.
I NEED YOU TO POINT YOUR FIST AT THE DOOR AND THEN VISUALIZE A BLUE FOUR-SIDED PYRAMID INSIDE A GLASS SPHERE.
WHAT?! LOOK, NONE OF THIS MAKES ANY--
YOU *MUST* DO JUST AS I SAY OR WE BOTH *DIE!* I WOULD DO IT MYSELF, BUT THE GAUNTLET CAN ONLY BE ENERGIZED BY SOMEONE OF *YOUR* BLOODLINE.
NOW QUICKLY! MAKE A FIST AND VISUALIZE A BLUE FOUR-SIDED PYRAMID INSIDE A GLASS SPHERE.
OKAY, *O-KAY.*
NOW, BENJAMIN, *NOW!*

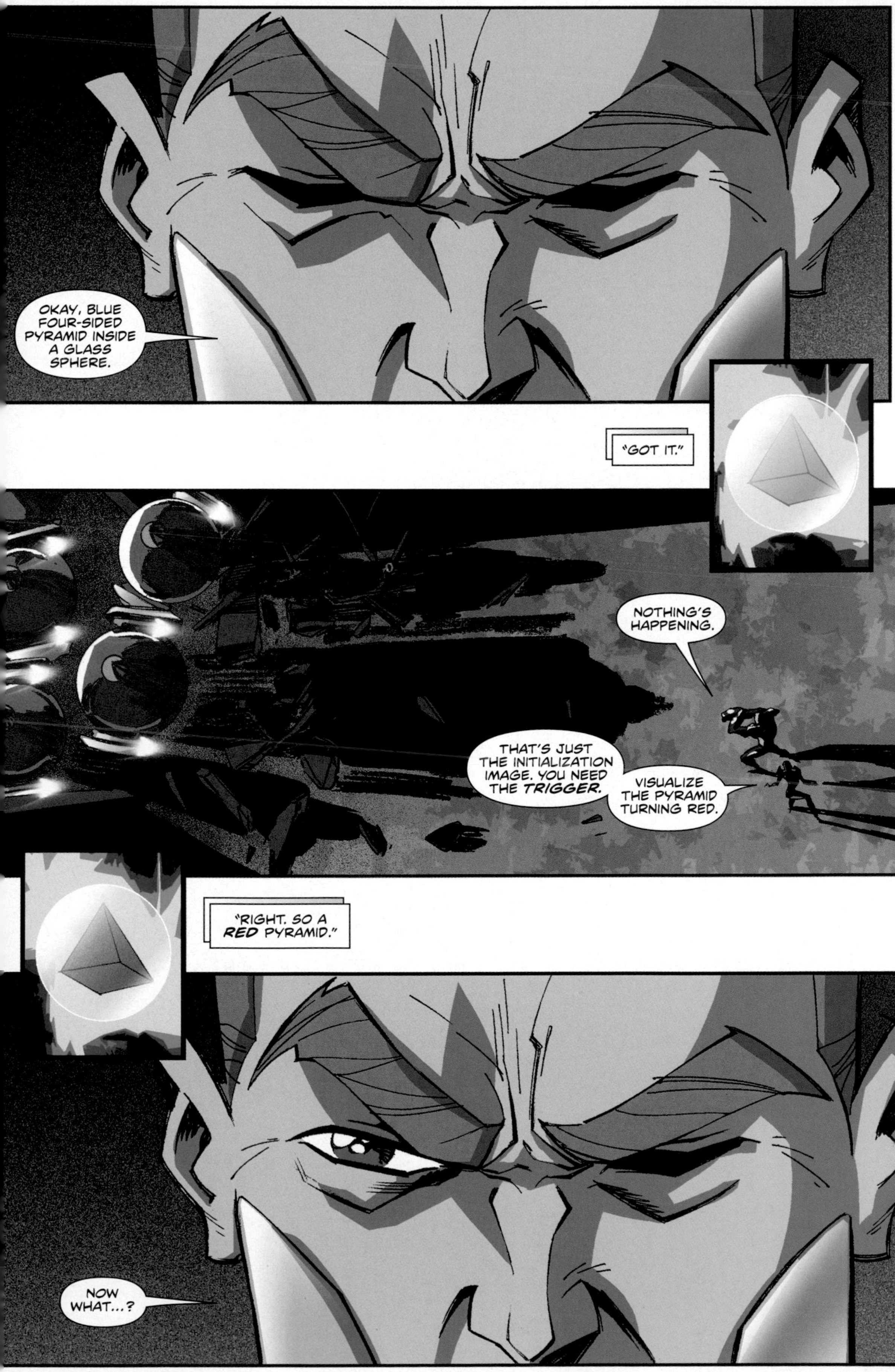
OKAY, BLUE FOUR-SIDED PYRAMID INSIDE A GLASS SPHERE.
"GOT IT."
NOTHING'S HAPPENING.
THAT'S JUST THE INITIALIZATION IMAGE. YOU NEED THE TRIGGER.
VISUALIZE THE PYRAMID TURNING RED.
"RIGHT. SO A RED PYRAMID."
NOW WHAT...?

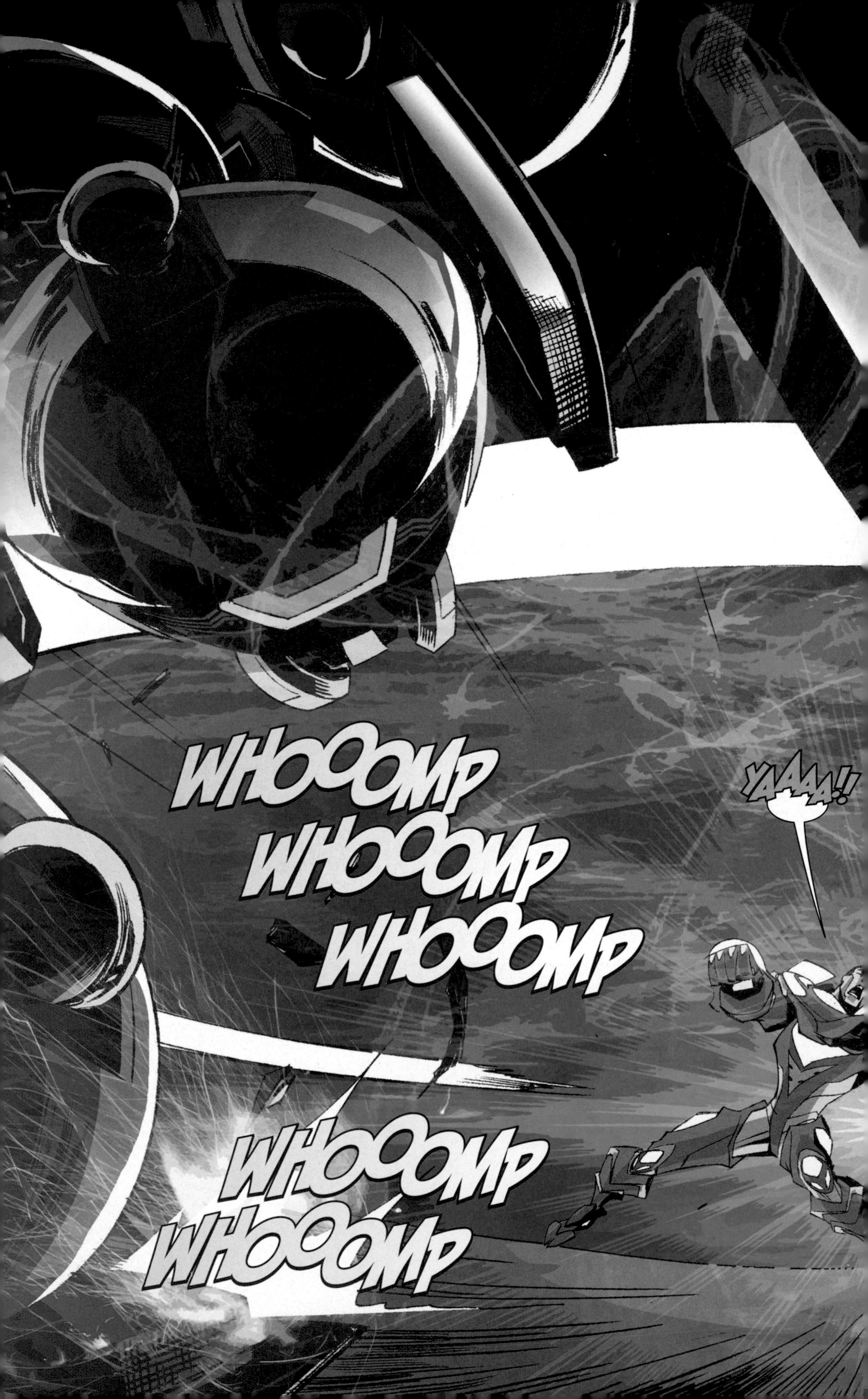
WHOOOMP
WHOOOMP
WHOOOMP
YAAAA!!
WHOOOMP
WHOOOMP

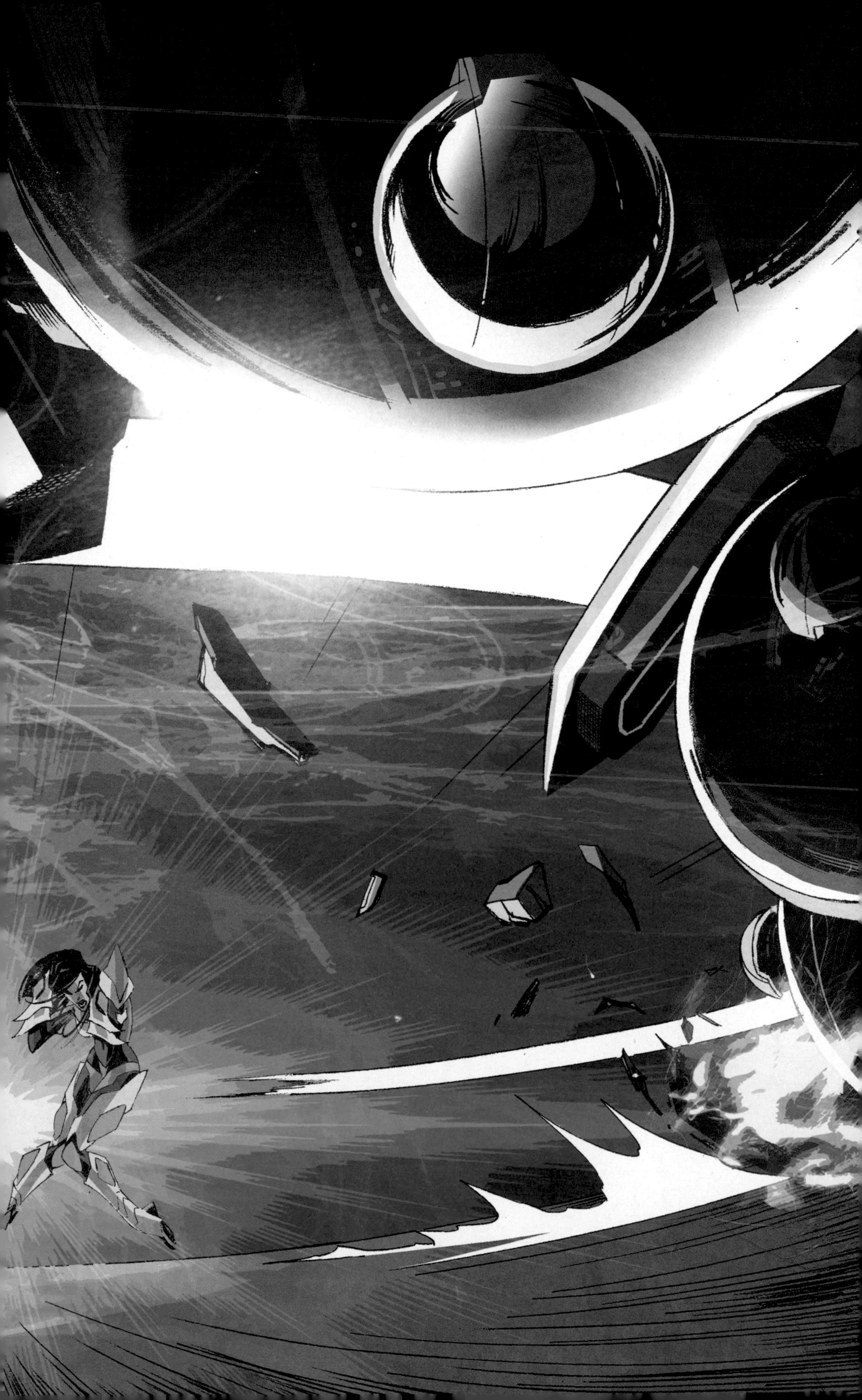

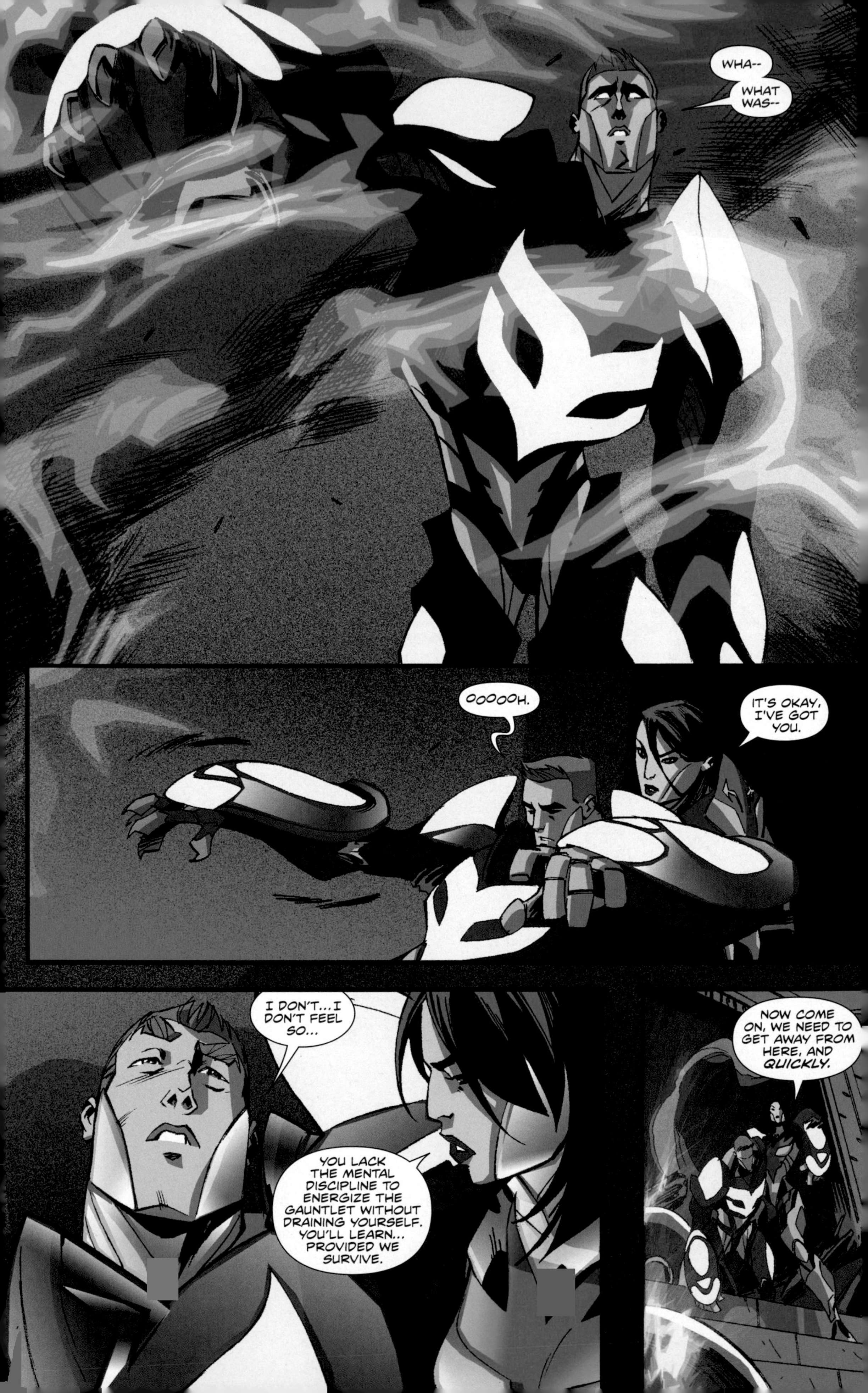
WHA--
WHAT WAS--
OOOOOH.
IT'S OKAY, I'VE GOT YOU.
I DON'T...I DON'T FEEL SO...
YOU LACK THE MENTAL DISCIPLINE TO ENERGIZE THE GAUNTLET WITHOUT DRAINING YOURSELF. YOU'LL LEARN... PROVIDED WE SURVIVE.
NOW COME ON, WE NEED TO GET AWAY FROM HERE, AND *QUICKLY*.

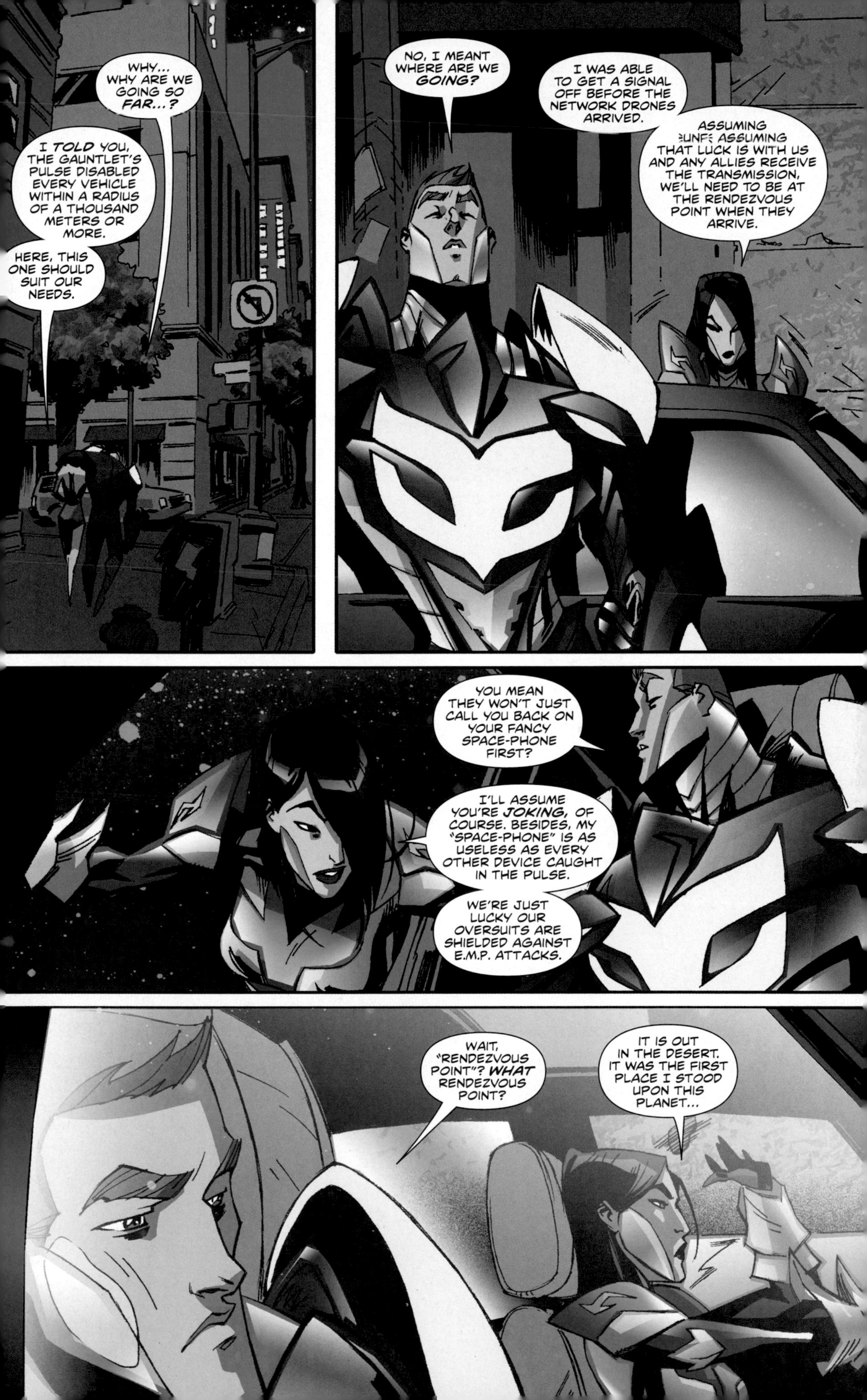
WHY... WHY ARE WE GOING SO FAR...?
I TOLD YOU, THE GAUNTLET'S PULSE DISABLED EVERY VEHICLE WITHIN A RADIUS OF A THOUSAND METERS OR MORE.
HERE, THIS ONE SHOULD SUIT OUR NEEDS.
NO, I MEANT WHERE ARE WE GOING?
I WAS ABLE TO GET A SIGNAL OFF BEFORE THE NETWORK DRONES ARRIVED.
ASSUMING ASSUMING THAT LUCK IS WITH US AND ANY ALLIES RECEIVE THE TRANSMISSION, WE'LL NEED TO BE AT THE RENDEZVOUS POINT WHEN THEY ARRIVE.
YOU MEAN THEY WON'T JUST CALL YOU BACK ON YOUR FANCY SPACE-PHONE FIRST?
I'LL ASSUME YOU'RE JOKING, OF COURSE. BESIDES, MY "SPACE-PHONE" IS AS USELESS AS EVERY OTHER DEVICE CAUGHT IN THE PULSE.
WE'RE JUST LUCKY OUR OVERSUITS ARE SHIELDED AGAINST E.M.P. ATTACKS.
WAIT, "RENDEZVOUS POINT"? WHAT RENDEZVOUS POINT?
IT IS OUT IN THE DESERT. IT WAS THE FIRST PLACE I STOOD UPON THIS PLANET...

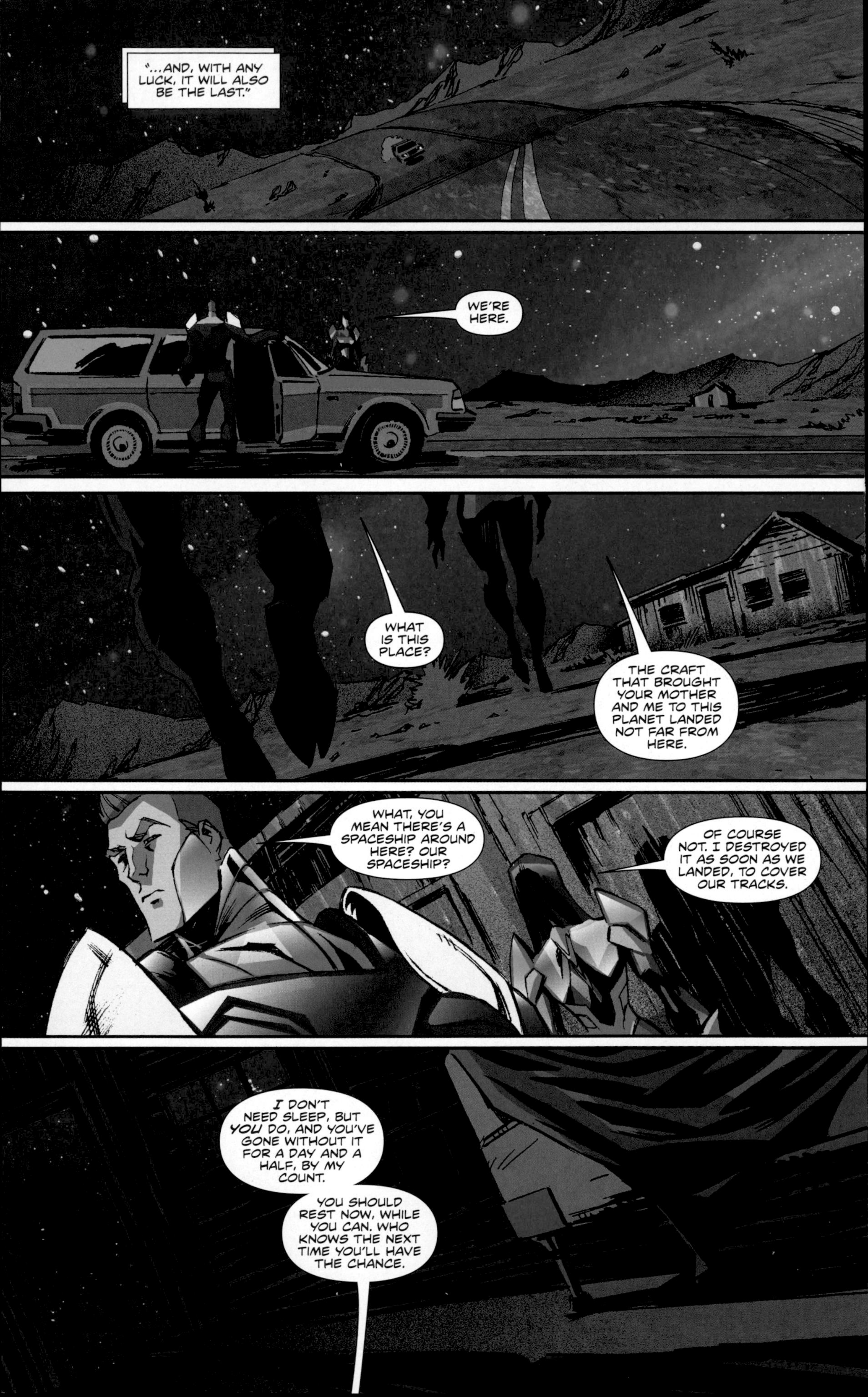
"...AND, WITH ANY LUCK, IT WILL ALSO BE THE LAST."
WE'RE HERE.
WHAT IS THIS PLACE?
THE CRAFT THAT BROUGHT YOUR MOTHER AND ME TO THIS PLANET LANDED NOT FAR FROM HERE.
WHAT, YOU MEAN THERE'S A SPACESHIP AROUND HERE? OUR SPACESHIP?
OF COURSE NOT. I DESTROYED IT AS SOON AS WE LANDED, TO COVER OUR TRACKS.
I DON'T NEED SLEEP, BUT YOU DO, AND YOU'VE GONE WITHOUT IT FOR A DAY AND A HALF, BY MY COUNT.
YOU SHOULD REST NOW, WHILE YOU CAN. WHO KNOWS THE NEXT TIME YOU'LL HAVE THE CHANCE.

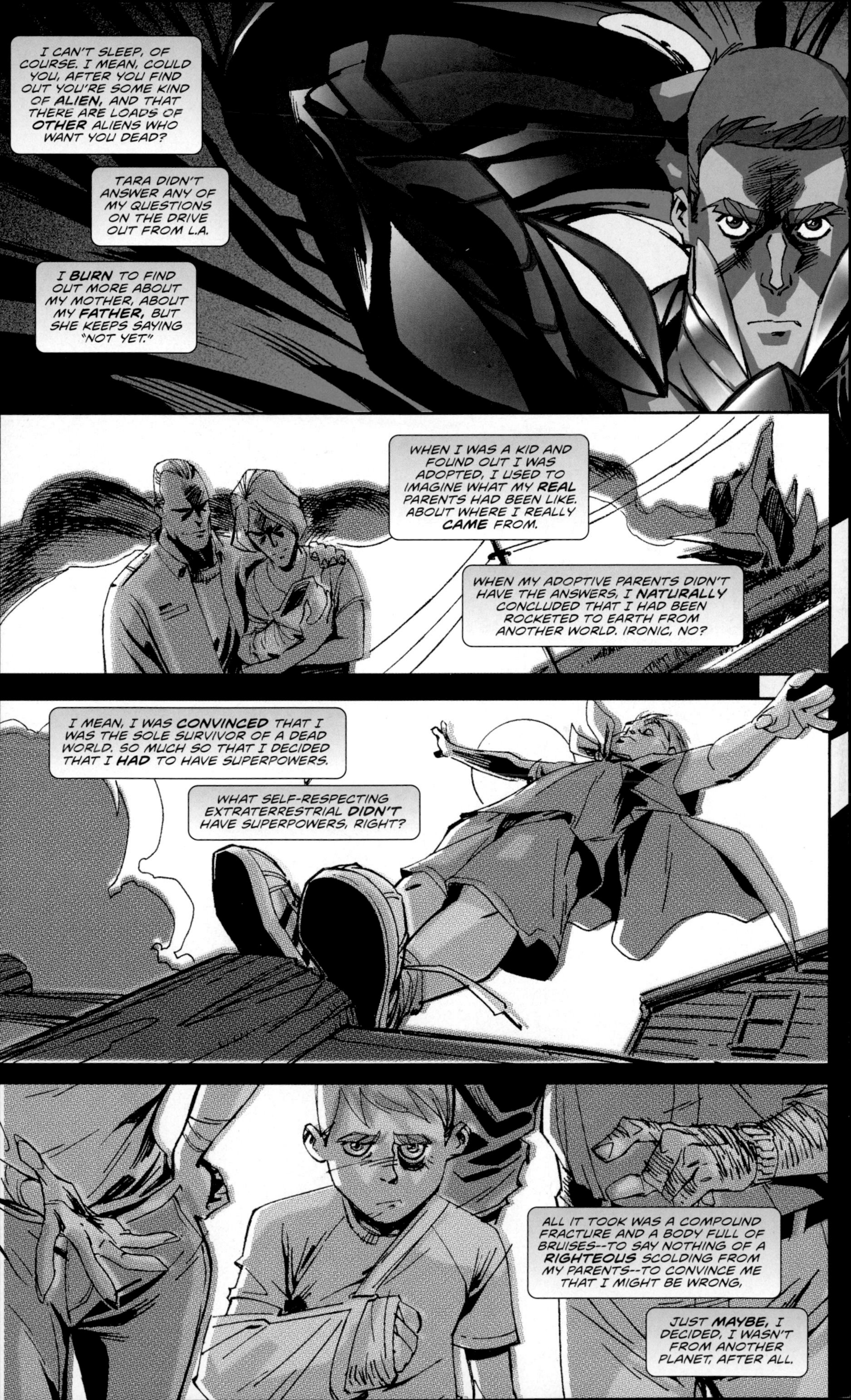
I CAN'T SLEEP, OF COURSE. I MEAN, COULD YOU, AFTER YOU FIND OUT YOU'RE SOME KIND OF ALIEN, AND THAT THERE ARE LOADS OF OTHER ALIENS WHO WANT YOU DEAD?
TARA DIDN'T ANSWER ANY OF MY QUESTIONS ON THE DRIVE OUT FROM L.A.
I BURN TO FIND OUT MORE ABOUT MY MOTHER, ABOUT MY FATHER, BUT SHE KEEPS SAYING "NOT YET."
WHEN I WAS A KID AND FOUND OUT I WAS ADOPTED, I USED TO IMAGINE WHAT MY REAL PARENTS HAD BEEN LIKE. ABOUT WHERE I REALLY CAME FROM.
WHEN MY ADOPTIVE PARENTS DIDN'T HAVE THE ANSWERS, I NATURALLY CONCLUDED THAT I HAD BEEN ROCKETED TO EARTH FROM ANOTHER WORLD. IRONIC, NO?
I MEAN, I WAS CONVINCED THAT I WAS THE SOLE SURVIVOR OF A DEAD WORLD. SO MUCH SO THAT I DECIDED THAT I HAD TO HAVE SUPERPOWERS.
WHAT SELF-RESPECTING EXTRATERRESTRIAL DIDN'T HAVE SUPERPOWERS, RIGHT?
ALL IT TOOK WAS A COMPOUND FRACTURE AND A BODY FULL OF BRUISES--TO SAY NOTHING OF A RIGHTEOUS SCOLDING FROM MY PARENTS--TO CONVINCE ME THAT I MIGHT BE WRONG,
JUST MAYBE, I DECIDED, I WASN'T FROM ANOTHER PLANET, AFTER ALL.

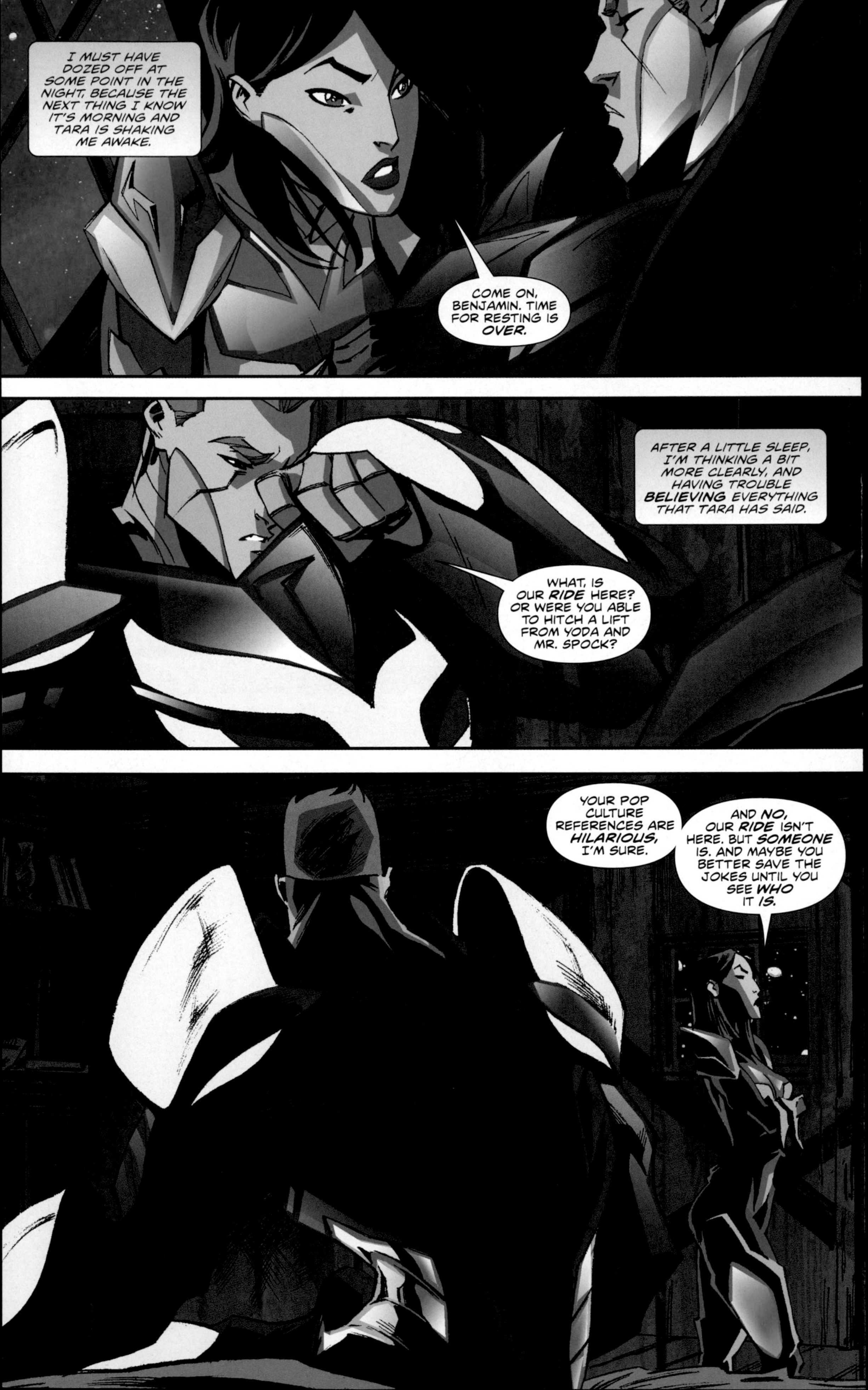
I MUST HAVE DOZED OFF AT SOME POINT IN THE NIGHT, BECAUSE THE NEXT THING I KNOW IT'S MORNING AND TARA IS SHAKING ME AWAKE.
COME ON, BENJAMIN. TIME FOR RESTING IS OVER.
AFTER A LITTLE SLEEP, I'M THINKING A BIT MORE CLEARLY, AND HAVING TROUBLE BELIEVING EVERYTHING THAT TARA HAS SAID.
WHAT, IS OUR RIDE HERE? OR WERE YOU ABLE TO HITCH A LIFT FROM YODA AND MR. SPOCK?
YOUR POP CULTURE REFERENCES ARE HILARIOUS, I'M SURE.
AND NO, OUR RIDE ISN'T HERE. BUT SOMEONE IS. AND MAYBE YOU BETTER SAVE THE JOKES UNTIL YOU SEE WHO IT IS.

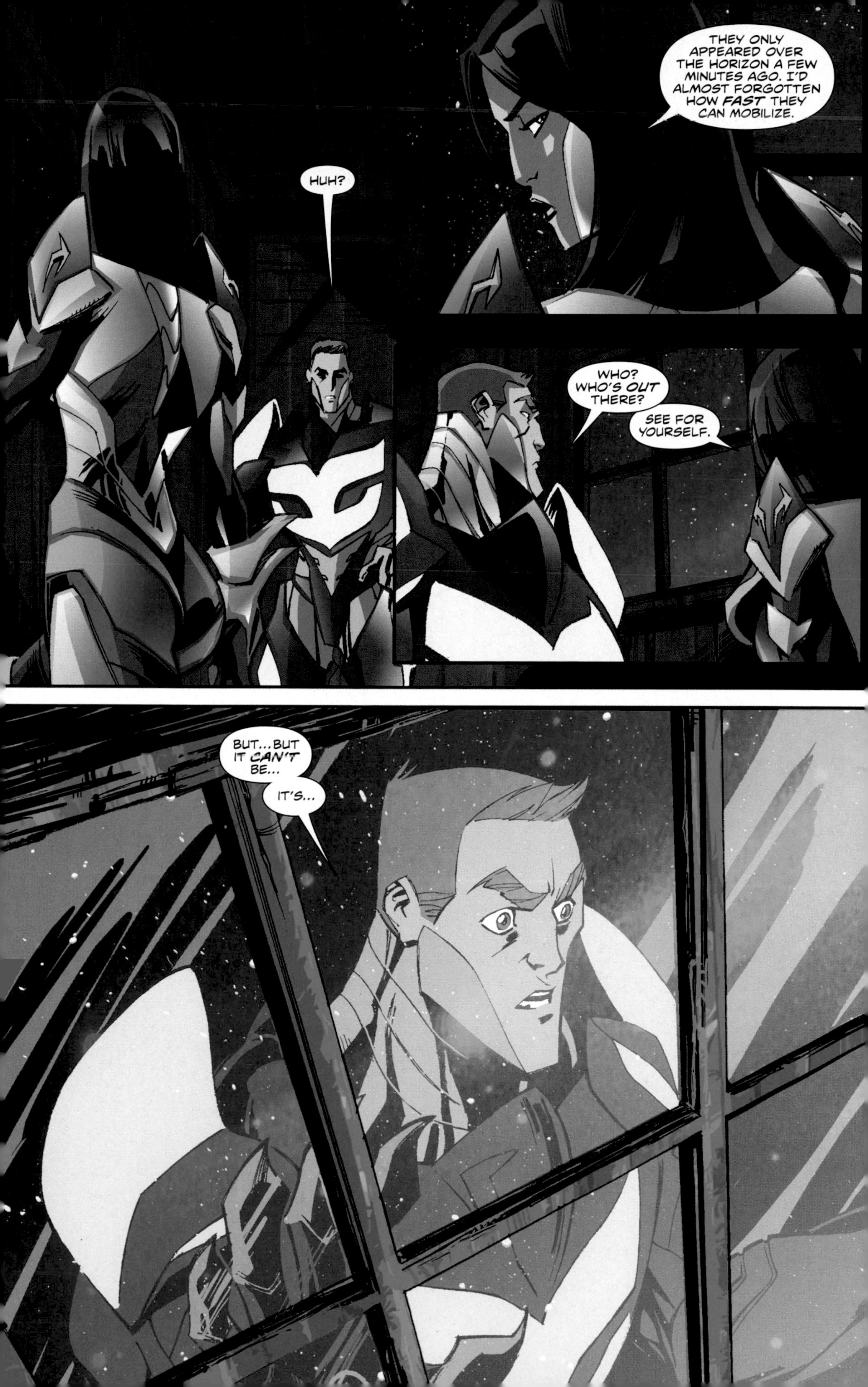
THEY ONLY APPEARED OVER THE HORIZON A FEW MINUTES AGO. I'D ALMOST FORGOTTEN HOW FAST THEY CAN MOBILIZE.
HUH?
WHO? WHO'S OUT THERE?
SEE FOR YOURSELF.
BUT... BUT IT CAN'T BE...
IT'S...

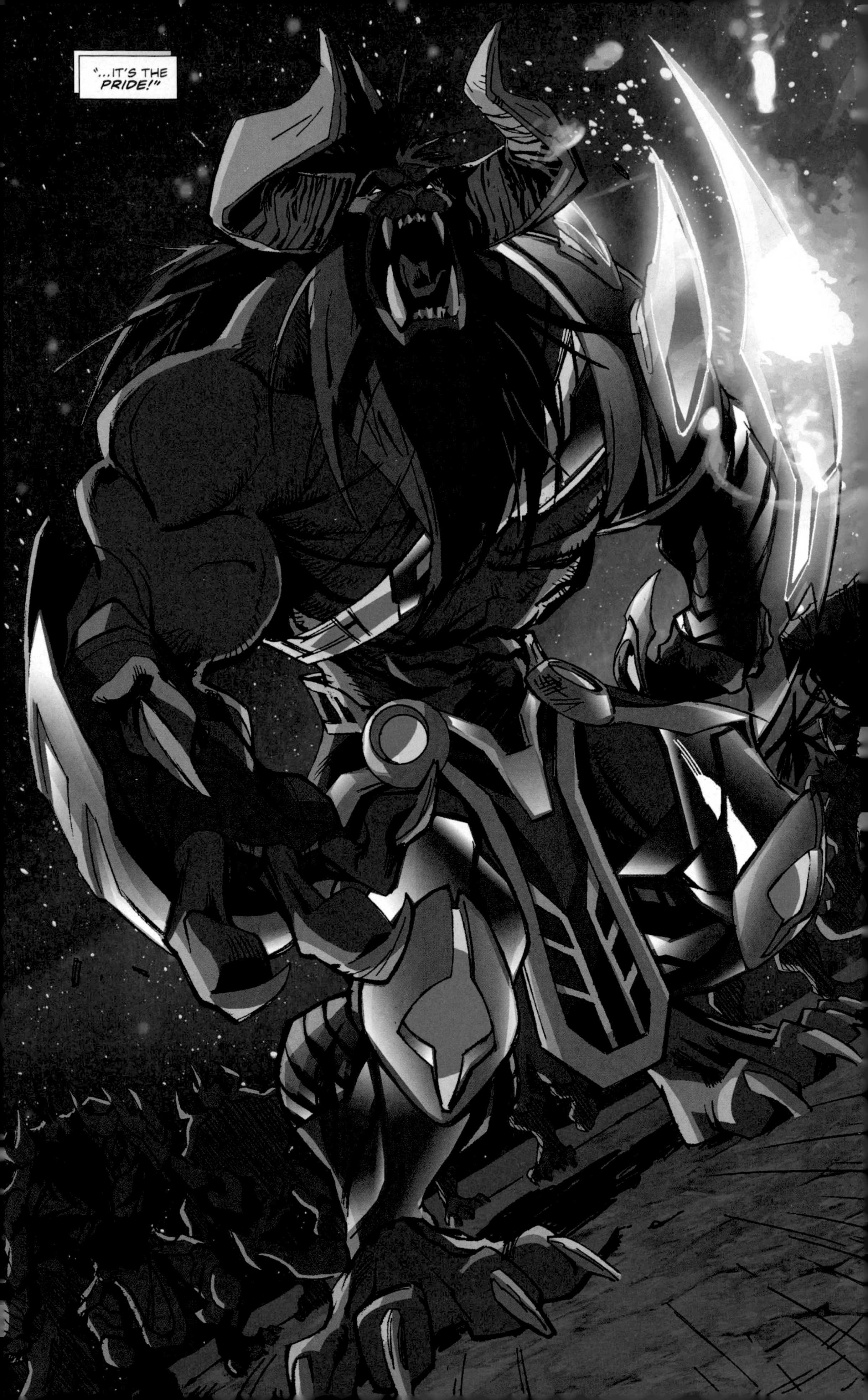
"...IT'S THE PRIDE!"

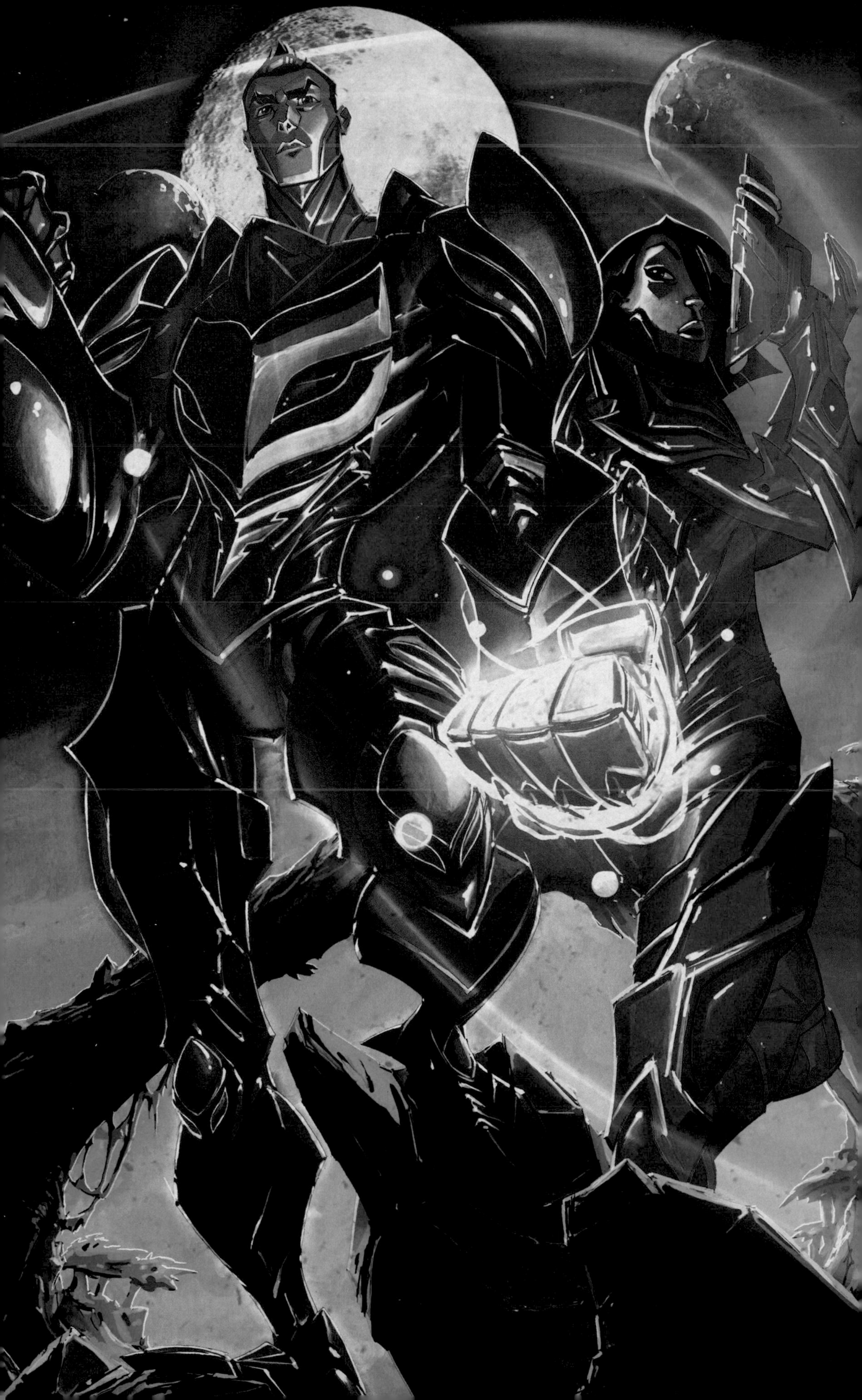

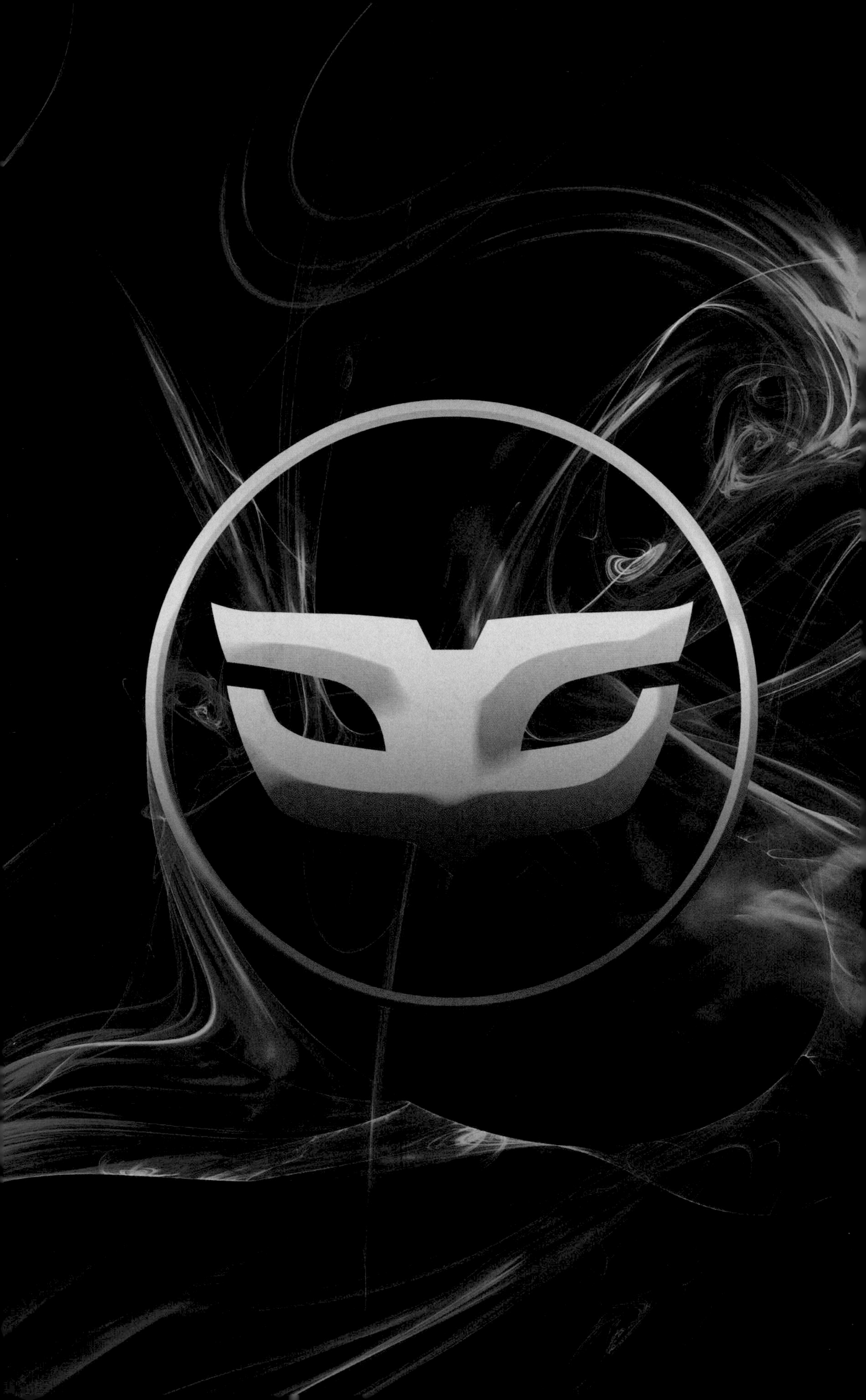

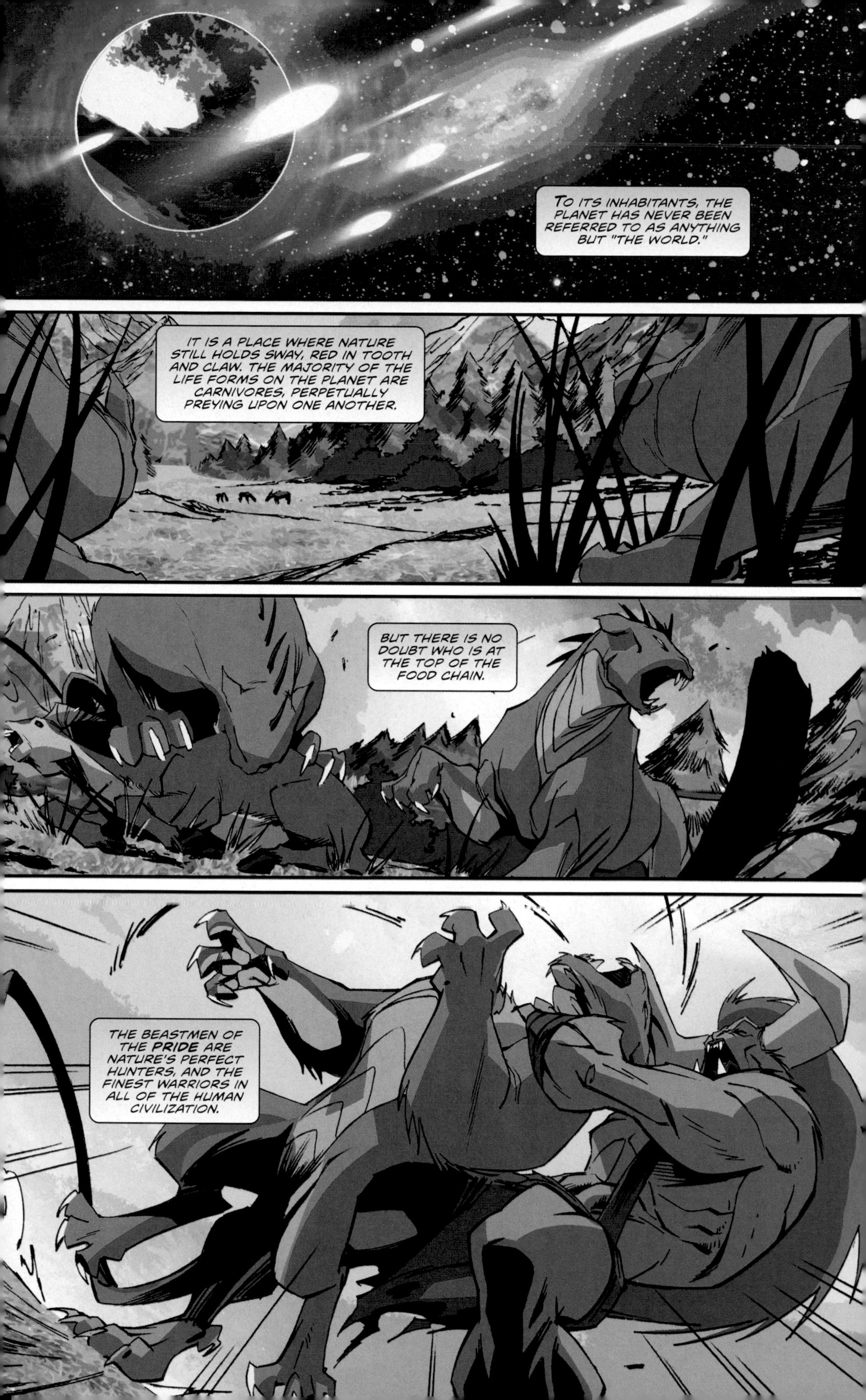

TO ITS INHABITANTS, THE PLANET HAS NEVER BEEN REFERRED TO AS ANYTHING BUT "THE WORLD."
IT IS A PLACE WHERE NATURE STILL HOLDS SWAY, RED IN TOOTH AND CLAW. THE MAJORITY OF THE LIFE FORMS ON THE PLANET ARE CARNIVORES, PERPETUALLY PREYING UPON ONE ANOTHER.
BUT THERE IS NO DOUBT WHO IS AT THE TOP OF THE FOOD CHAIN.
THE BEASTMEN OF THE **PRIDE** ARE NATURE'S PERFECT HUNTERS, AND THE FINEST WARRIORS IN ALL OF THE HUMAN CIVILIZATION.

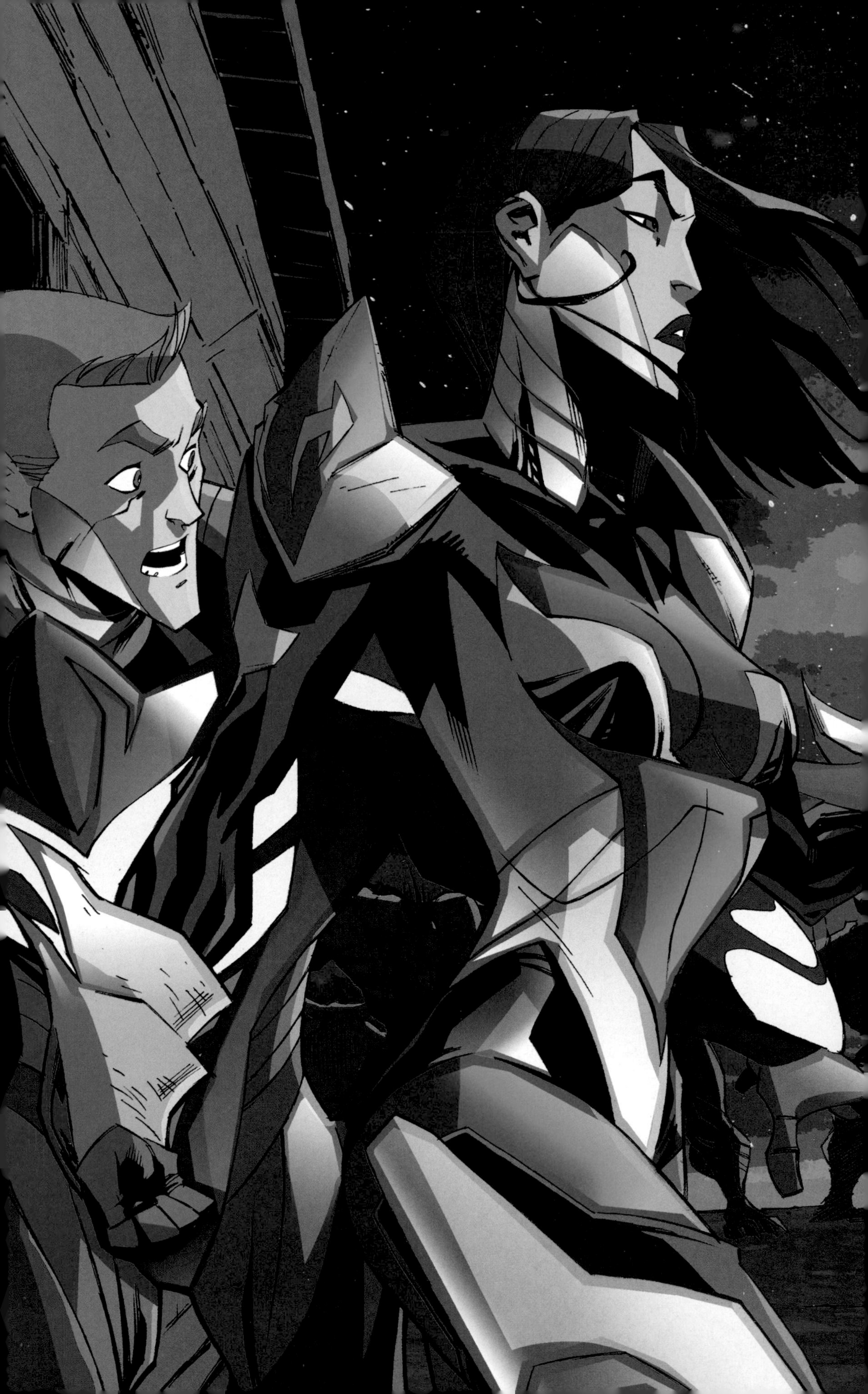

AT LEAST, THAT'S THE WAY IT IS IN MY STORIES.
I DON'T KNOW WHY I SHOULD BE SURPRISED THAT THE PRIDE IS REAL, JUST LIKE EVERYTHING ELSE IN MY MADE-UP WORLD SEEMS TO BE. BUT I AM, ALL THE SAME.
WHAT DO YOU WANT, MONGRELS?
HAND OVER THE HEIR TO THE HOUSE OF BIN AND WE MAY LET YOU LIVE, SHAPE-SHIFTER.
RESIST, AND YOU DIE WITH HIM.

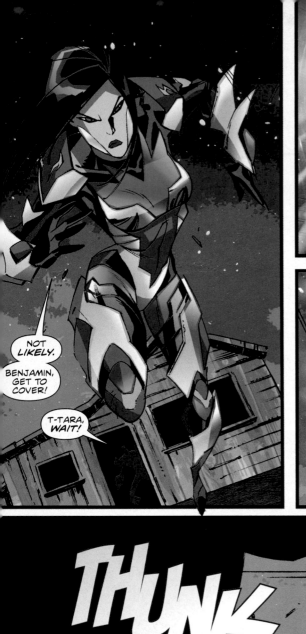

NOT *LIKELY.*

BENJAMIN, GET TO COVER!

T-TARA, WAIT!

KZZAK

THUNK

UNG.

OKAY. WHO'S NEXT?

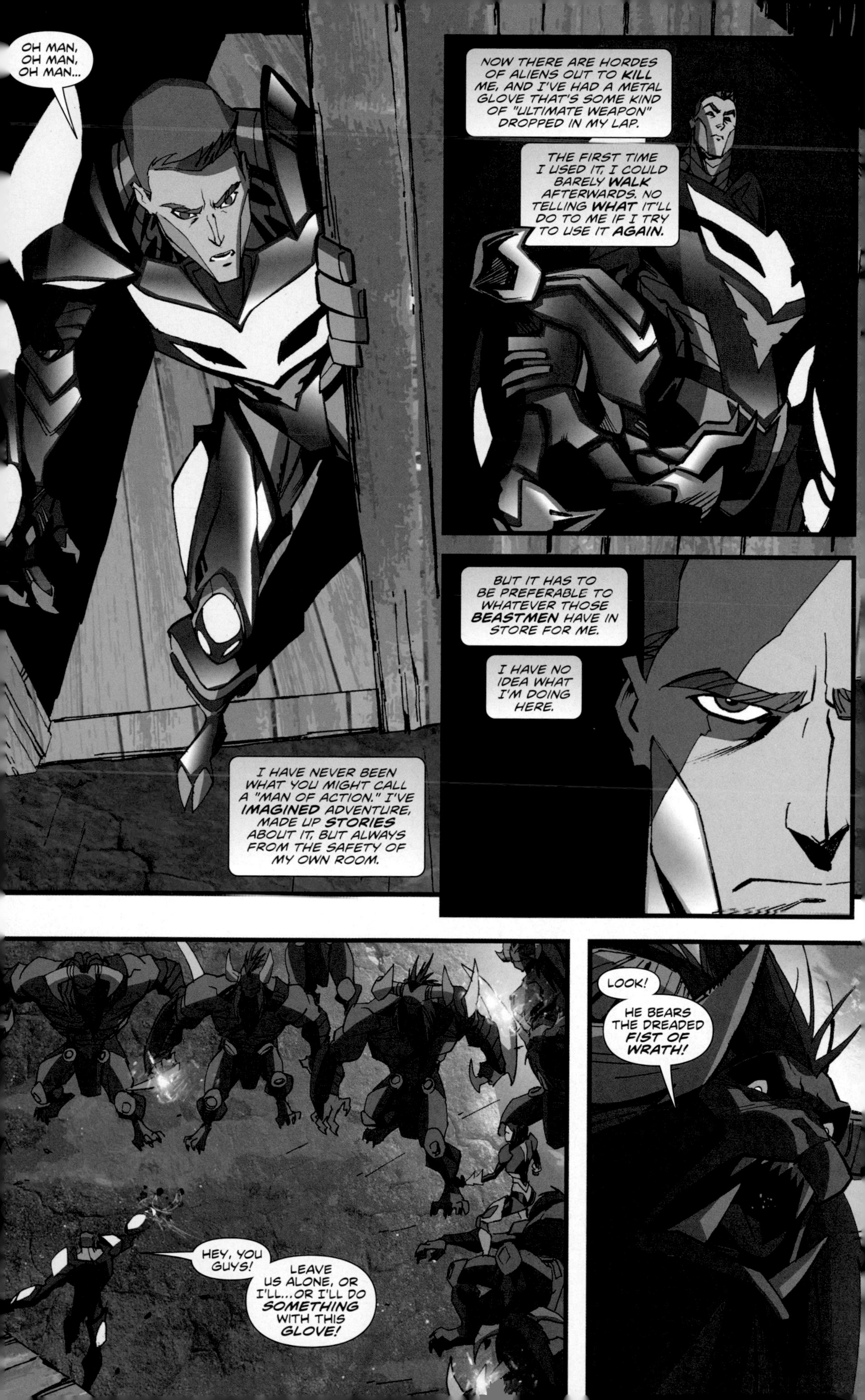
OH MAN, OH MAN, OH MAN...
I HAVE NEVER BEEN WHAT YOU MIGHT CALL A "MAN OF ACTION." I'VE IMAGINED ADVENTURE, MADE UP STORIES ABOUT IT, BUT ALWAYS FROM THE SAFETY OF MY OWN ROOM.
NOW THERE ARE HORDES OF ALIENS OUT TO KILL ME, AND I'VE HAD A METAL GLOVE THAT'S SOME KIND OF "ULTIMATE WEAPON" DROPPED IN MY LAP.
THE FIRST TIME I USED IT, I COULD BARELY WALK AFTERWARDS. NO TELLING WHAT IT'LL DO TO ME IF I TRY TO USE IT AGAIN.
BUT IT HAS TO BE PREFERABLE TO WHATEVER THOSE BEASTMEN HAVE IN STORE FOR ME.
I HAVE NO IDEA WHAT I'M DOING HERE.
HEY, YOU GUYS!
LEAVE US ALONE, OR I'LL...OR I'LL DO SOMETHING WITH THIS GLOVE!
LOOK!
HE BEARS THE DREADED FIST OF WRATH!

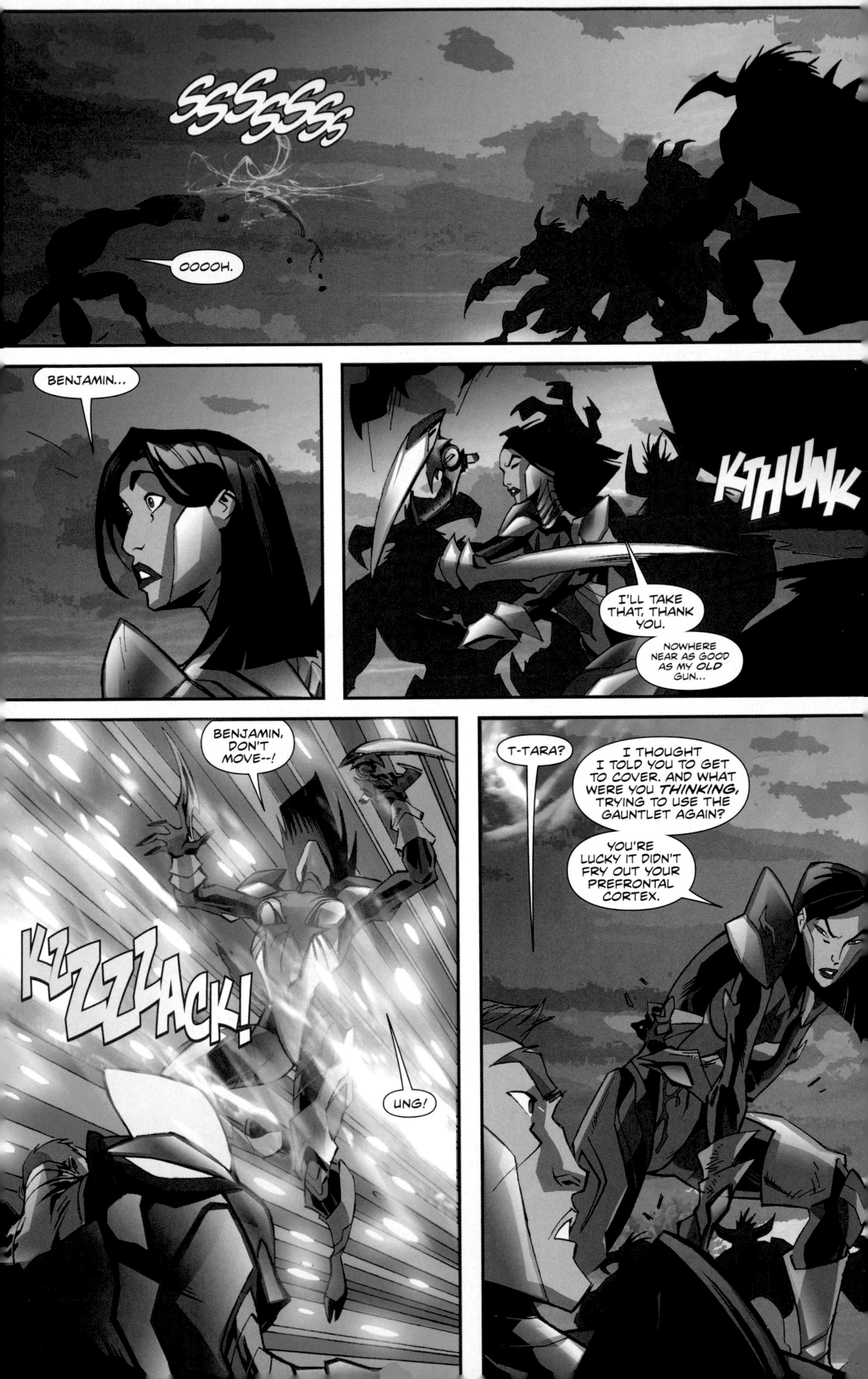
SSSSSSSS
OOOOH.
BENJAMIN...
KTHUNK
I'LL TAKE THAT, THANK YOU.
NOWHERE NEAR AS GOOD AS MY *OLD* GUN...
BENJAMIN, DON'T MOVE--!
KZZZZACK!
UNG!
T-TARA?
I THOUGHT I TOLD YOU TO GET TO COVER. AND WHAT WERE YOU *THINKING*, TRYING TO USE THE GAUNTLET AGAIN?
YOU'RE LUCKY IT DIDN'T FRY OUT YOUR PREFRONTAL CORTEX.

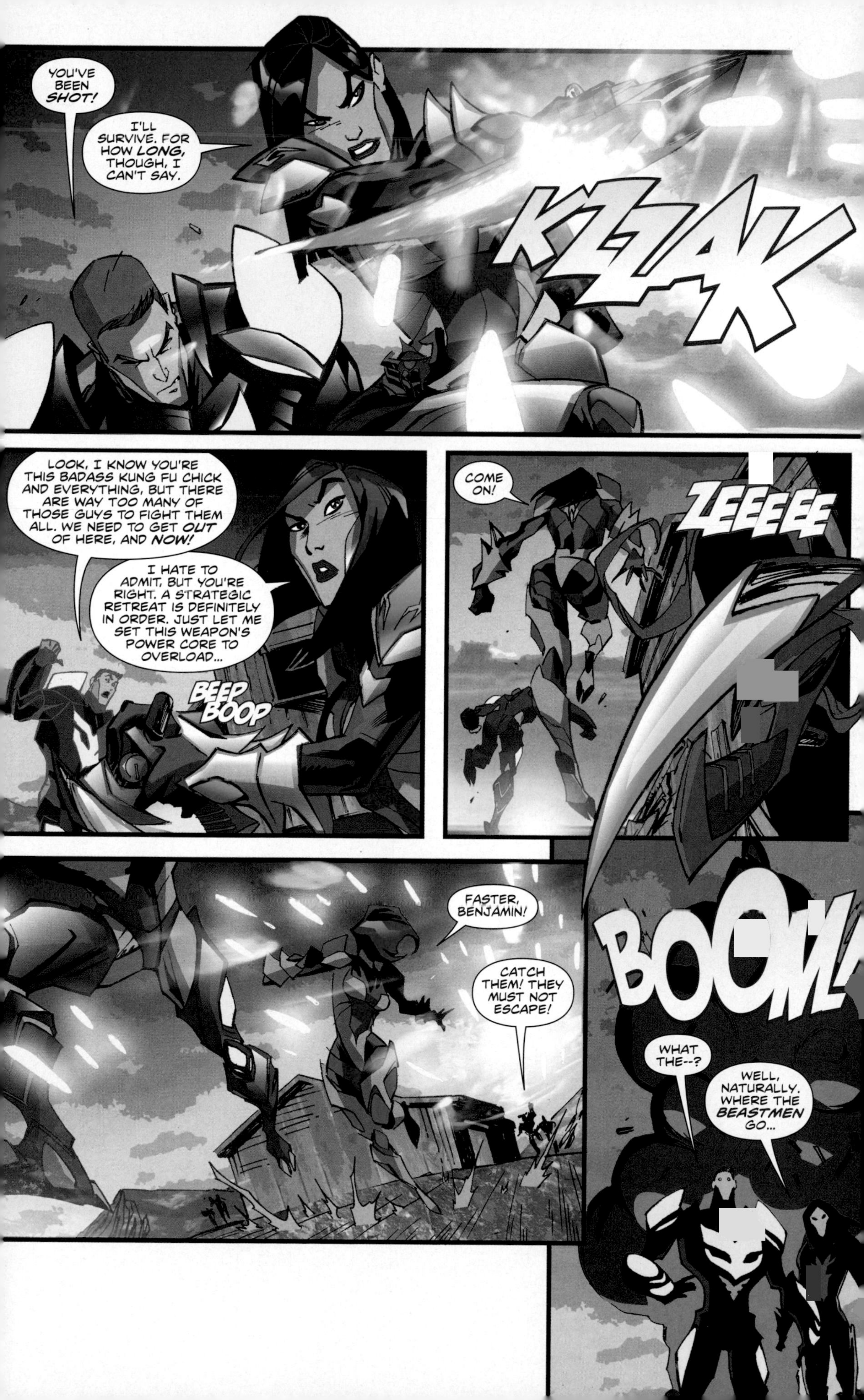
YOU'VE BEEN SHOT!
I'LL SURVIVE. FOR HOW LONG, THOUGH, I CAN'T SAY.
KZZAK
LOOK, I KNOW YOU'RE THIS BADASS KUNG FU CHICK AND EVERYTHING, BUT THERE ARE WAY TOO MANY OF THOSE GUYS TO FIGHT THEM ALL. WE NEED TO GET OUT OF HERE, AND NOW!
I HATE TO ADMIT, BUT YOU'RE RIGHT. A STRATEGIC RETREAT IS DEFINITELY IN ORDER. JUST LET ME SET THIS WEAPON'S POWER CORE TO OVERLOAD...
BEEP BOOP
COME ON!
ZEEEEE
FASTER, BENJAMIN!
CATCH THEM! THEY MUST NOT ESCAPE!
BOOM!
WHAT THE--?
WELL, NATURALLY. WHERE THE BEASTMEN GO...

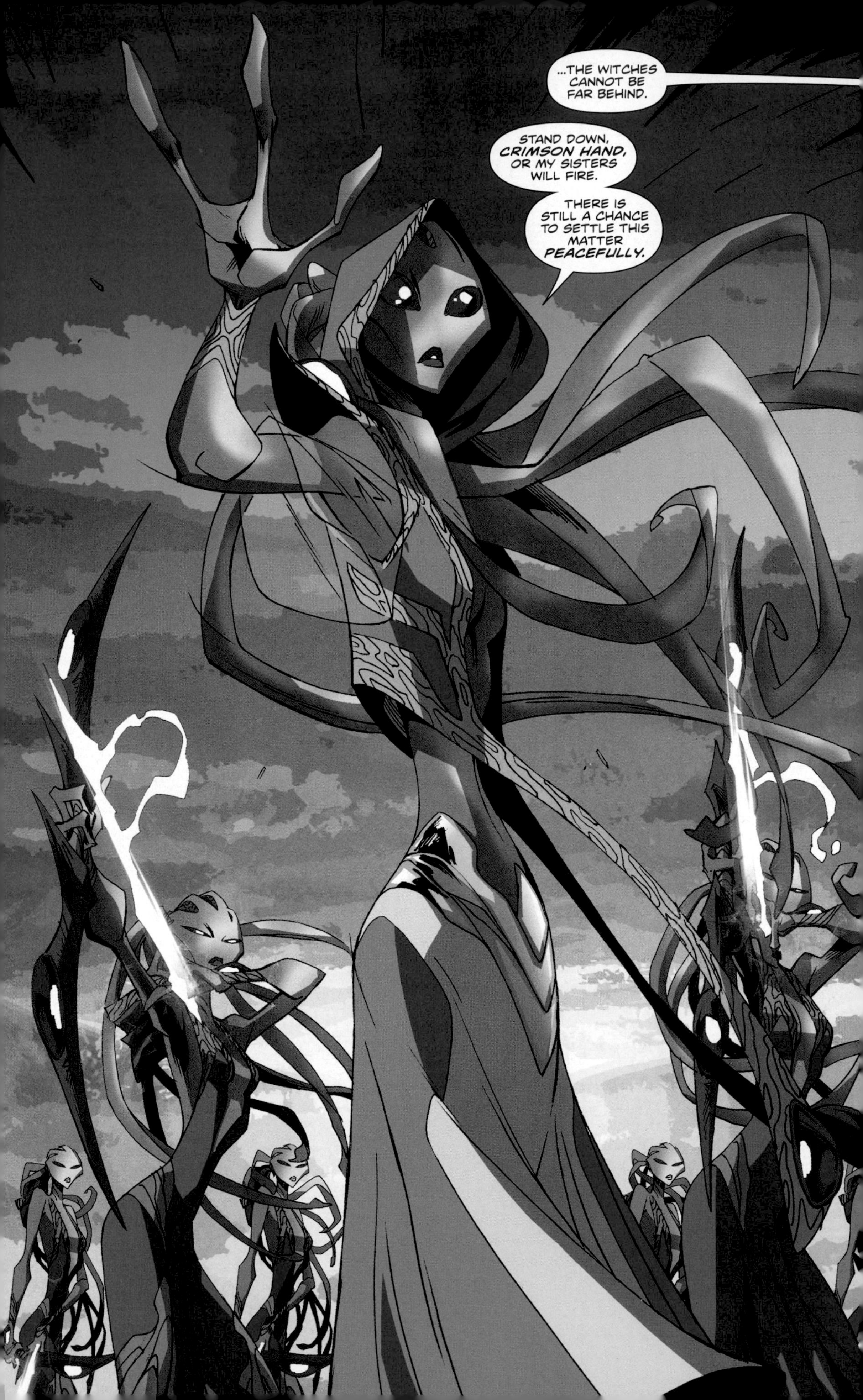
...THE WITCHES CANNOT BE FAR BEHIND.
STAND DOWN, *CRIMSON HAND,* OR MY SISTERS WILL FIRE.
THERE IS STILL A CHANCE TO SETTLE THIS MATTER *PEACEFULLY.*

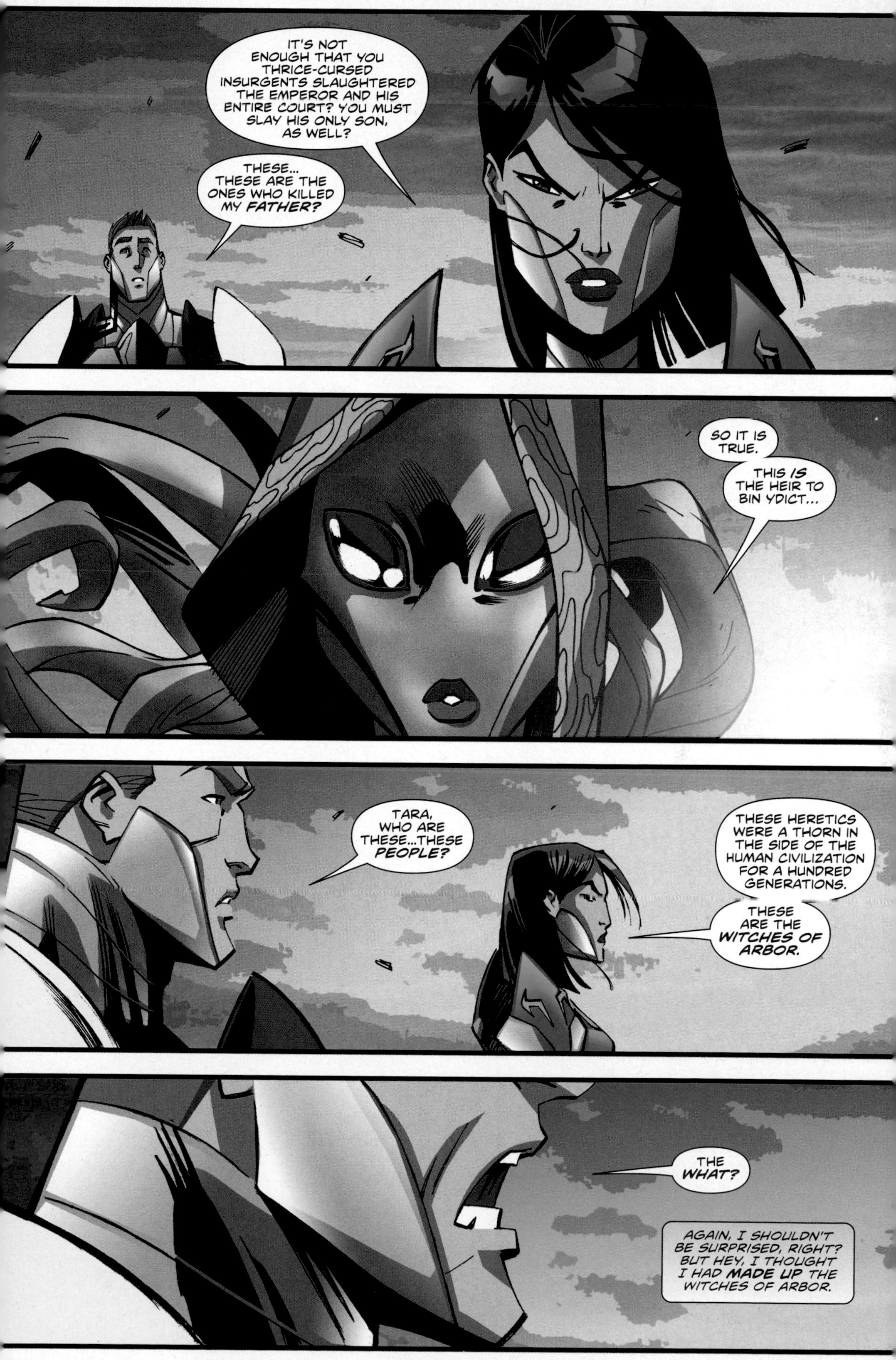
IT'S NOT ENOUGH THAT YOU THRICE-CURSED INSURGENTS SLAUGHTERED THE EMPEROR AND HIS ENTIRE COURT? YOU MUST SLAY HIS ONLY SON, AS WELL?
THESE... THESE ARE THE ONES WHO KILLED MY FATHER?
SO IT IS TRUE.
THIS IS THE HEIR TO BIN YDICT...
TARA, WHO ARE THESE...THESE PEOPLE?
THESE HERETICS WERE A THORN IN THE SIDE OF THE HUMAN CIVILIZATION FOR A HUNDRED GENERATIONS.
THESE ARE THE WITCHES OF ARBOR.
THE WHAT?
AGAIN, I SHOULDN'T BE SURPRISED, RIGHT? BUT HEY, I THOUGHT I HAD MADE UP THE WITCHES OF ARBOR.

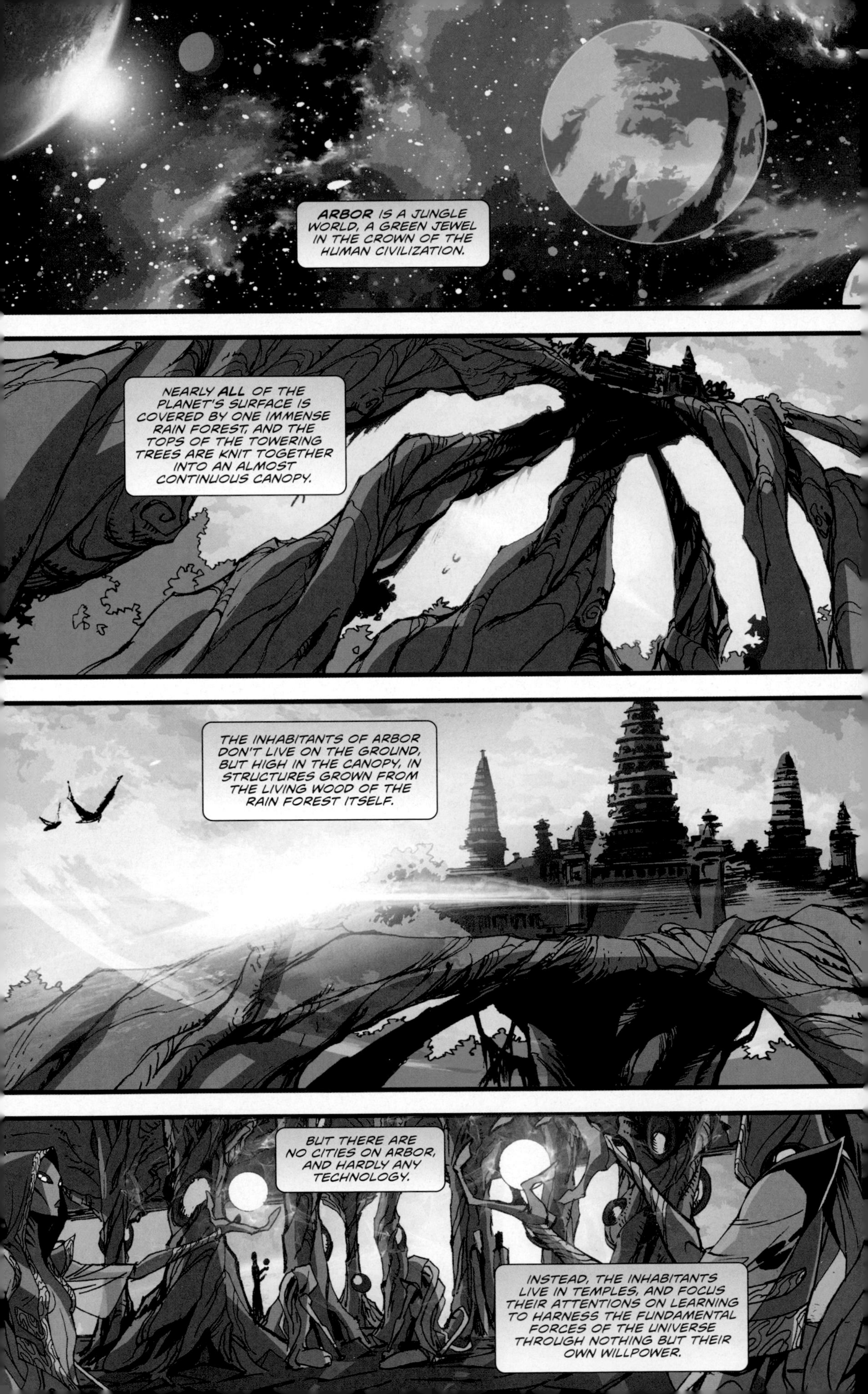
ARBOR IS A JUNGLE WORLD, A GREEN JEWEL IN THE CROWN OF THE HUMAN CIVILIZATION.
NEARLY ALL OF THE PLANET'S SURFACE IS COVERED BY ONE IMMENSE RAIN FOREST, AND THE TOPS OF THE TOWERING TREES ARE KNIT TOGETHER INTO AN ALMOST CONTINUOUS CANOPY.
THE INHABITANTS OF ARBOR DON'T LIVE ON THE GROUND, BUT HIGH IN THE CANOPY, IN STRUCTURES GROWN FROM THE LIVING WOOD OF THE RAIN FOREST ITSELF.
BUT THERE ARE NO CITIES ON ARBOR, AND HARDLY ANY TECHNOLOGY.
INSTEAD, THE INHABITANTS LIVE IN TEMPLES, AND FOCUS THEIR ATTENTIONS ON LEARNING TO HARNESS THE FUNDAMENTAL FORCES OF THE UNIVERSE THROUGH NOTHING BUT THEIR OWN WILLPOWER.

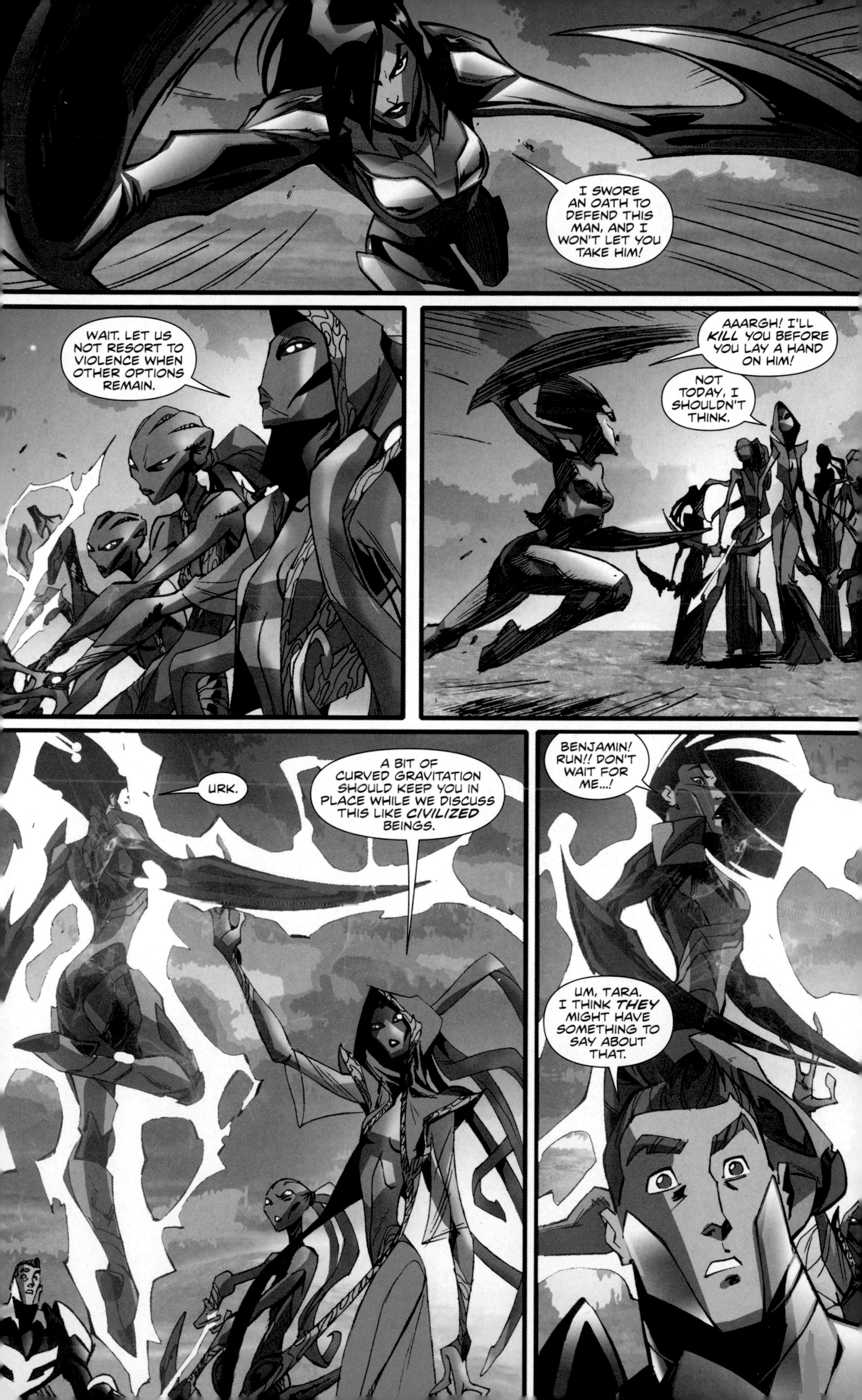
I SWORE AN OATH TO DEFEND THIS MAN, AND I WON'T LET YOU TAKE HIM!
WAIT. LET US NOT RESORT TO VIOLENCE WHEN OTHER OPTIONS REMAIN.
AAARGH! I'LL KILL YOU BEFORE YOU LAY A HAND ON HIM!
NOT TODAY, I SHOULDN'T THINK.
URK.
A BIT OF CURVED GRAVITATION SHOULD KEEP YOU IN PLACE WHILE WE DISCUSS THIS LIKE CIVILIZED BEINGS.
BENJAMIN! RUN!! DON'T WAIT FOR ME...!
UM, TARA. I THINK THEY MIGHT HAVE SOMETHING TO SAY ABOUT THAT.

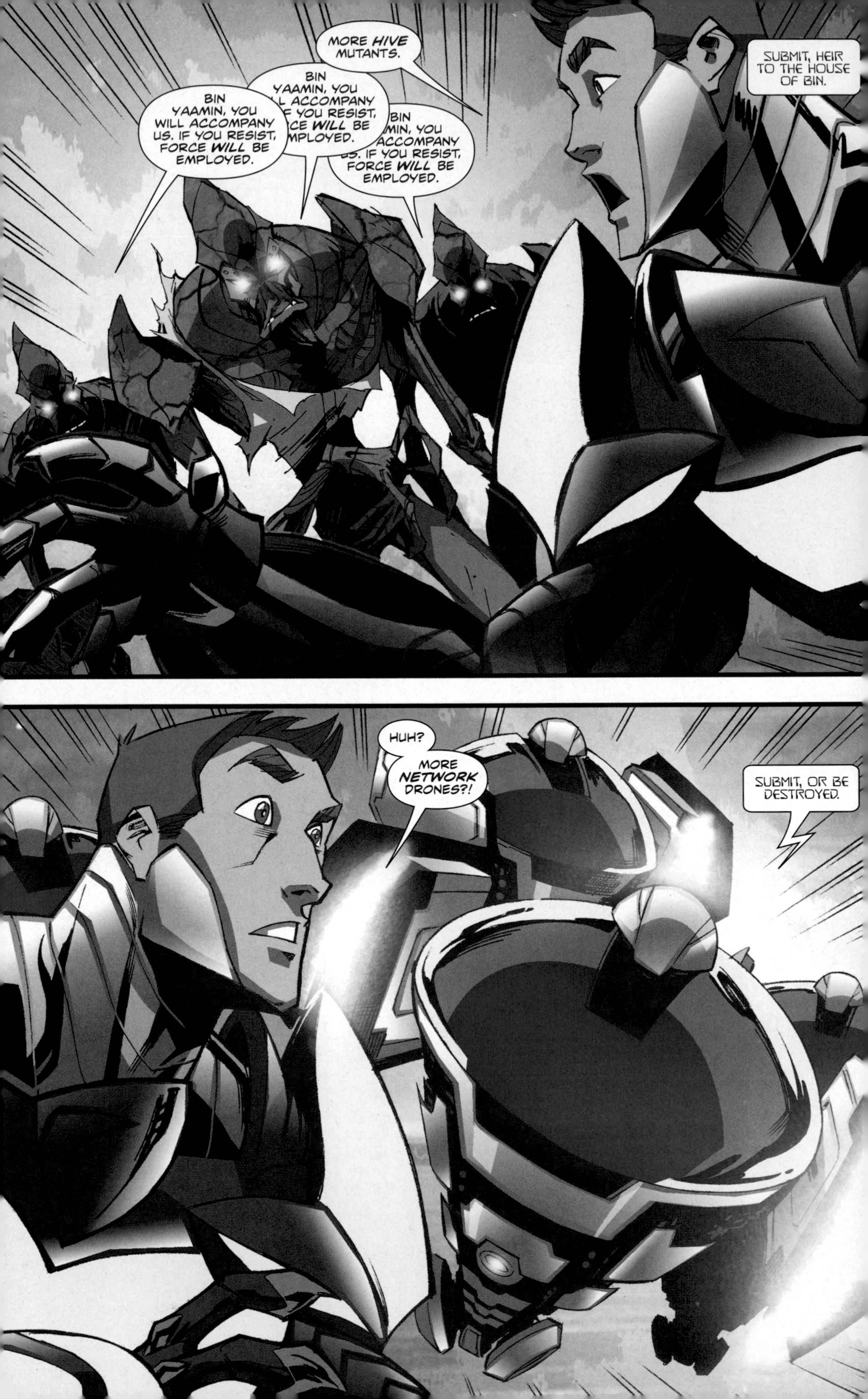
MORE HIVE MUTANTS.
BIN YAAMIN, YOU WILL ACCOMPANY US. IF YOU RESIST, FORCE WILL BE EMPLOYED.
BIN YAAMIN, YOU LL ACCOMPANY F YOU RESIST, ORCE WILL BE EMPLOYED.
BIN AMIN, YOU ACCOMPANY S. IF YOU RESIST, FORCE WILL BE EMPLOYED.
SUBMIT, HEIR TO THE HOUSE OF BIN.
HUH?
MORE NETWORK DRONES?!
SUBMIT, OR BE DESTROYED.

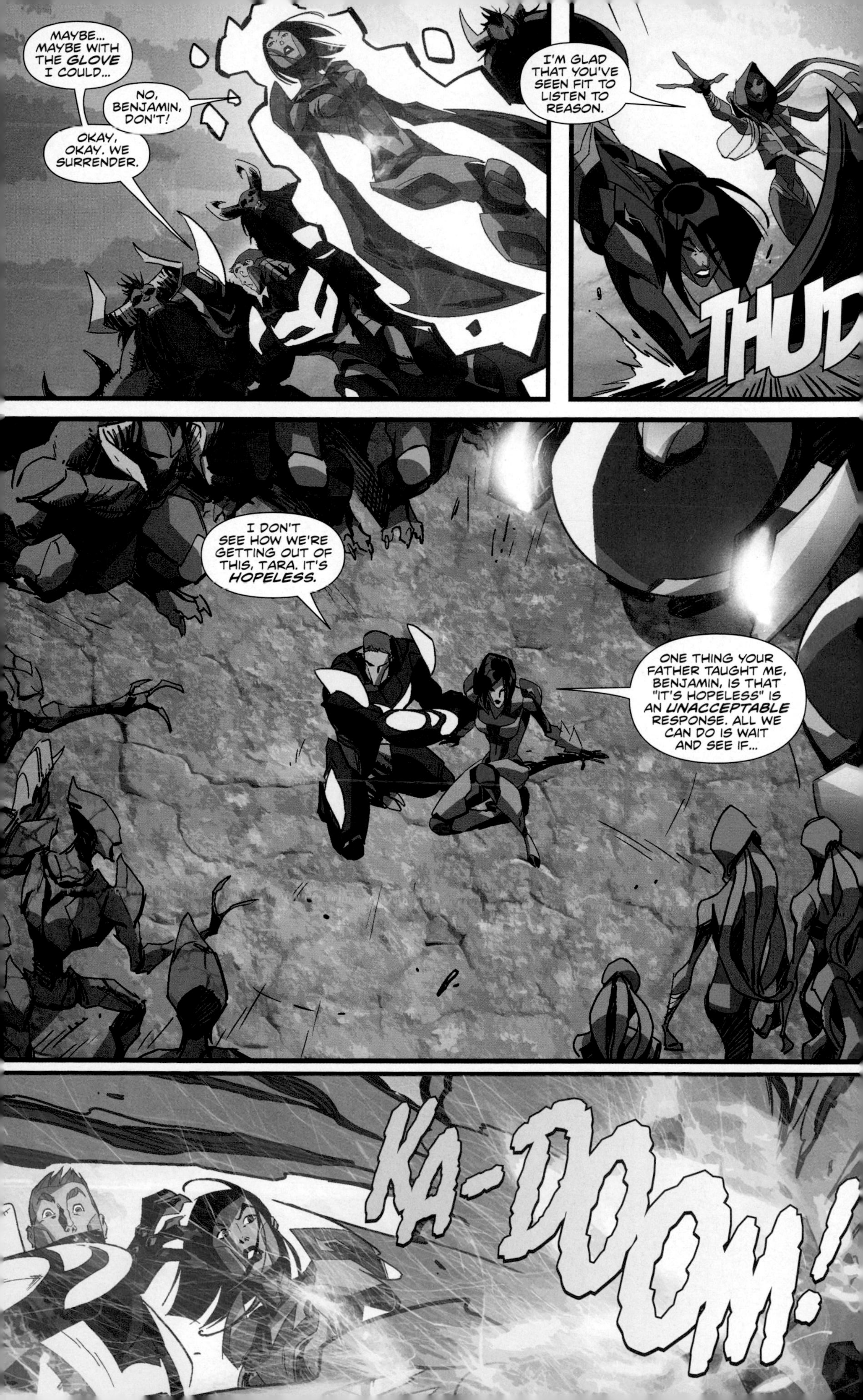
MAYBE... MAYBE WITH THE GLOVE I COULD...
NO, BENJAMIN, DON'T!
OKAY, OKAY. WE SURRENDER.
I'M GLAD THAT YOU'VE SEEN FIT TO LISTEN TO REASON.
THUD
I DON'T SEE HOW WE'RE GETTING OUT OF THIS, TARA. IT'S HOPELESS.
ONE THING YOUR FATHER TAUGHT ME, BENJAMIN, IS THAT "IT'S HOPELESS" IS AN UNACCEPTABLE RESPONSE. ALL WE CAN DO IS WAIT AND SEE IF...
KA-DOOOM!

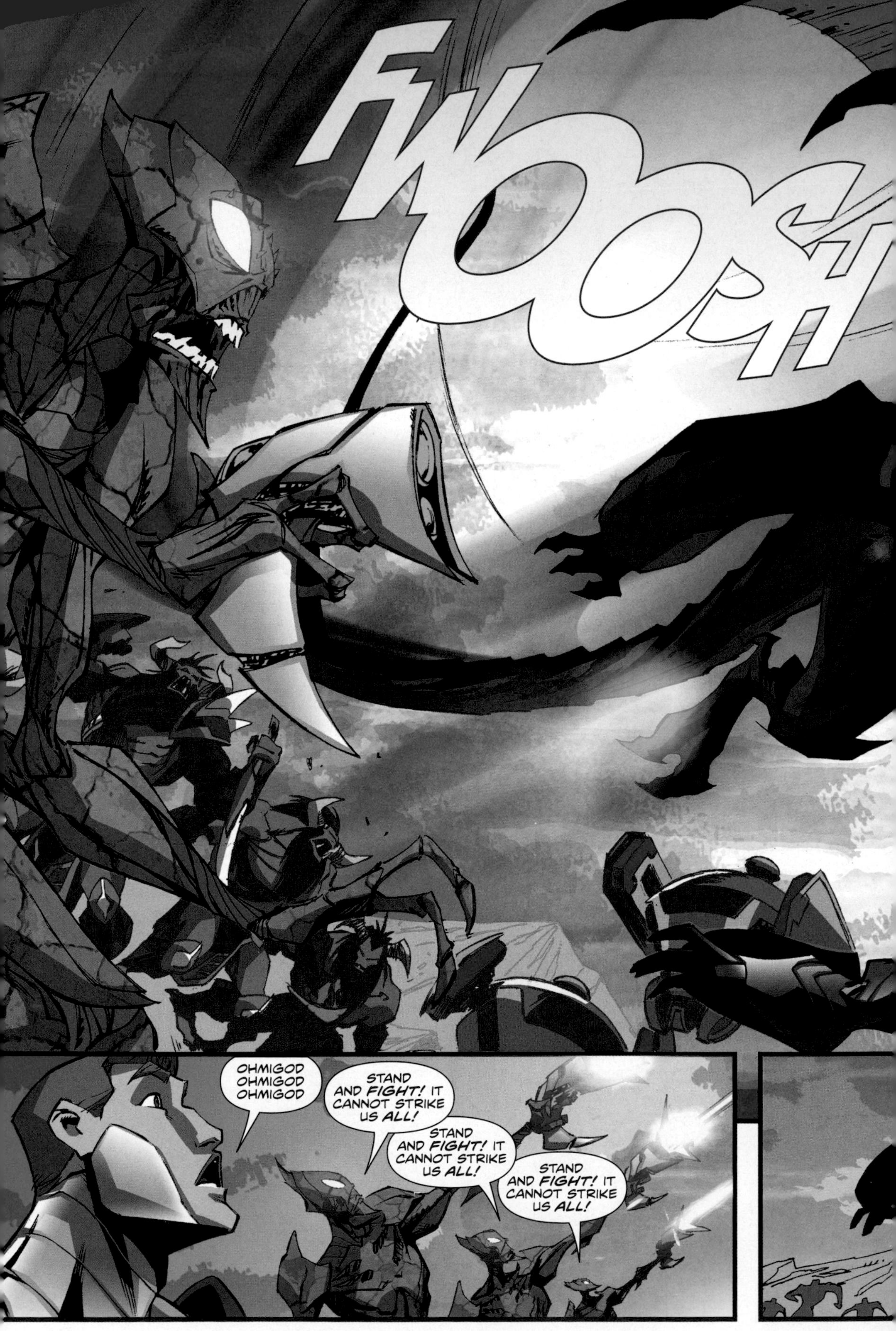
FWOOSH
OHMIGOD OHMIGOD OHMIGOD
STAND AND FIGHT! IT CANNOT STRIKE US ALL!
STAND AND FIGHT! IT CANNOT STRIKE US ALL!
STAND AND FIGHT! IT CANNOT STRIKE US ALL!

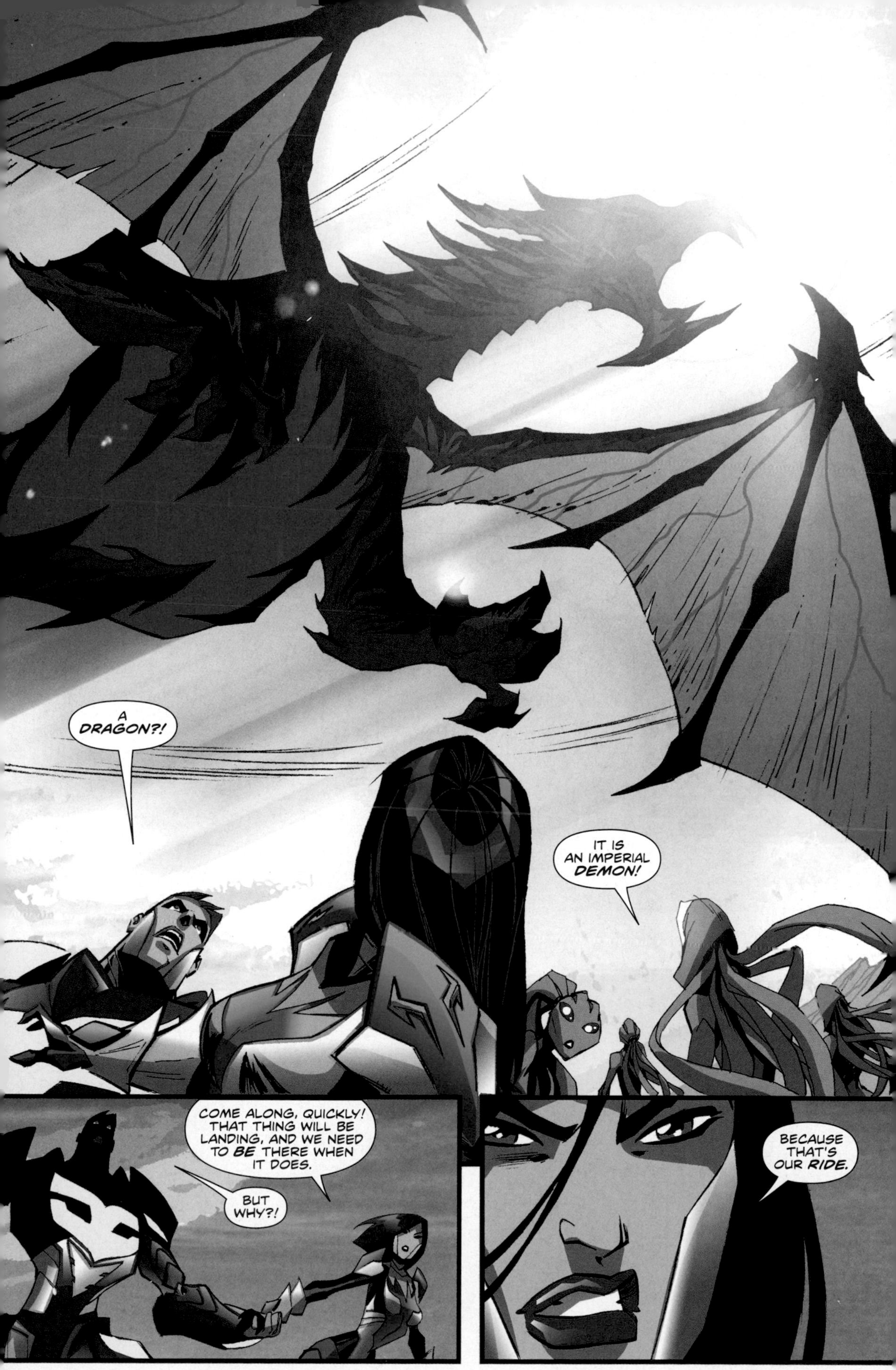
A DRAGON?!
IT IS AN IMPERIAL DEMON!
COME ALONG, QUICKLY! THAT THING WILL BE LANDING, AND WE NEED TO BE THERE WHEN IT DOES.
BUT WHY?!
BECAUSE THAT'S OUR RIDE.

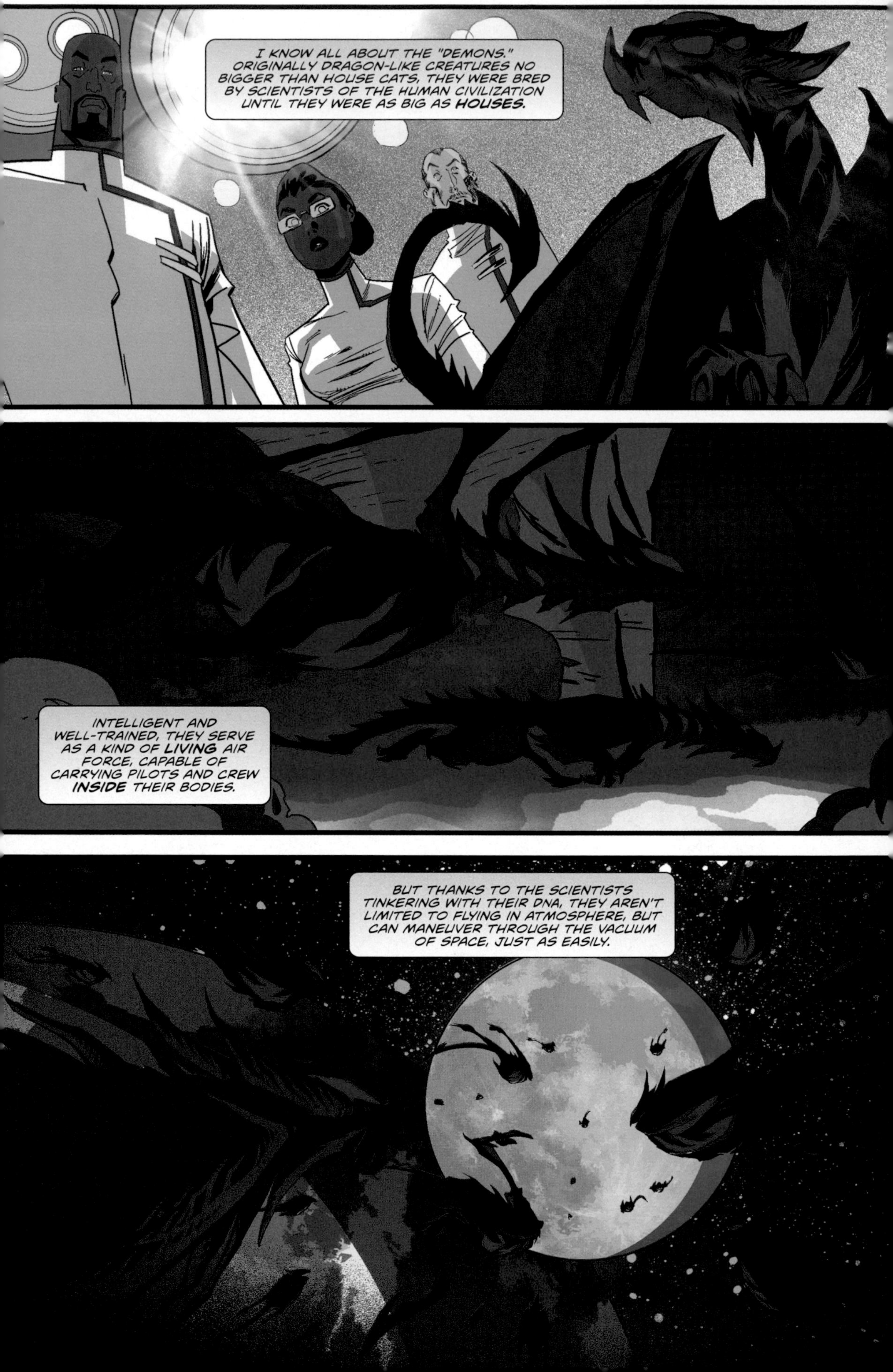
I KNOW ALL ABOUT THE "DEMONS." ORIGINALLY DRAGON-LIKE CREATURES NO BIGGER THAN HOUSE CATS, THEY WERE BRED BY SCIENTISTS OF THE HUMAN CIVILIZATION UNTIL THEY WERE AS BIG AS **HOUSES.**
INTELLIGENT AND WELL-TRAINED, THEY SERVE AS A KIND OF **LIVING** AIR FORCE, CAPABLE OF CARRYING PILOTS AND CREW **INSIDE** THEIR BODIES.
BUT THANKS TO THE SCIENTISTS TINKERING WITH THEIR DNA, THEY AREN'T LIMITED TO FLYING IN ATMOSPHERE, BUT CAN MANEUVER THROUGH THE VACUUM OF SPACE, JUST AS EASILY.

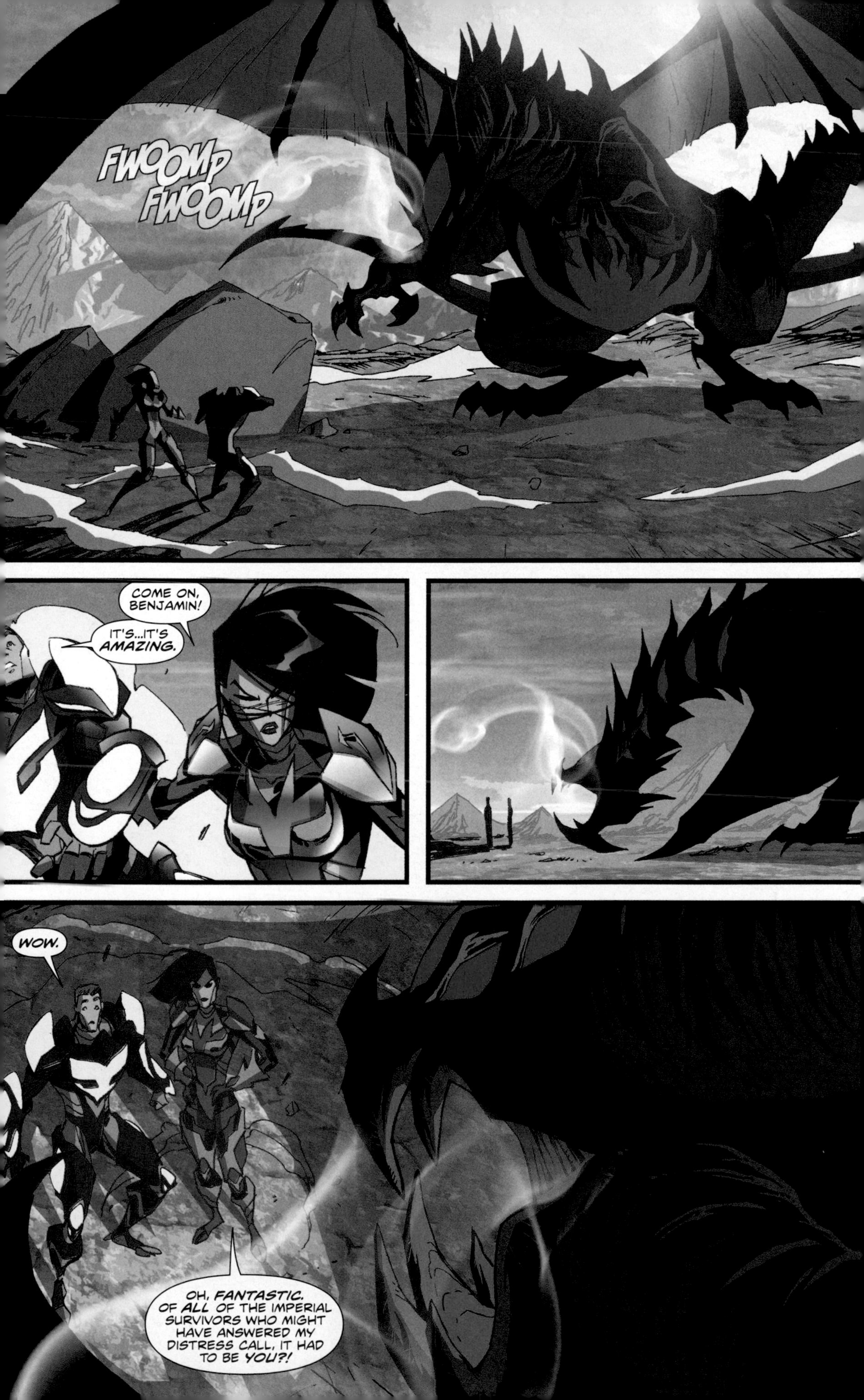
FWOOMP FWOOMP
COME ON, BENJAMIN!
IT'S...IT'S AMAZING.
WOW.
OH, FANTASTIC. OF ALL OF THE IMPERIAL SURVIVORS WHO MIGHT HAVE ANSWERED MY DISTRESS CALL, IT HAD TO BE YOU?!

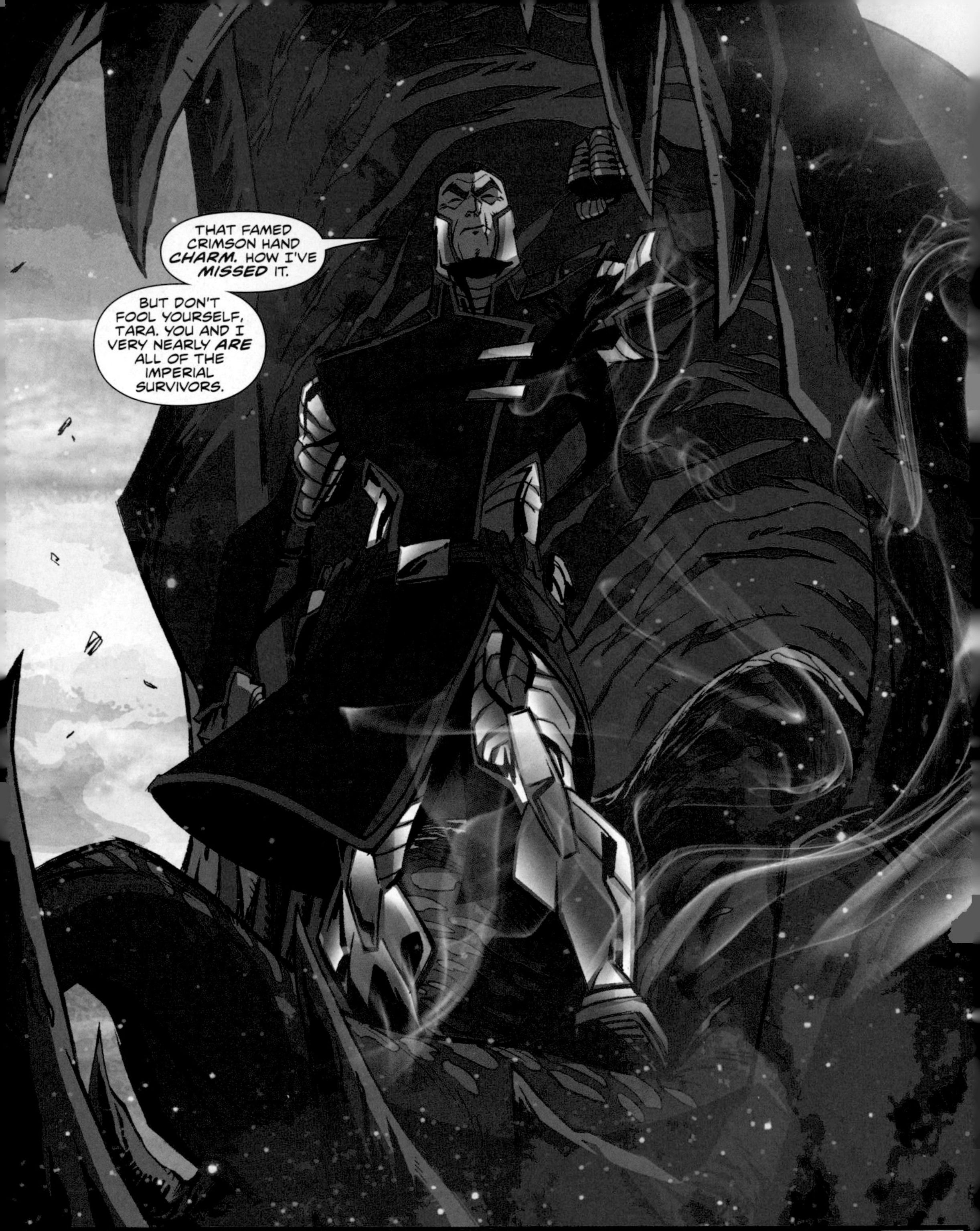
THAT FAMED CRIMSON HAND CHARM. HOW I'VE MISSED IT.
BUT DON'T FOOL YOURSELF, TARA. YOU AND I VERY NEARLY ARE ALL OF THE IMPERIAL SURVIVORS.

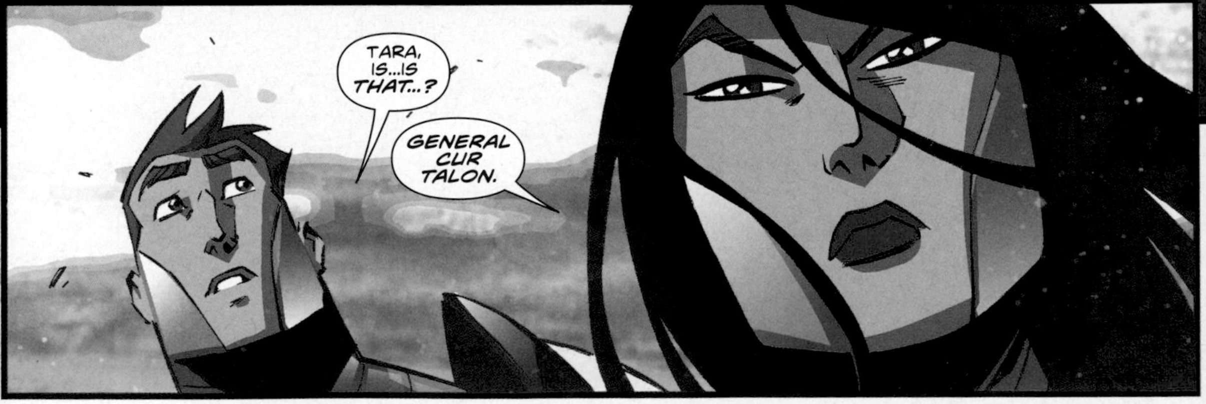
TARA, IS...IS THAT...?
GENERAL CUR TALON.

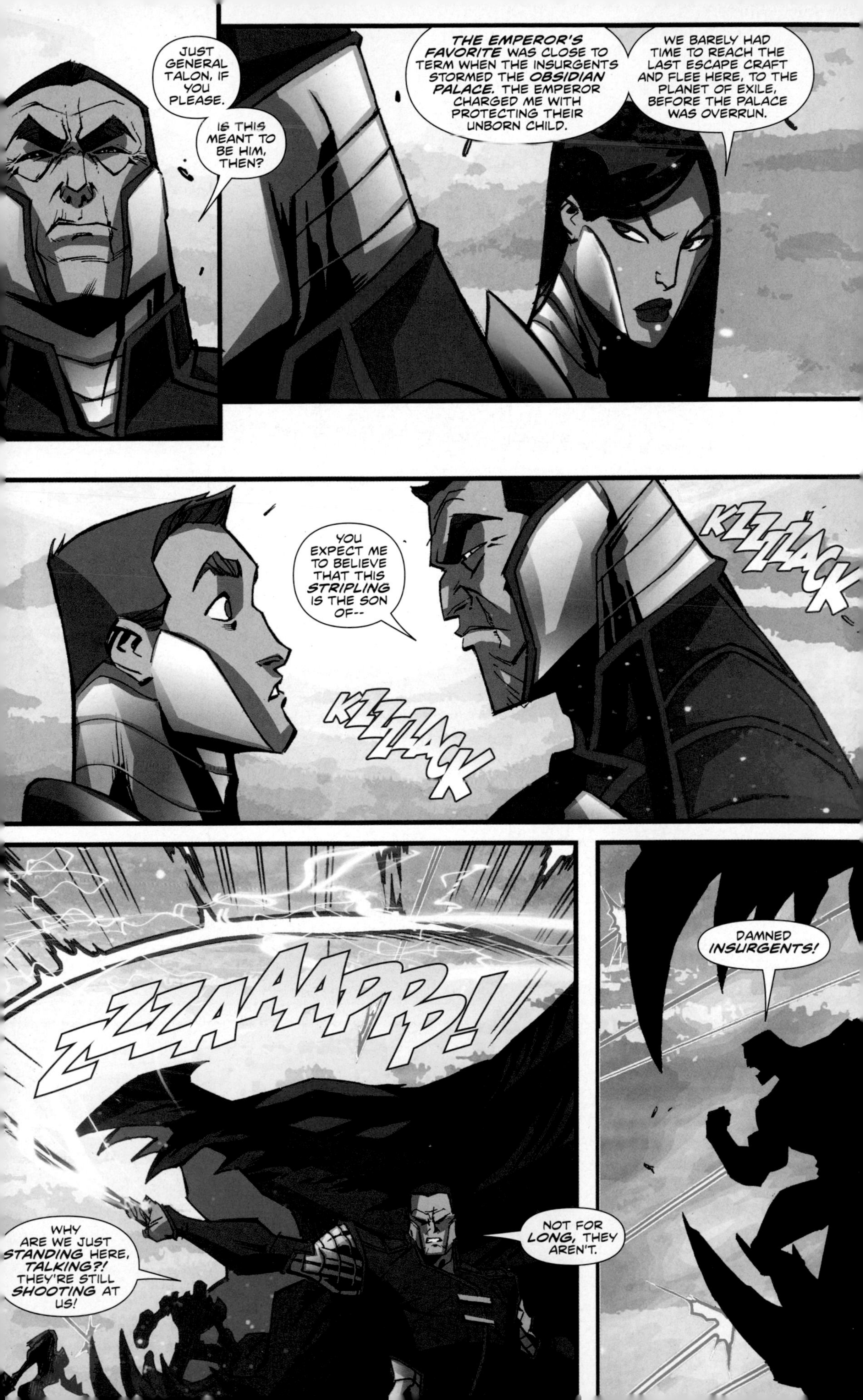
JUST GENERAL TALON, IF YOU PLEASE.
IS THIS MEANT TO BE HIM, THEN?
THE EMPEROR'S FAVORITE WAS CLOSE TO TERM WHEN THE INSURGENTS STORMED THE OBSIDIAN PALACE. THE EMPEROR CHARGED ME WITH PROTECTING THEIR UNBORN CHILD.
WE BARELY HAD TIME TO REACH THE LAST ESCAPE CRAFT AND FLEE HERE, TO THE PLANET OF EXILE, BEFORE THE PALACE WAS OVERRUN.
YOU EXPECT ME TO BELIEVE THAT THIS STRIPLING IS THE SON OF--
KZZZLACK
KZZZLACK
ZZZAAAPPP!
WHY ARE WE JUST STANDING HERE, TALKING?! THEY'RE STILL SHOOTING AT US!
NOT FOR LONG, THEY AREN'T.
DAMNED INSURGENTS!

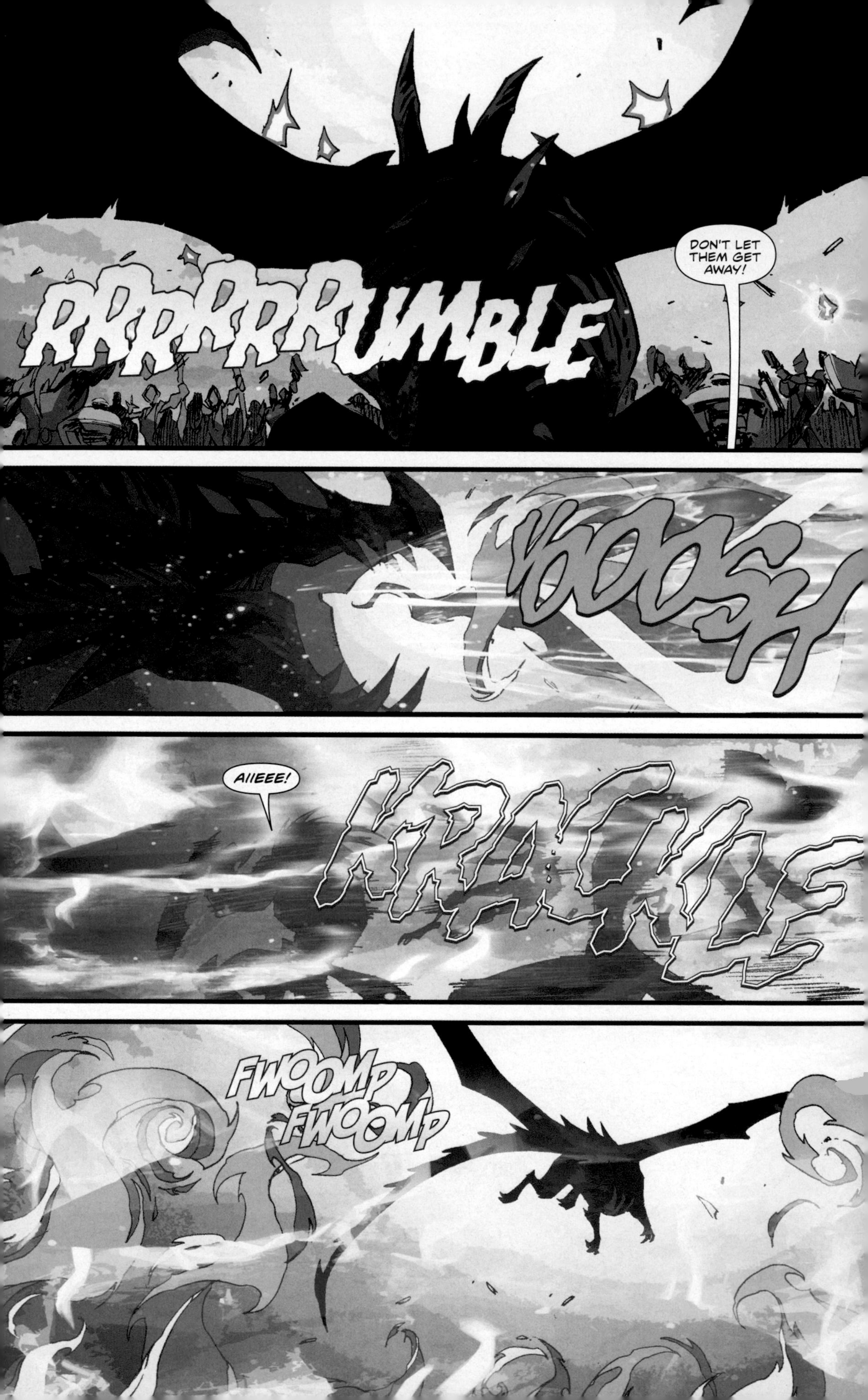
RRRRRRUMBLE
DON'T LET THEM GET AWAY!
WOOOSH
AIIEEE!
KRACKLE
FWOOMP
FWOOMP

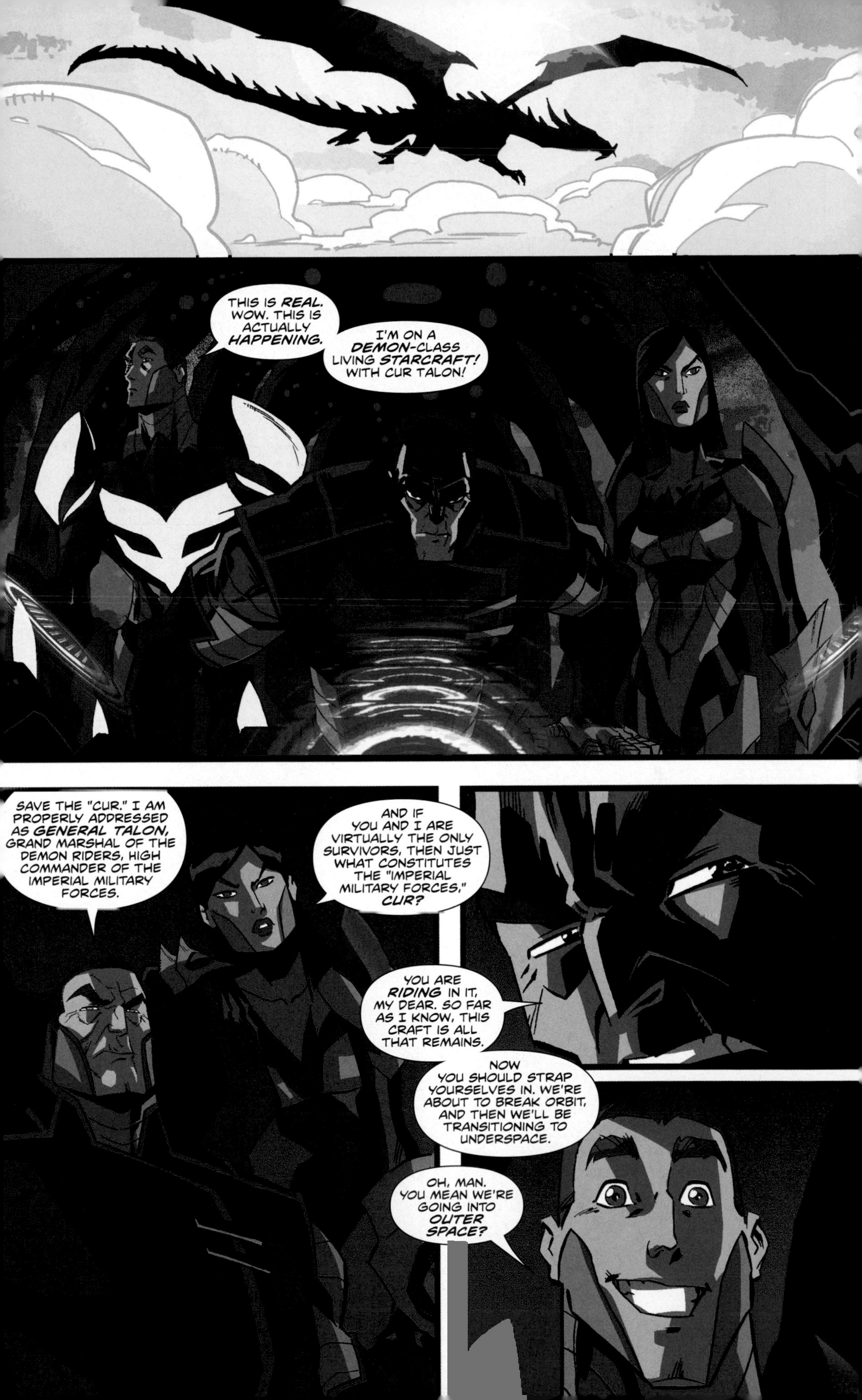
THIS IS REAL. WOW. THIS IS ACTUALLY HAPPENING.
I'M ON A DEMON-CLASS LIVING STARCRAFT! WITH CUR TALON!
SAVE THE "CUR." I AM PROPERLY ADDRESSED AS GENERAL TALON, GRAND MARSHAL OF THE DEMON RIDERS, HIGH COMMANDER OF THE IMPERIAL MILITARY FORCES.
AND IF YOU AND I ARE VIRTUALLY THE ONLY SURVIVORS, THEN JUST WHAT CONSTITUTES THE "IMPERIAL MILITARY FORCES," CUR?
YOU ARE RIDING IN IT, MY DEAR. SO FAR AS I KNOW, THIS CRAFT IS ALL THAT REMAINS.
NOW YOU SHOULD STRAP YOURSELVES IN. WE'RE ABOUT TO BREAK ORBIT, AND THEN WE'LL BE TRANSITIONING TO UNDERSPACE.
OH, MAN. YOU MEAN WE'RE GOING INTO OUTER SPACE?

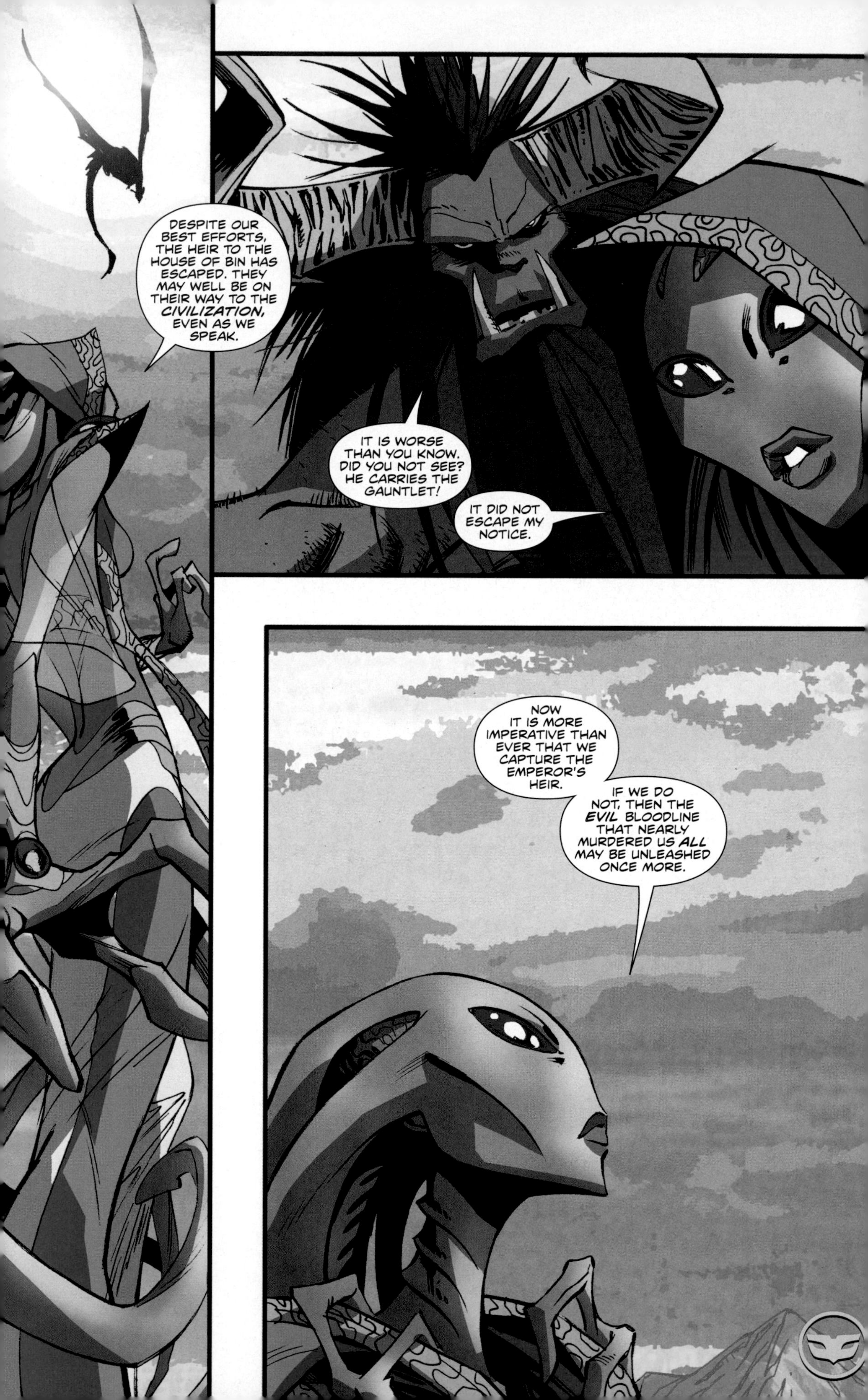
DESPITE OUR BEST EFFORTS, THE HEIR TO THE HOUSE OF BIN HAS ESCAPED. THEY MAY WELL BE ON THEIR WAY TO THE *CIVILIZATION*, EVEN AS WE SPEAK.
IT IS WORSE THAN YOU KNOW. DID YOU NOT SEE? HE CARRIES THE GAUNTLET!
IT DID NOT ESCAPE MY NOTICE.
NOW IT IS MORE IMPERATIVE THAN EVER THAT WE CAPTURE THE EMPEROR'S HEIR.
IF WE DO NOT, THEN THE *EVIL* BLOODLINE THAT NEARLY MURDERED US *ALL* MAY BE UNLEASHED ONCE MORE.

STARBORN

STAN LEE

CHRIS ROBERSON

KHARY RANDOLPH

MATTEO SCALERA

VOLUME TWO

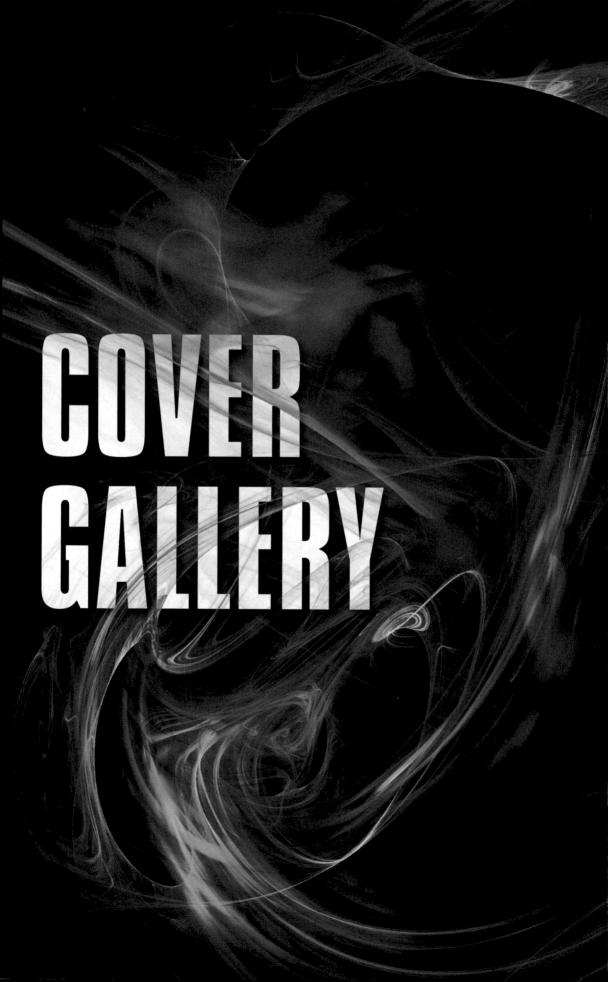

COVER GALLERY

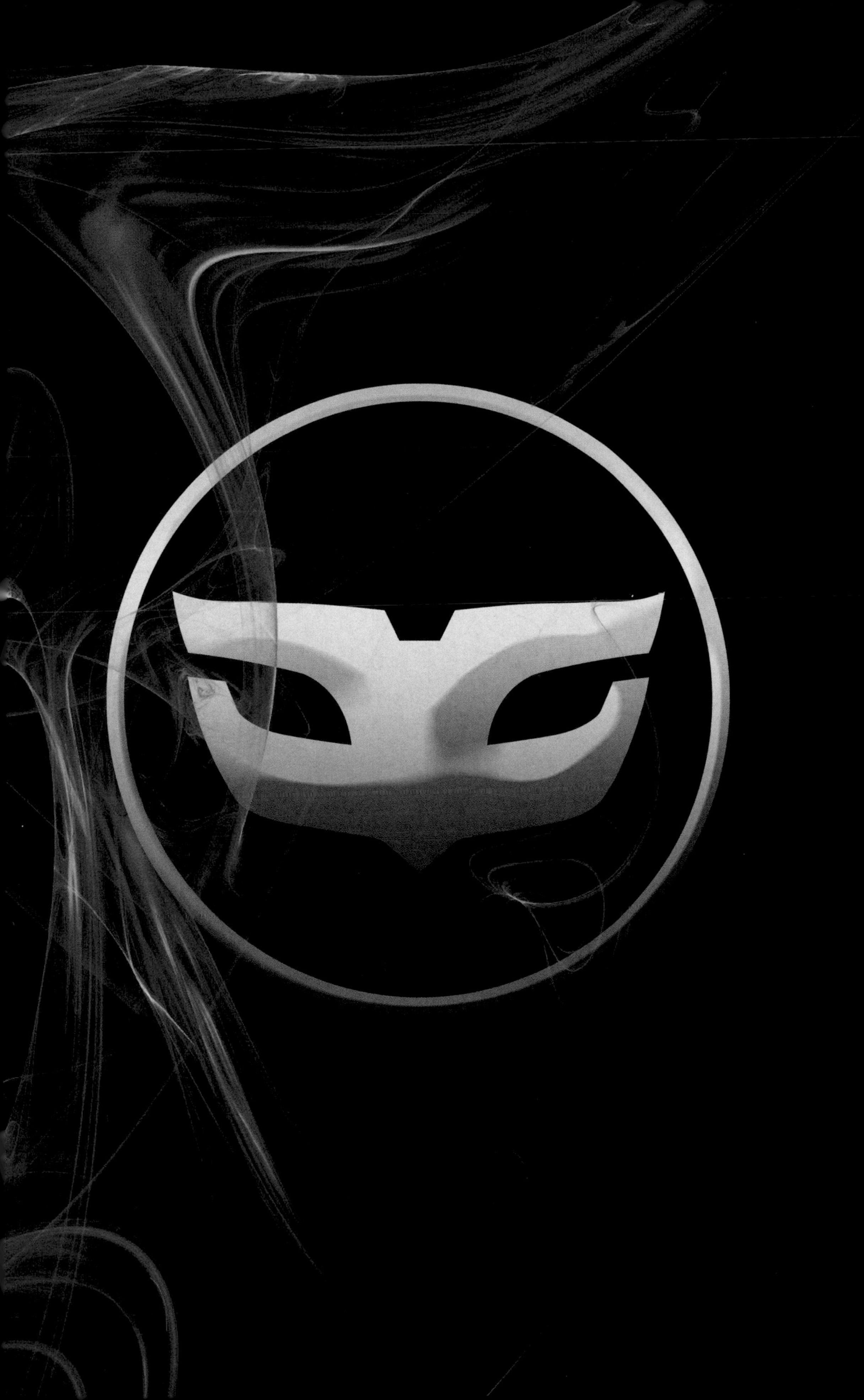

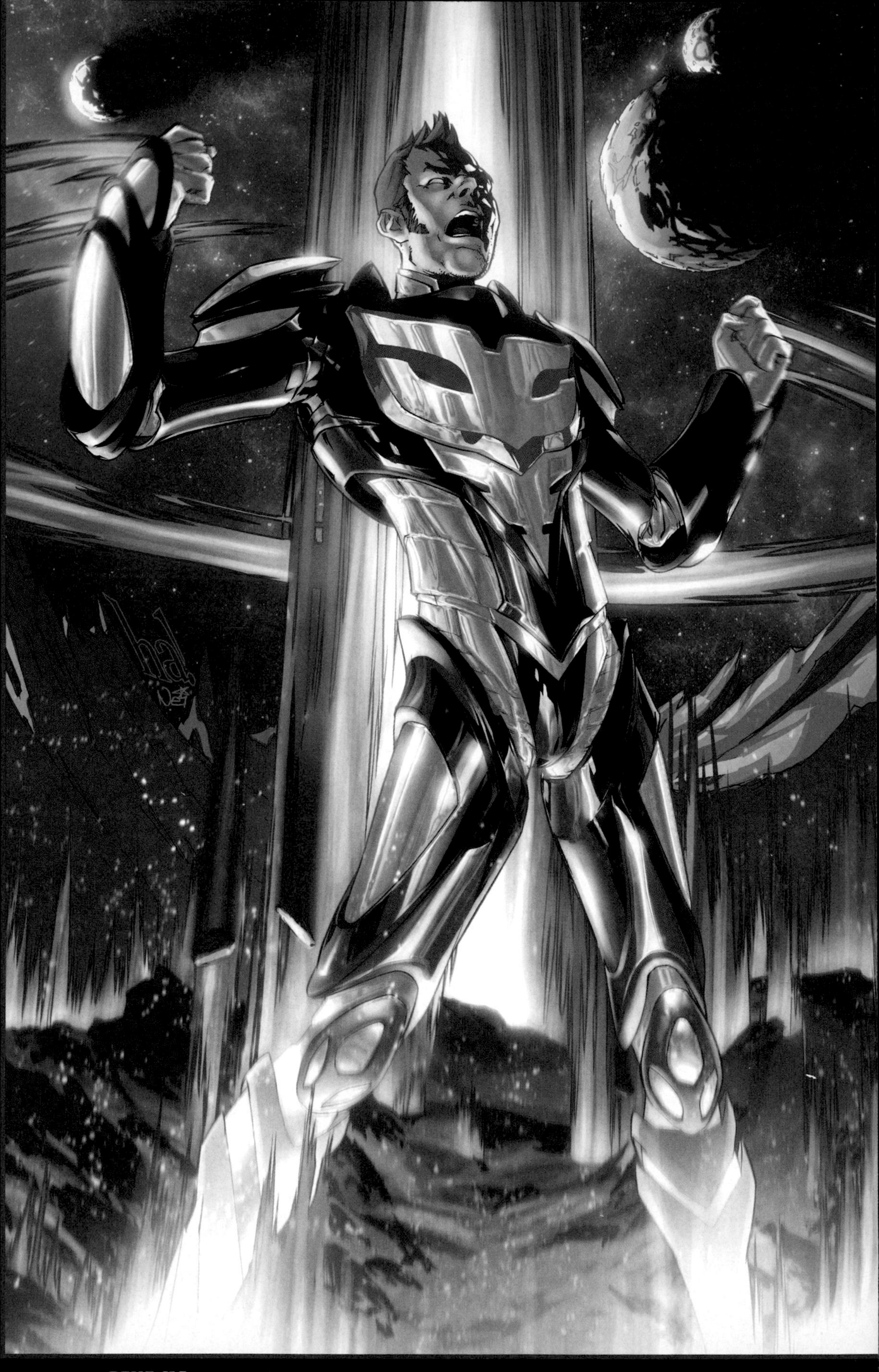

ISSUE ONE: GENE HA
WITH NEI RUFFINO

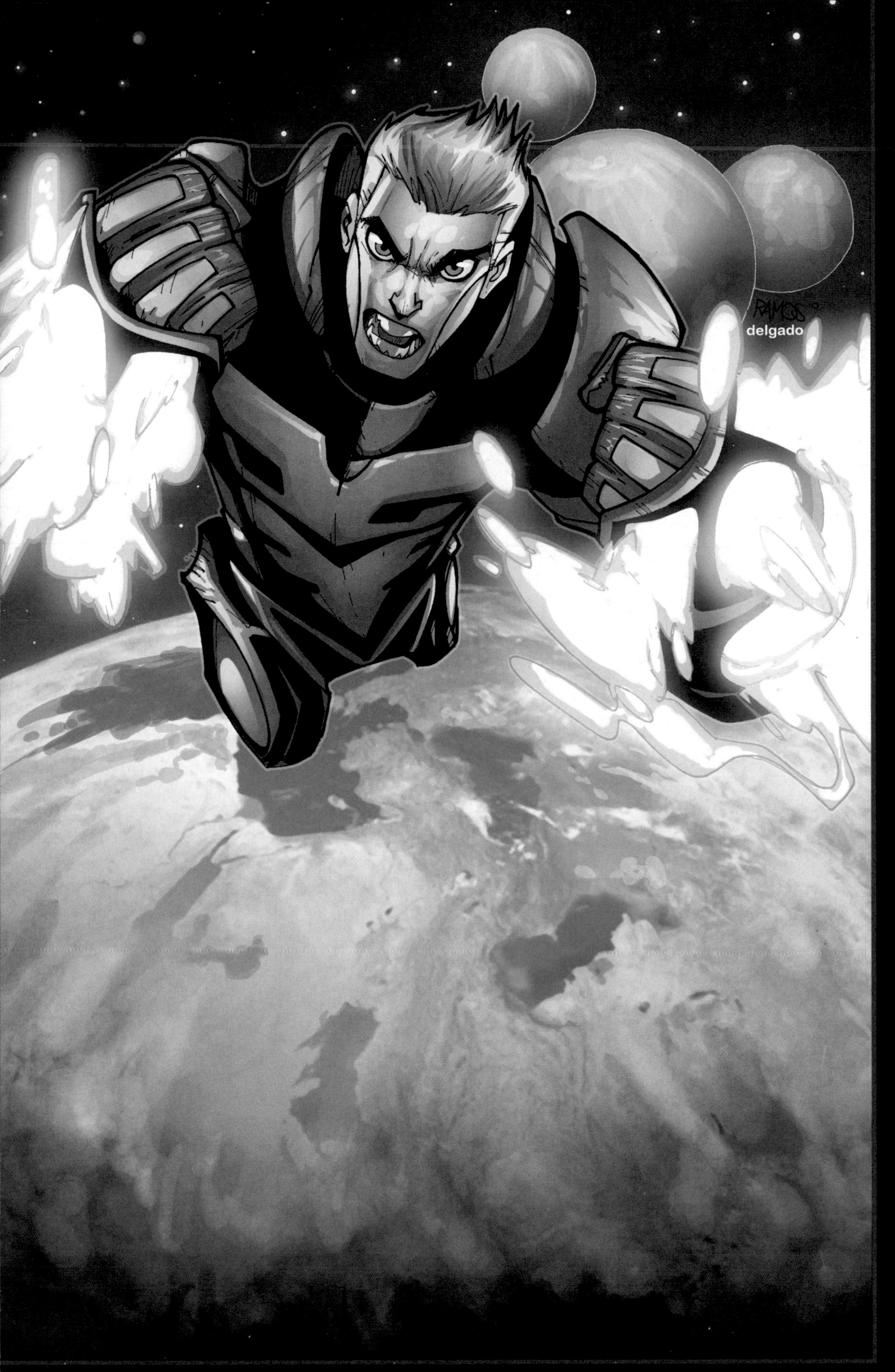
RAMOS '09
delgado

ISSUE ONE: HUMBERTO RAMOS

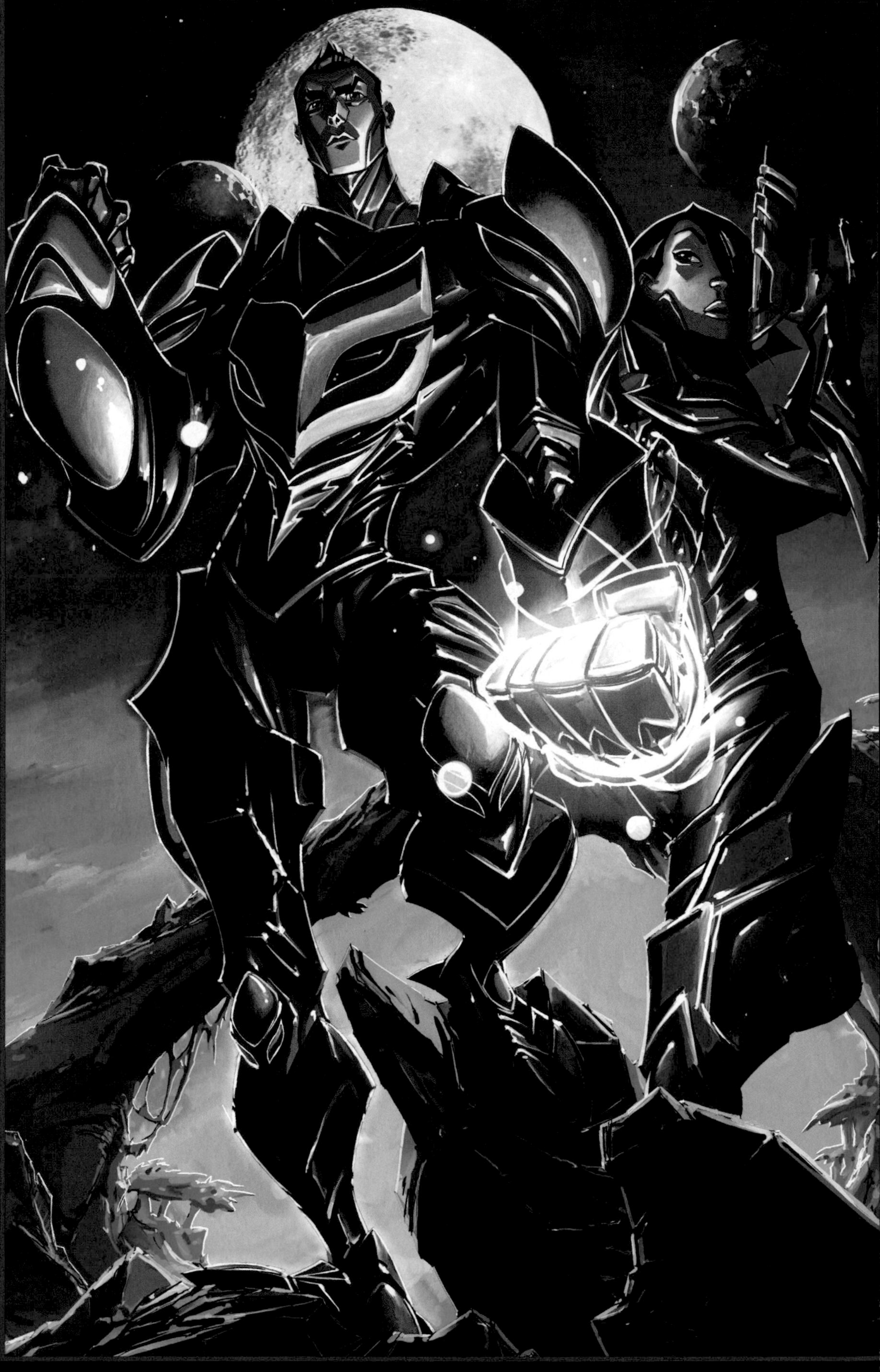

ISSUE ONE: **KHARY RANDOLPH**
WITH ETIENNE ST LAURENT

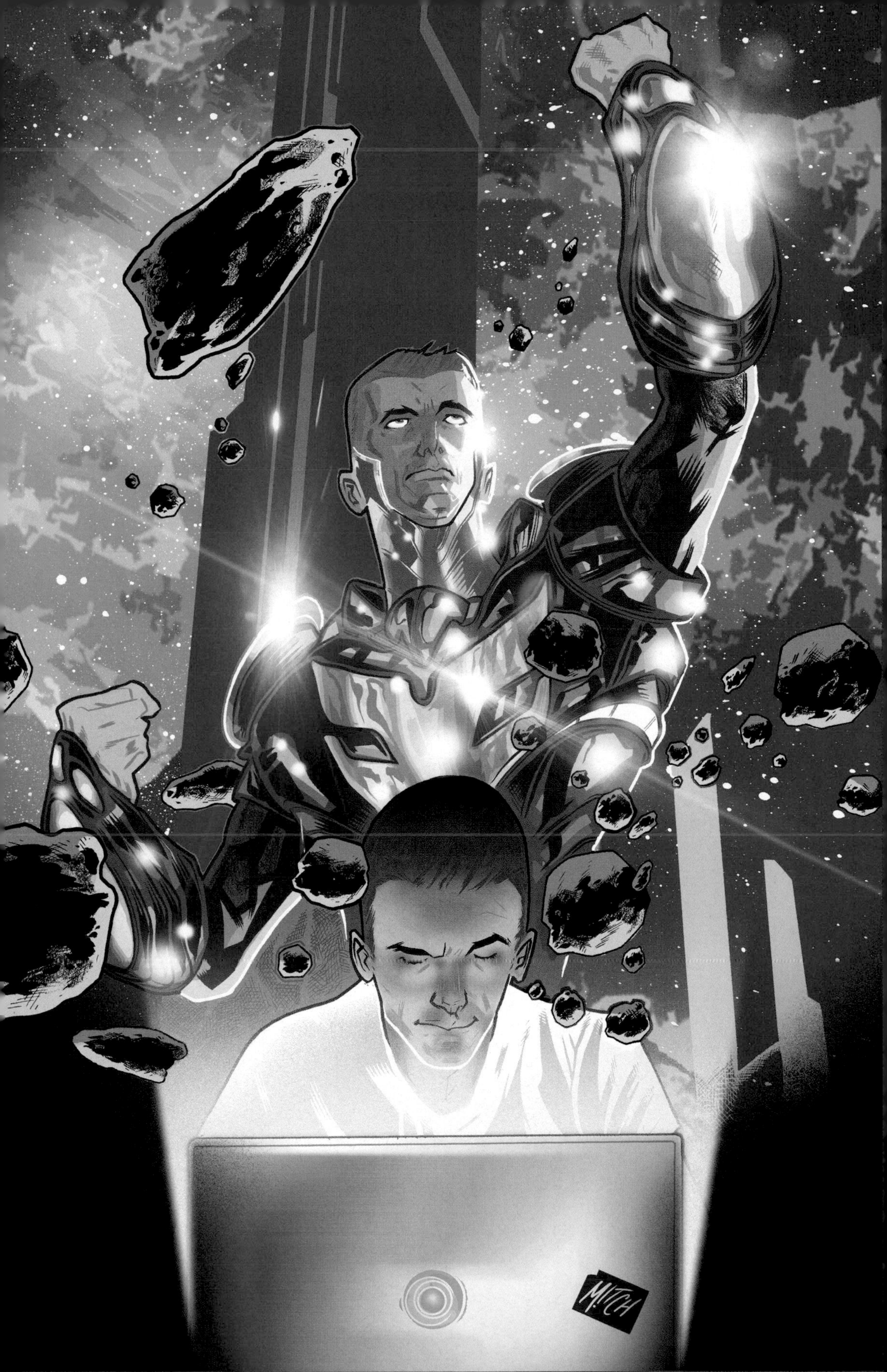
M!TCH

ISSUE ONE RETAILER INCENTIVE VARIANT: MITCH GERADS

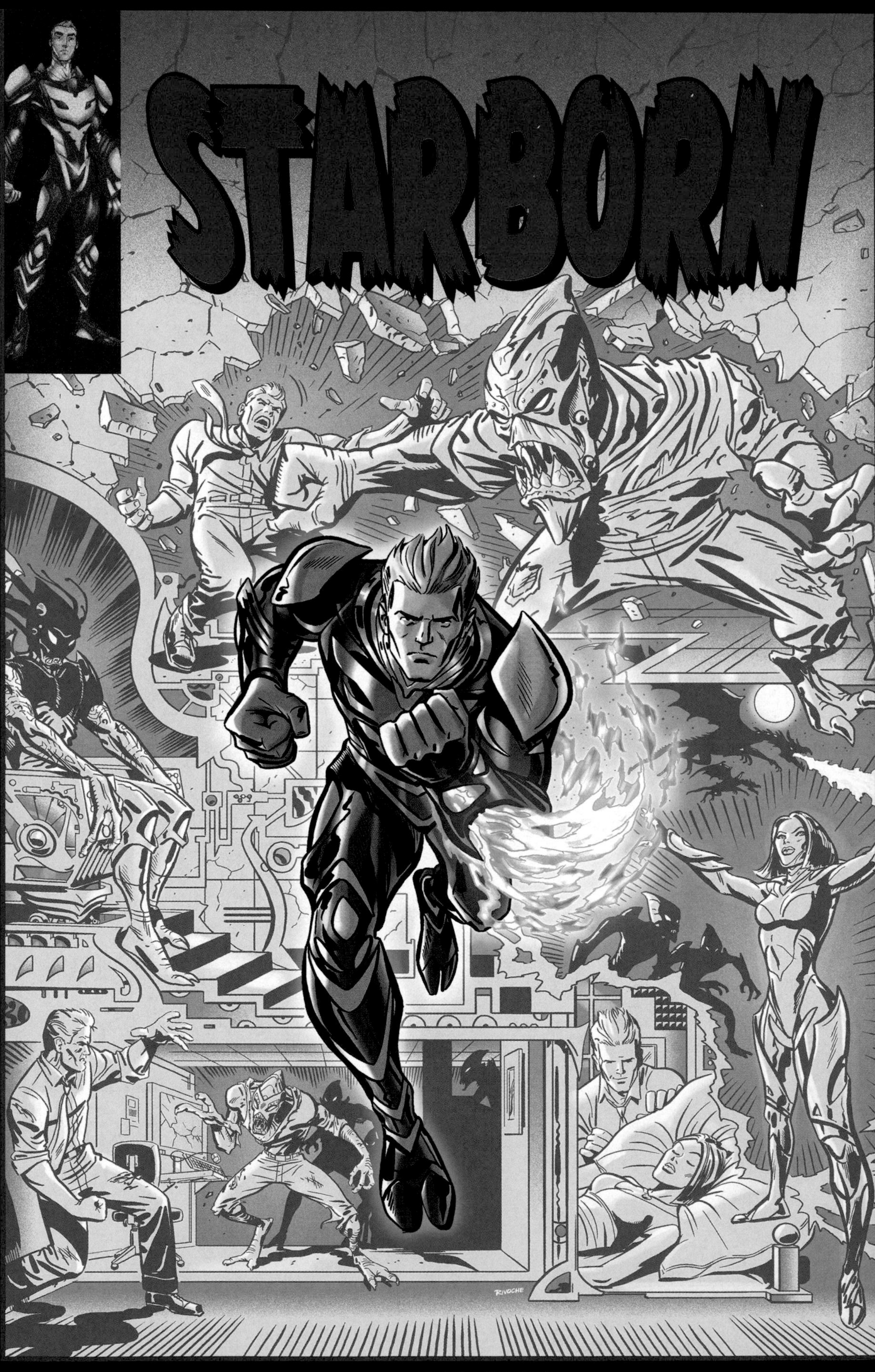
STARBORN
RIVOCHE

ISSUE ONE MIDTOWN COMICS EXCLUSIVE VARIANT: PAUL RIVOCHE

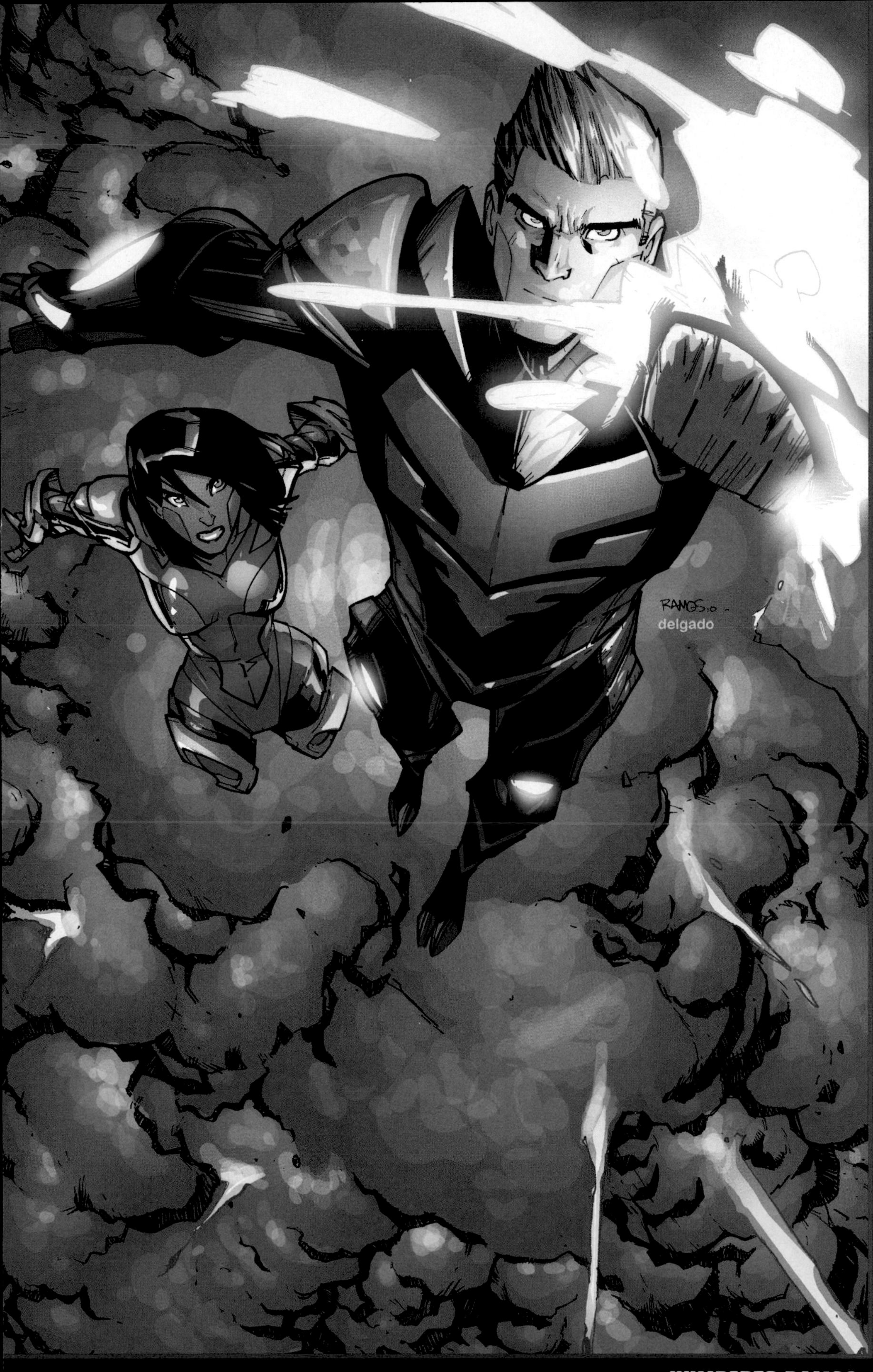
RAMOS.10
delgado

ISSUE TWO: HUMBERTO RAMOS

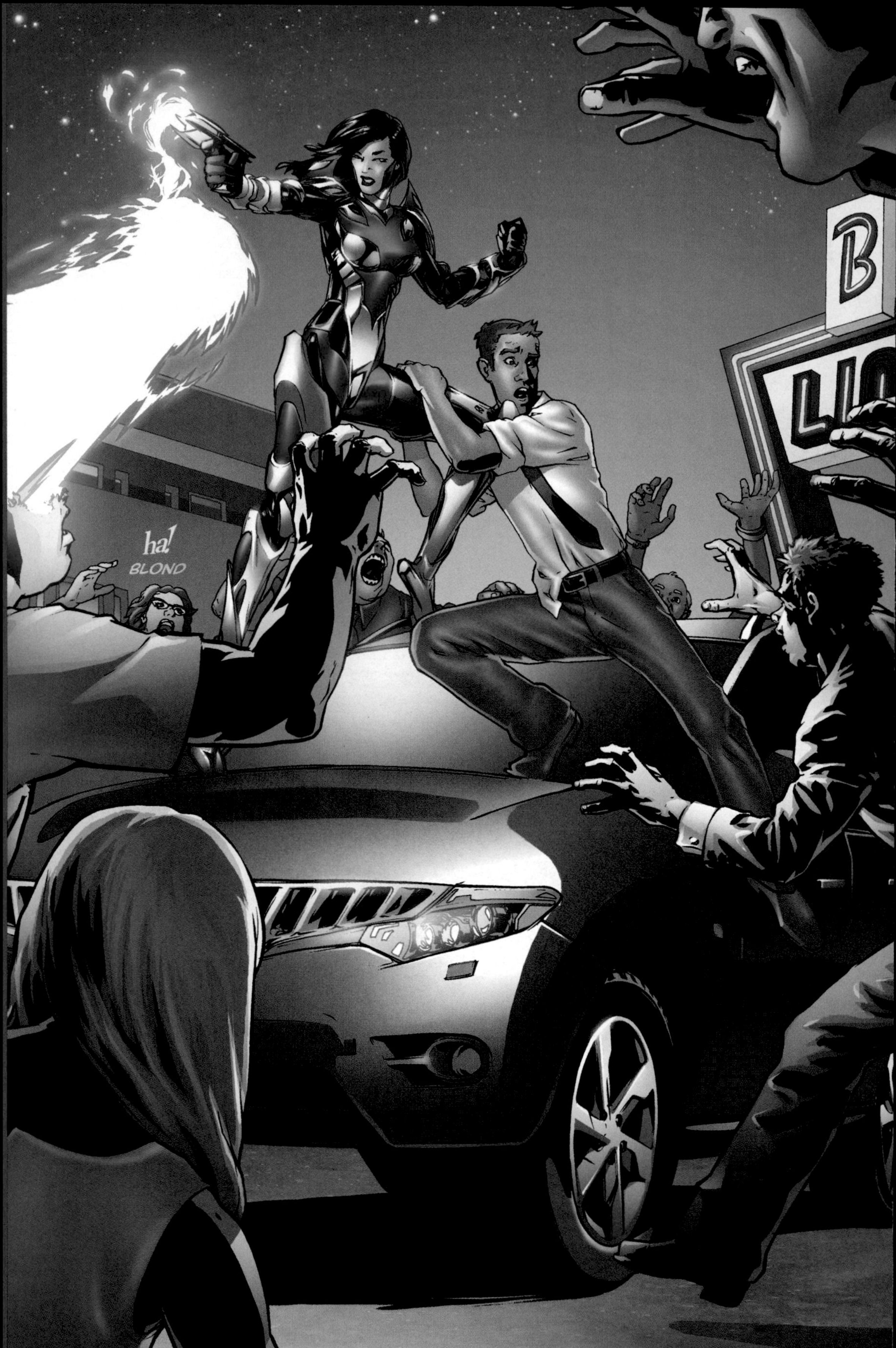
ha!
BLOND

ISSUE TWO: GENE HA
WITH BLOND

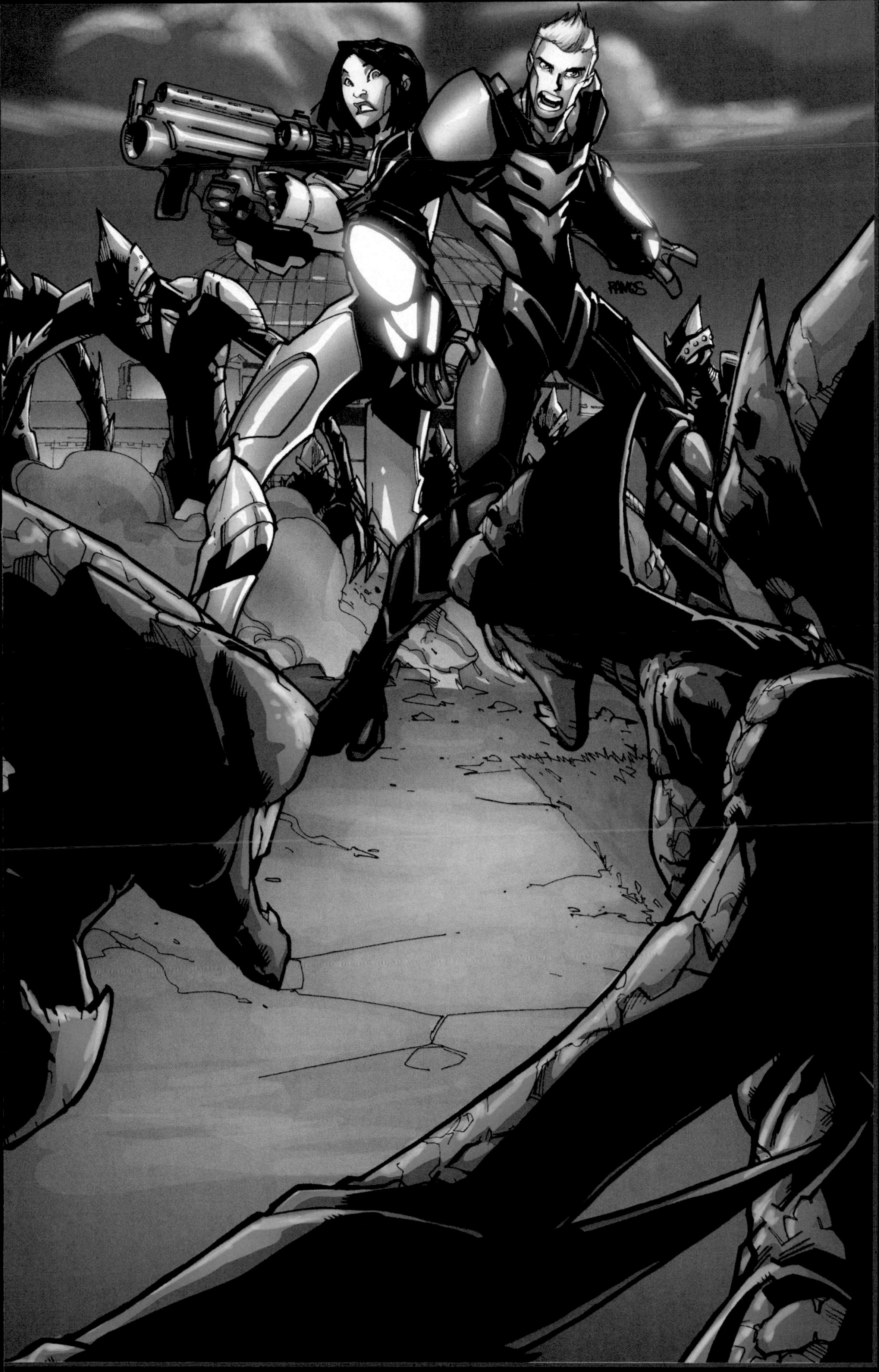
RAMOS

ISSUE THREE: **HUMBERTO RAMOS**
WITH EDGAR DELGADO

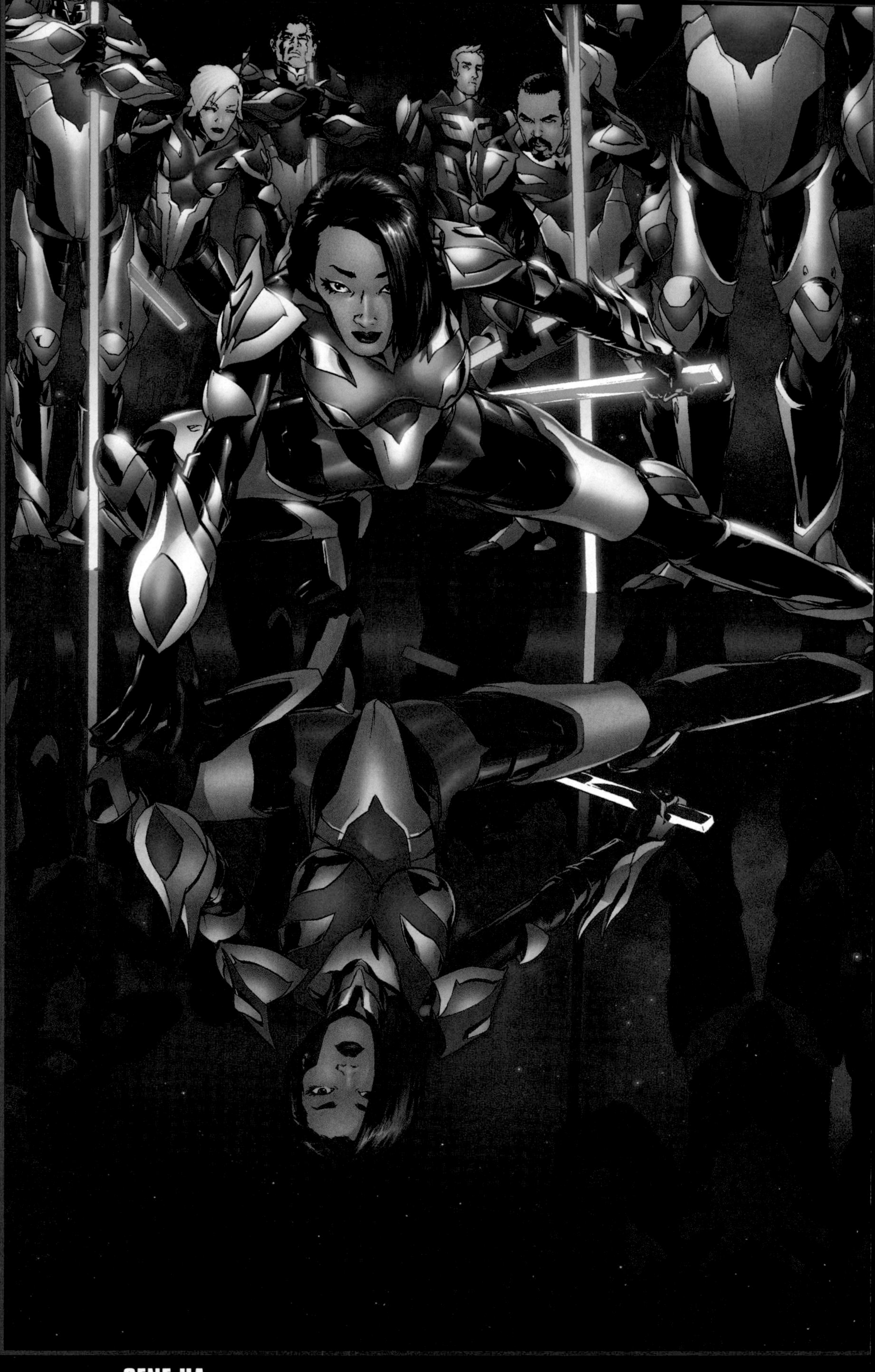

ISSUE THREE: **GENE HA**
WITH BLOND

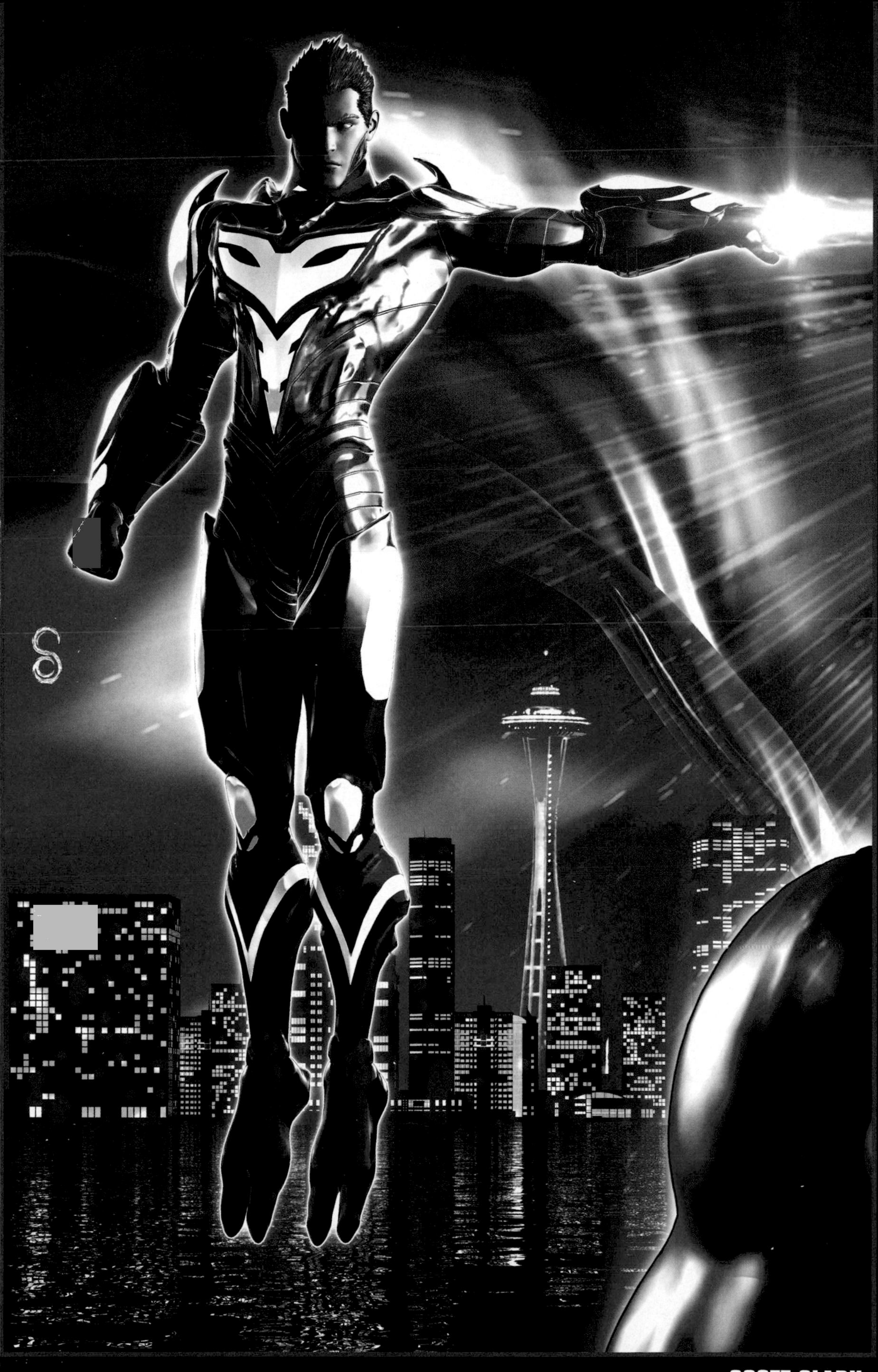

ISSUE THREE ECCC EXCLUSIVE VARIANT: SCOTT CLARK

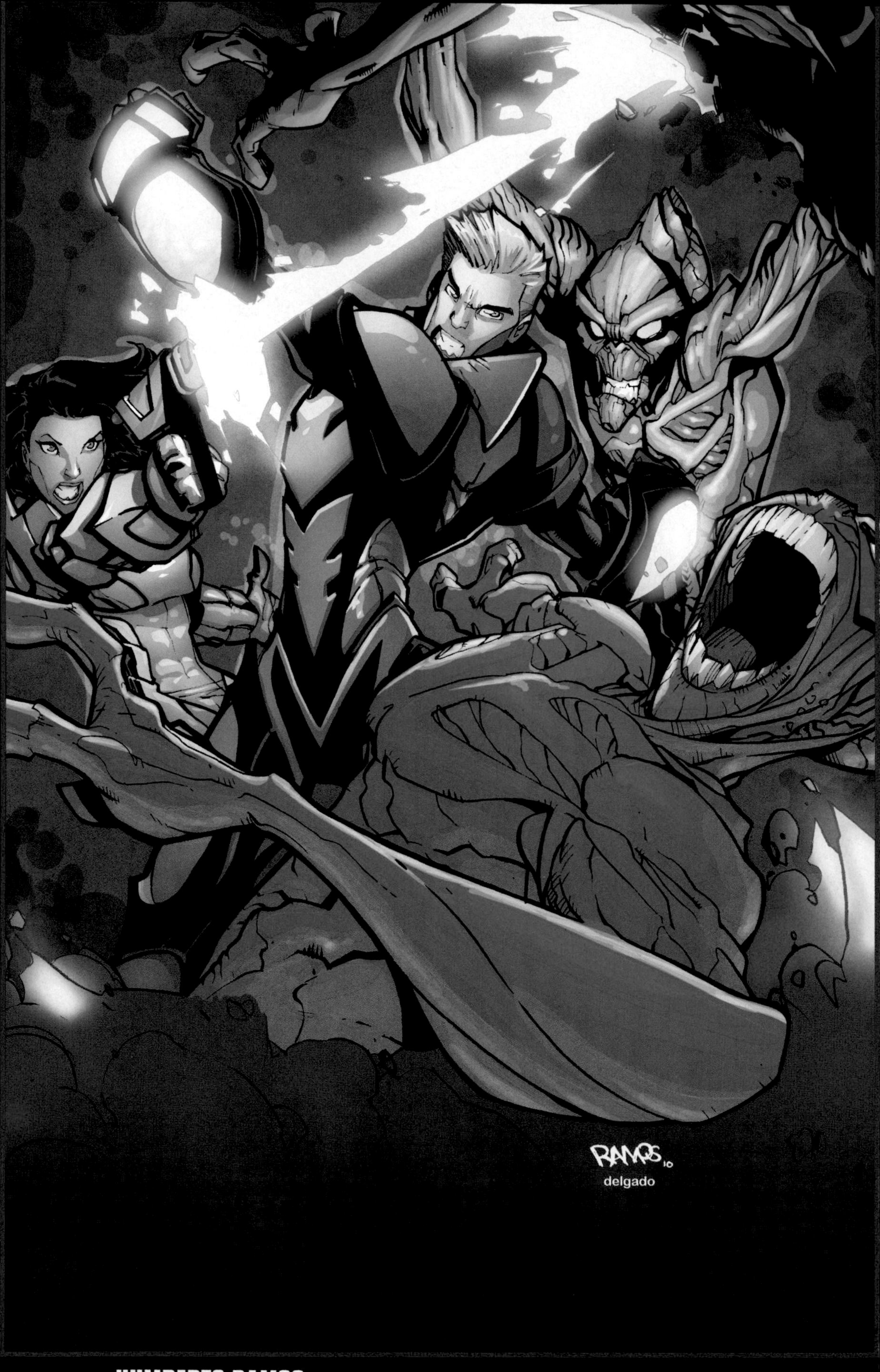
RAMOS 10
delgado

ISSUE FOUR: **HUMBERTO RAMOS**
WITH EDGAR DELGADO

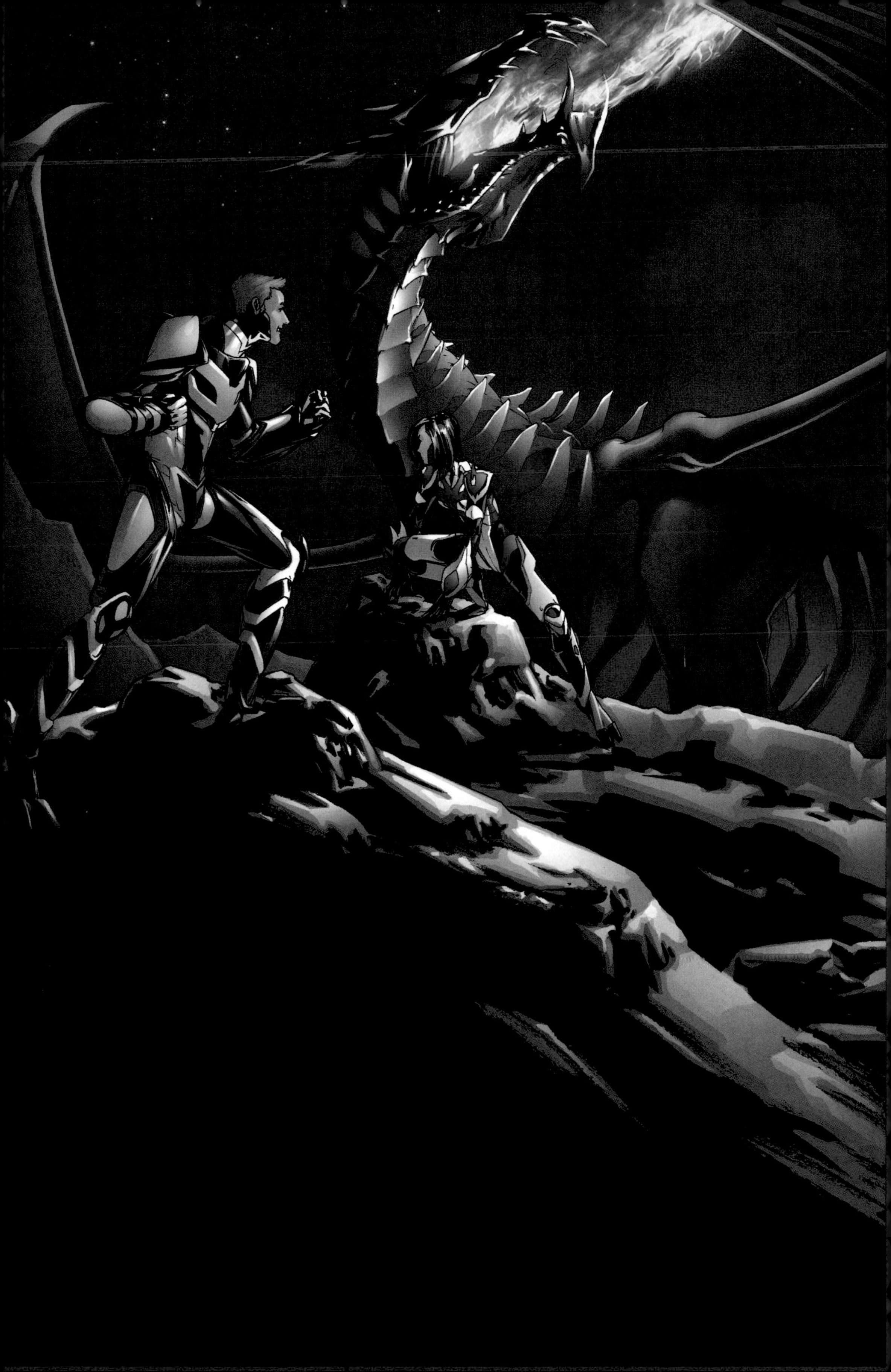

ISSUE FOUR: GENE HA
WITH BLOND

ARTIST GALLERY

DESIGNS AND SKETCHES FROM
KHARY RANDOLPH
WITH COLORS BY JUAN MANUEL TUMBURÚS

STARBORN
CHARACTER DESIGNS

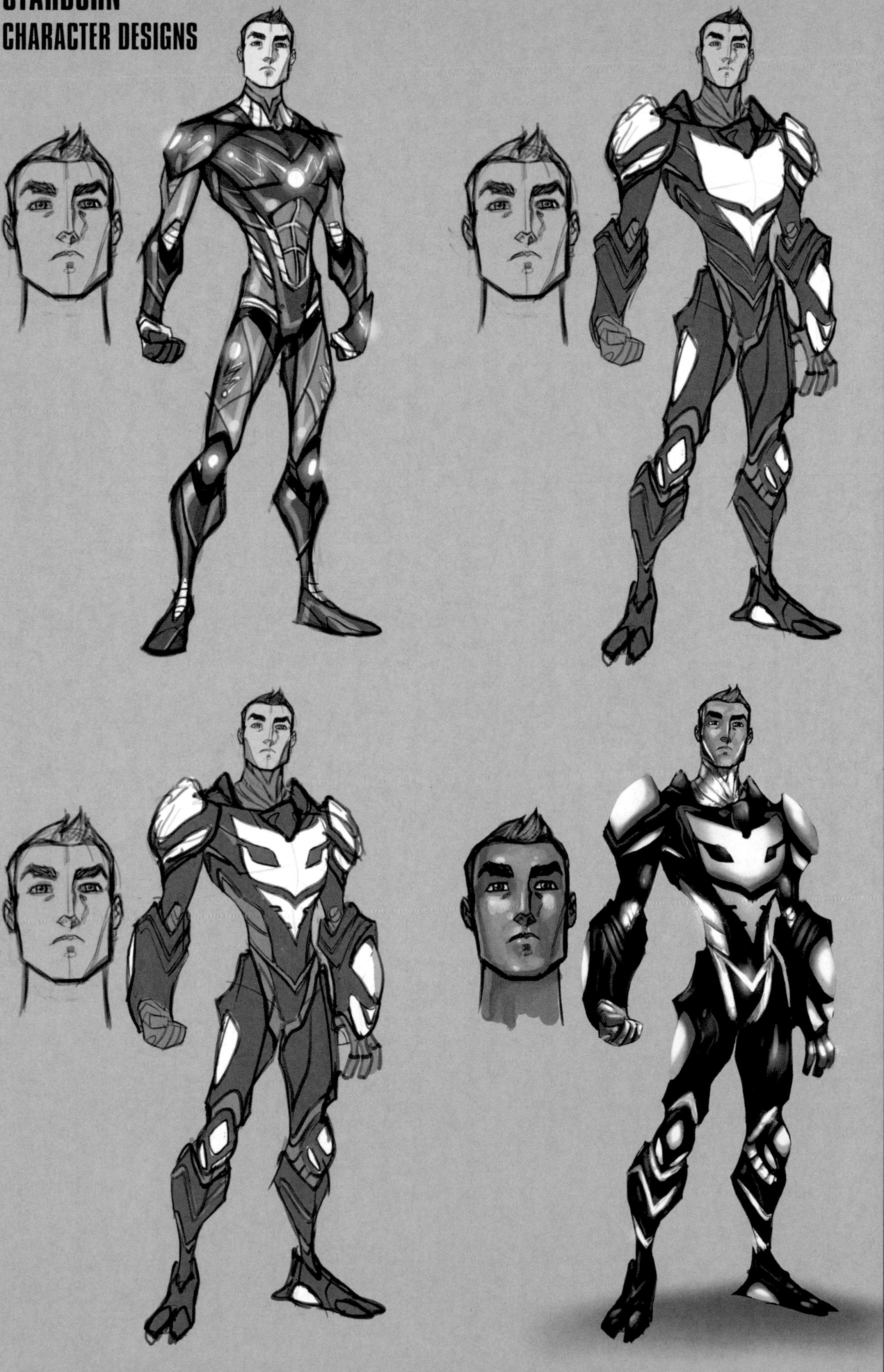

TARA TAKAMOTO
CHARACTER DESIGNS

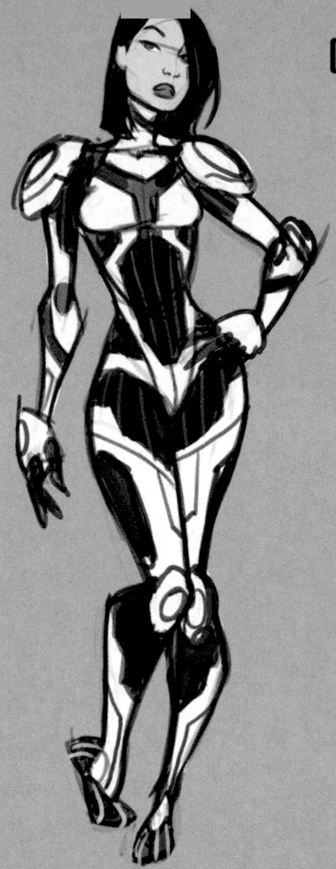

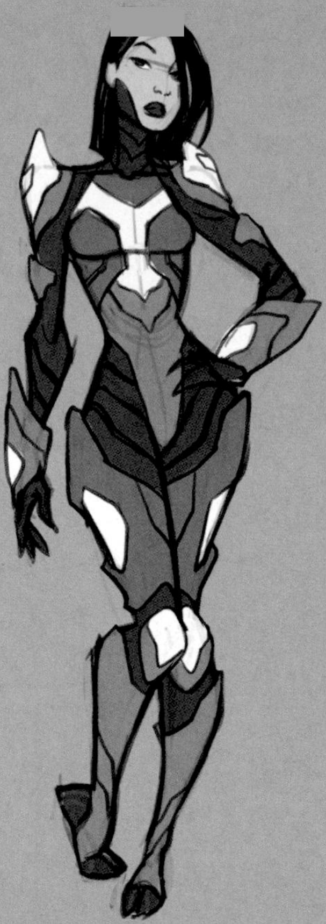

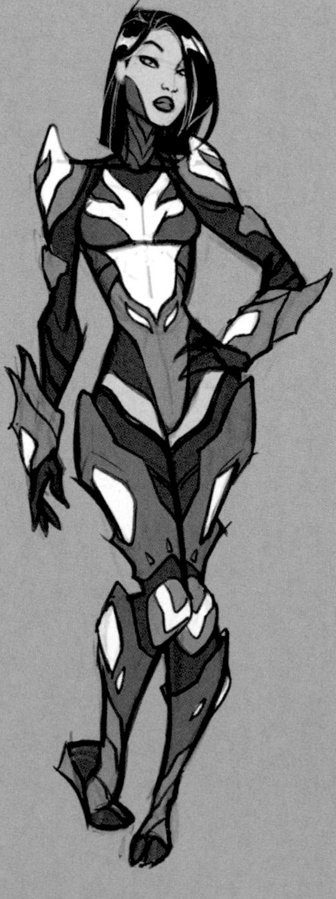

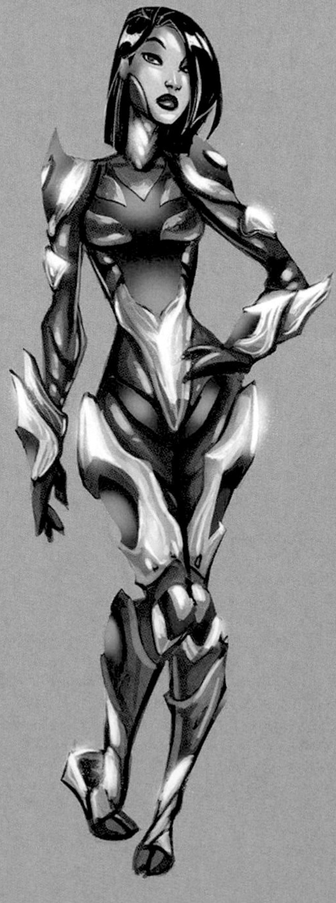

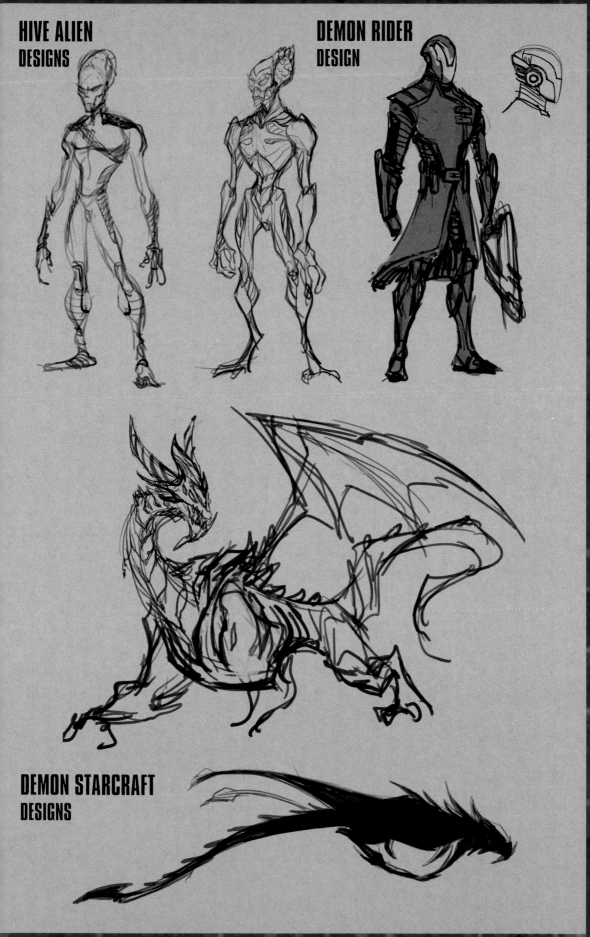

HIVE ALIEN
DESIGNS

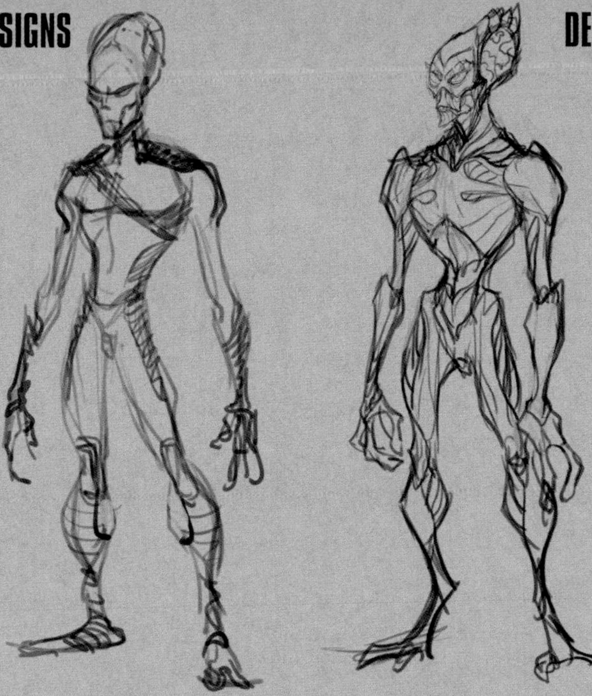

DEMON RIDER
DESIGN

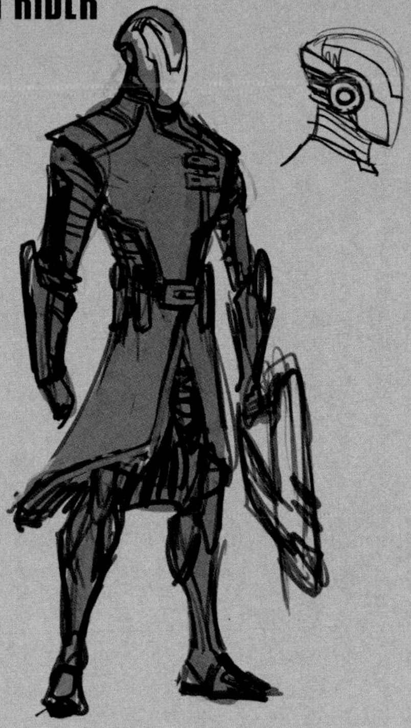

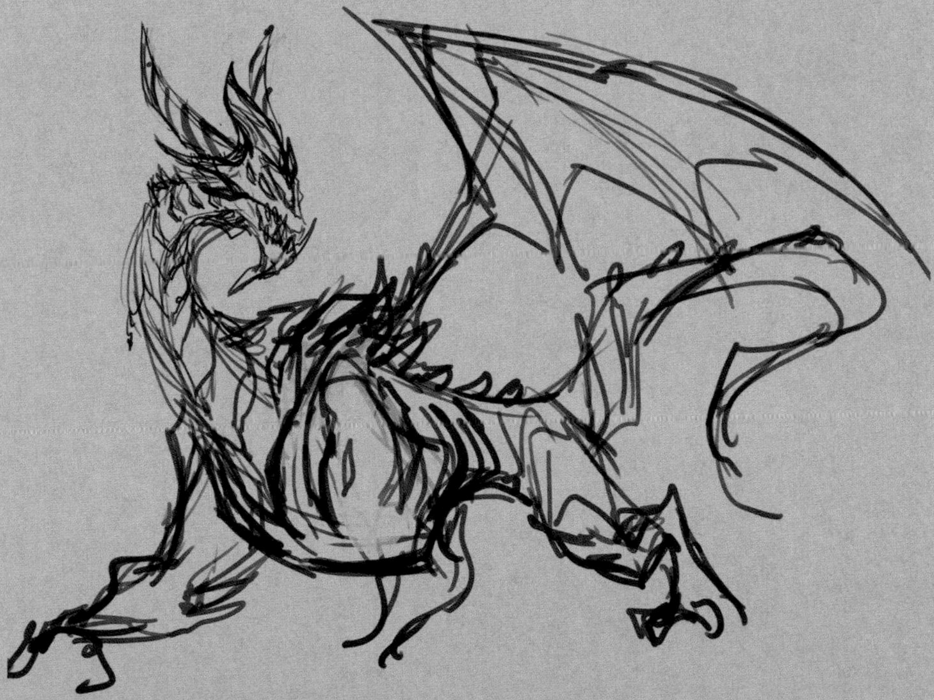

DEMON STARCRAFT
DESIGNS

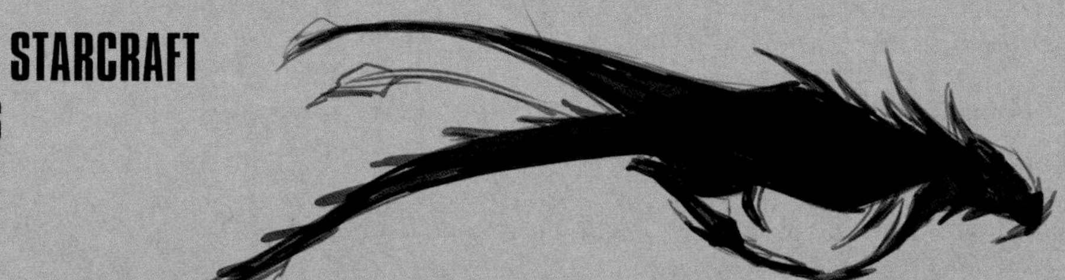

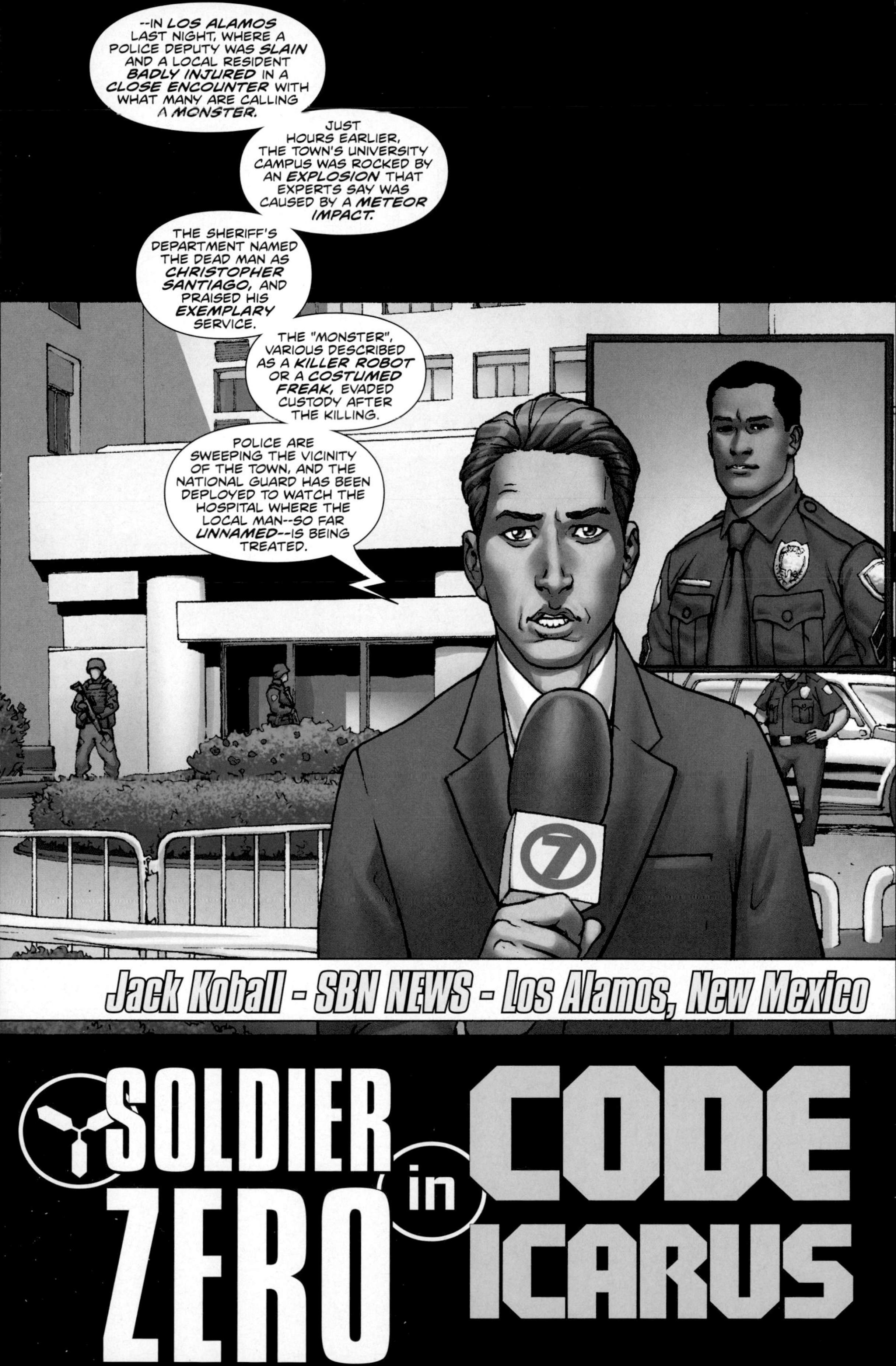
--IN LOS ALAMOS LAST NIGHT, WHERE A POLICE DEPUTY WAS SLAIN AND A LOCAL RESIDENT BADLY INJURED IN A CLOSE ENCOUNTER WITH WHAT MANY ARE CALLING A MONSTER.
JUST HOURS EARLIER, THE TOWN'S UNIVERSITY CAMPUS WAS ROCKED BY AN EXPLOSION THAT EXPERTS SAY WAS CAUSED BY A METEOR IMPACT.
THE SHERIFF'S DEPARTMENT NAMED THE DEAD MAN AS CHRISTOPHER SANTIAGO, AND PRAISED HIS EXEMPLARY SERVICE.
THE "MONSTER", VARIOUS DESCRIBED AS A KILLER ROBOT OR A COSTUMED FREAK, EVADED CUSTODY AFTER THE KILLING.
POLICE ARE SWEEPING THE VICINITY OF THE TOWN, AND THE NATIONAL GUARD HAS BEEN DEPLOYED TO WATCH THE HOSPITAL WHERE THE LOCAL MAN--SO FAR UNNAMED--IS BEING TREATED.
7
Jack Koball - SBN NEWS - Los Alamos, New Mexico
SOLDIER ZERO in CODE ICARUS

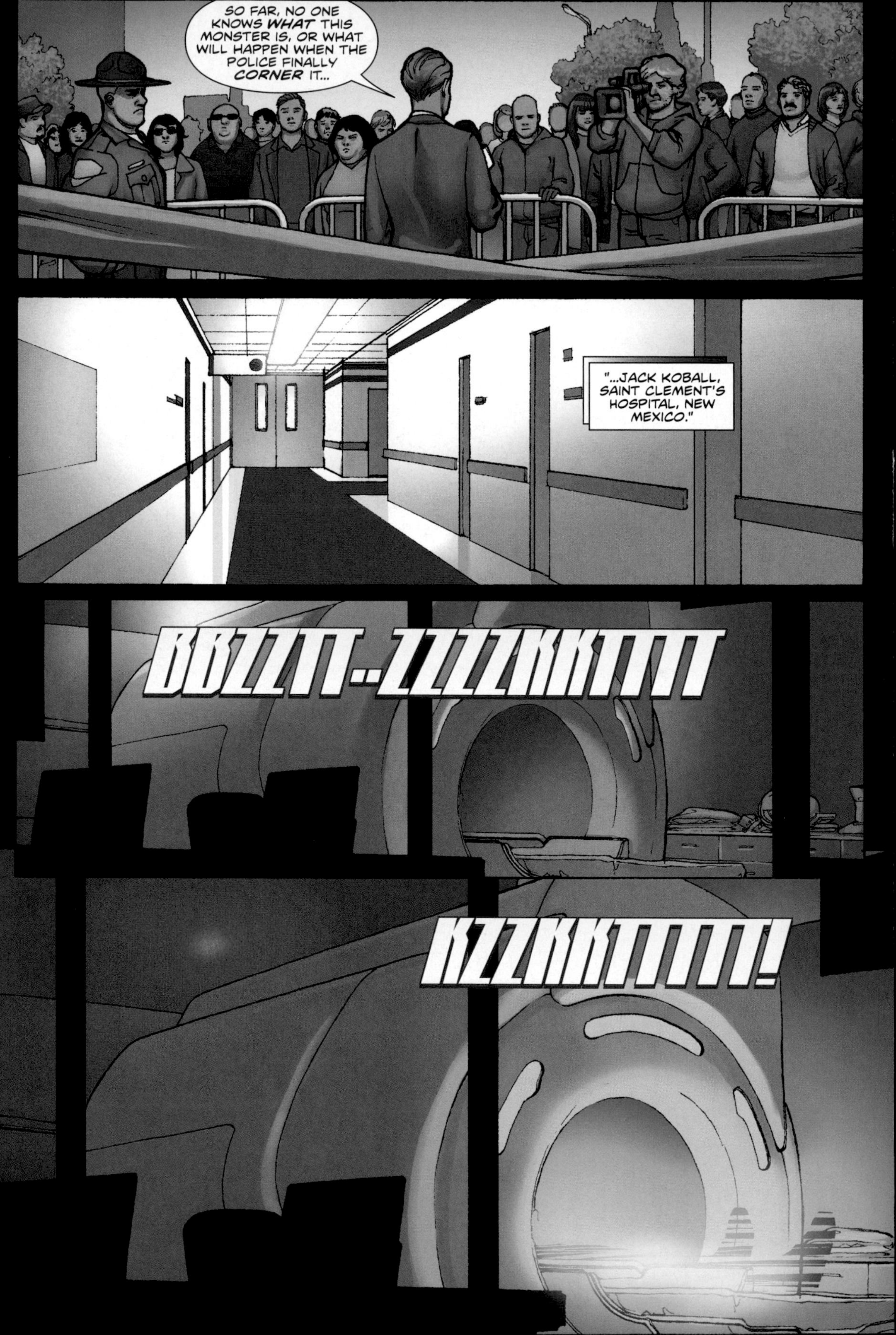
SO FAR, NO ONE KNOWS WHAT THIS MONSTER IS, OR WHAT WILL HAPPEN WHEN THE POLICE FINALLY CORNER IT...
"...JACK KOBALL, SAINT CLEMENT'S HOSPITAL, NEW MEXICO."
BBZZTT--ZZZZKKTTTT
KZZKKTTTTT!

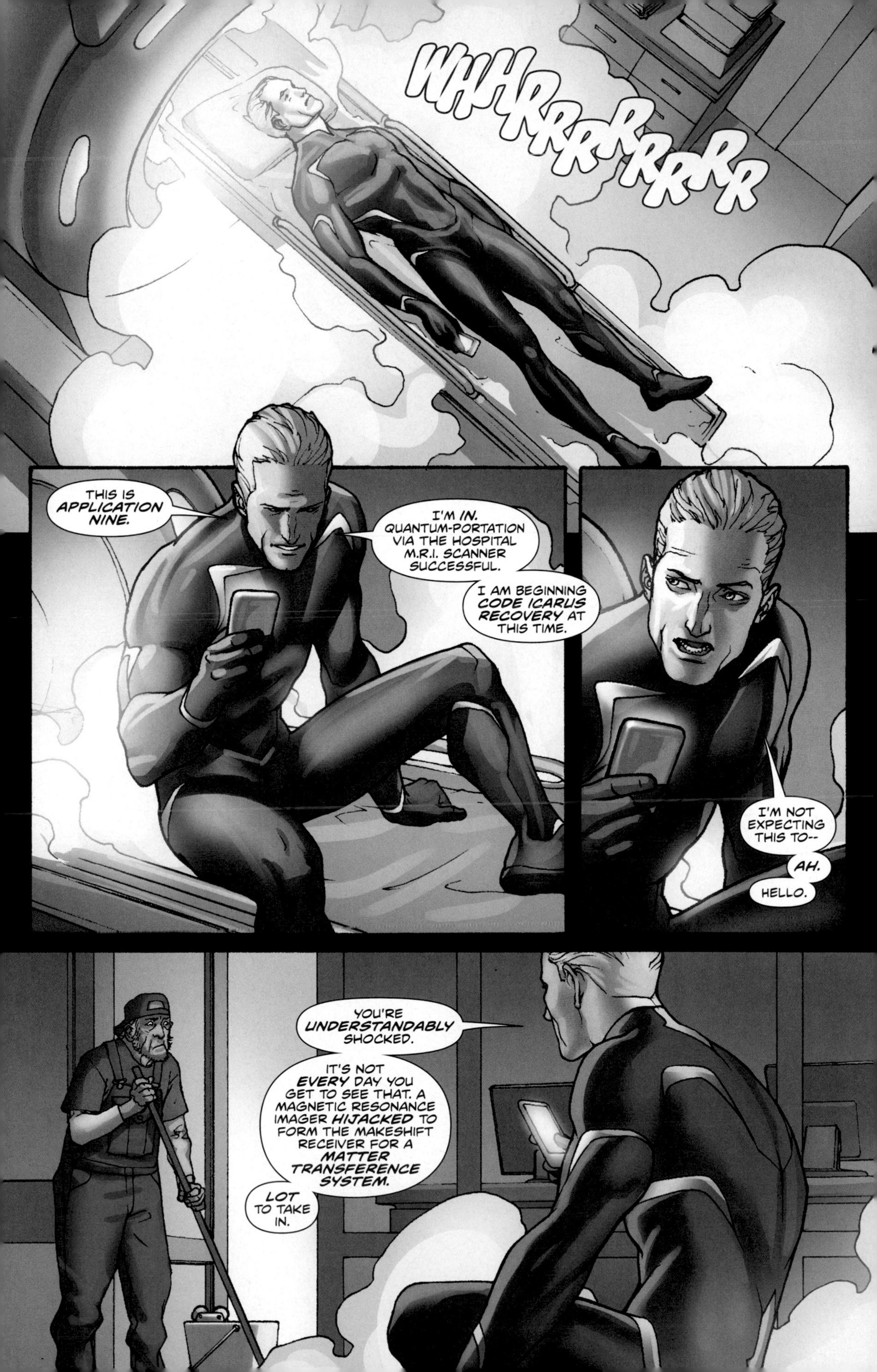
WHHRRRRRRRRR
THIS IS APPLICATION NINE.
I'M IN. QUANTUM-PORTATION VIA THE HOSPITAL M.R.I. SCANNER SUCCESSFUL.
I AM BEGINNING CODE ICARUS RECOVERY AT THIS TIME.
I'M NOT EXPECTING THIS TO--
AH.
HELLO.
YOU'RE UNDERSTANDABLY SHOCKED.
IT'S NOT EVERY DAY YOU GET TO SEE THAT. A MAGNETIC RESONANCE IMAGER HIJACKED TO FORM THE MAKESHIFT RECEIVER FOR A MATTER TRANSFERENCE SYSTEM.
LOT TO TAKE IN.

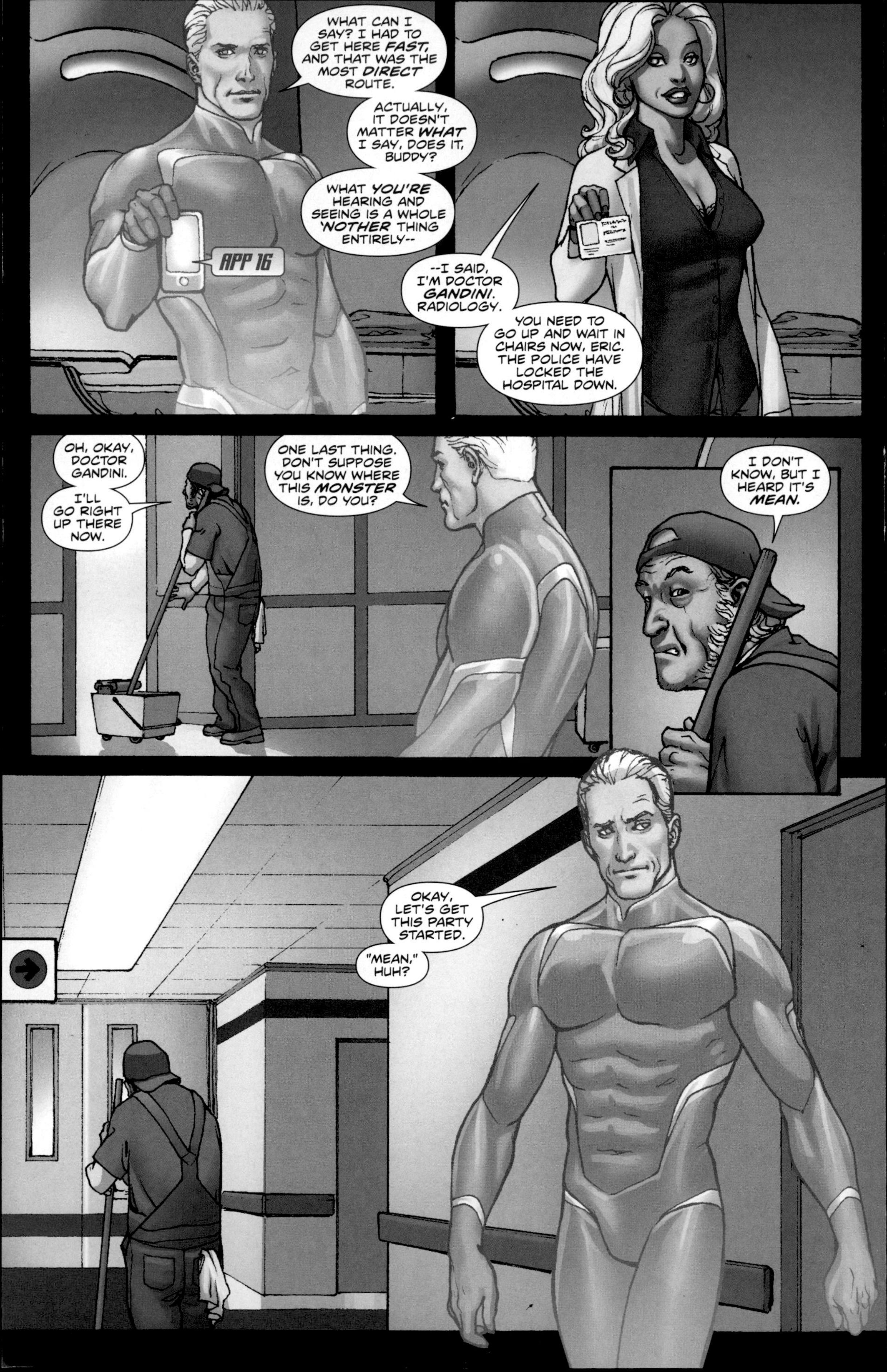
WHAT CAN I SAY? I HAD TO GET HERE FAST, AND THAT WAS THE MOST DIRECT ROUTE.
ACTUALLY, IT DOESN'T MATTER WHAT I SAY, DOES IT, BUDDY?
WHAT YOU'RE HEARING AND SEEING IS A WHOLE 'NOTHER THING ENTIRELY--
APP 16
--I SAID, I'M DOCTOR GANDINI. RADIOLOGY.
YOU NEED TO GO UP AND WAIT IN CHAIRS NOW, ERIC. THE POLICE HAVE LOCKED THE HOSPITAL DOWN.
OH, OKAY, DOCTOR GANDINI.
I'LL GO RIGHT UP THERE NOW.
ONE LAST THING. DON'T SUPPOSE YOU KNOW WHERE THIS MONSTER IS, DO YOU?
I DON'T KNOW, BUT I HEARD IT'S MEAN.
OKAY, LET'S GET THIS PARTY STARTED.
"MEAN," HUH?

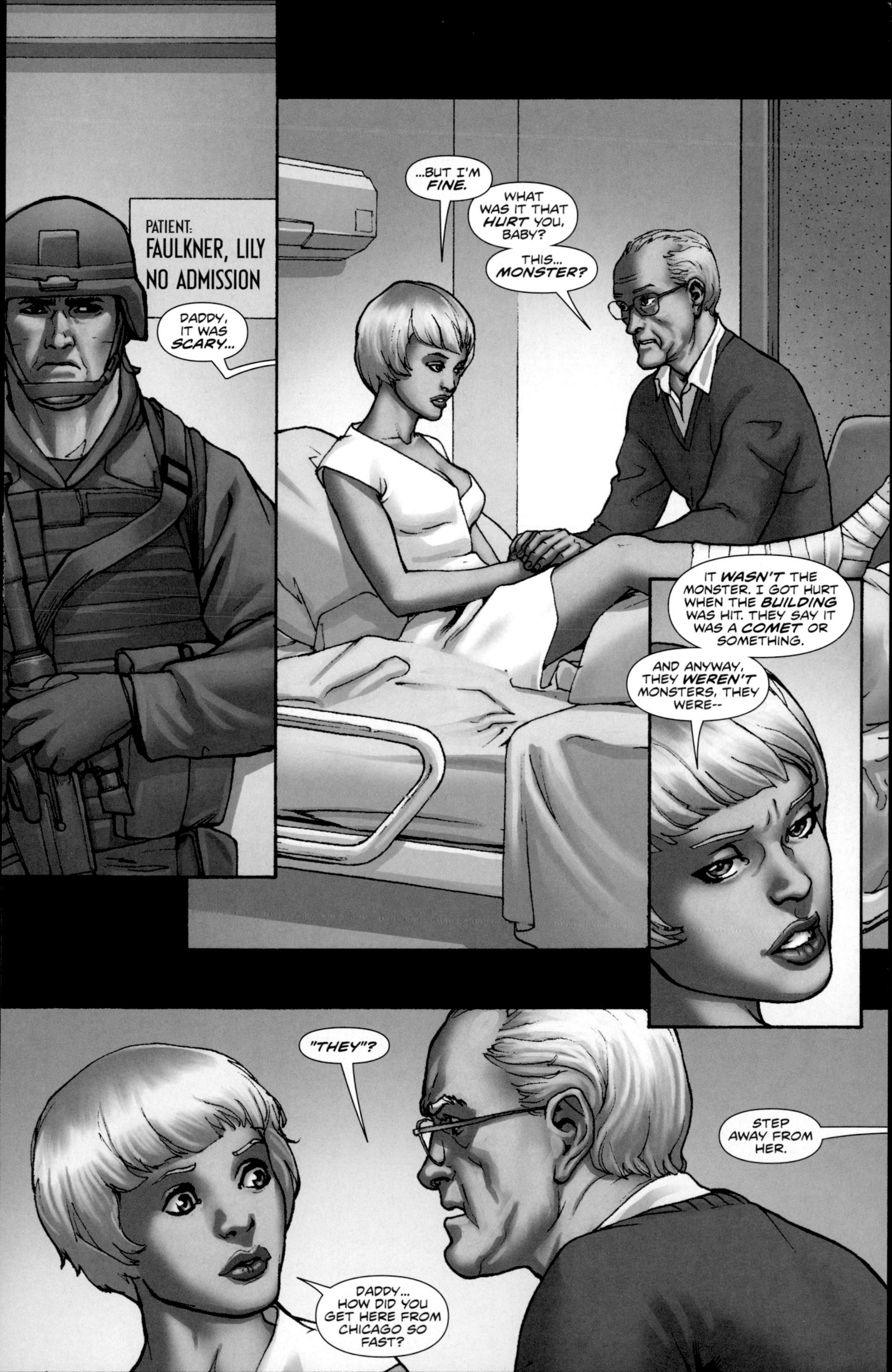
PATIENT: FAULKNER, LILY NO ADMISSION
DADDY, IT WAS SCARY...
...BUT I'M FINE.
WHAT WAS IT THAT HURT YOU, BABY?
THIS... MONSTER?
IT WASN'T THE MONSTER. I GOT HURT WHEN THE BUILDING WAS HIT. THEY SAY IT WAS A COMET OR SOMETHING.
AND ANYWAY, THEY WEREN'T MONSTERS, THEY WERE--
"THEY"?
STEP AWAY FROM HER.
DADDY... HOW DID YOU GET HERE FROM CHICAGO SO FAST?

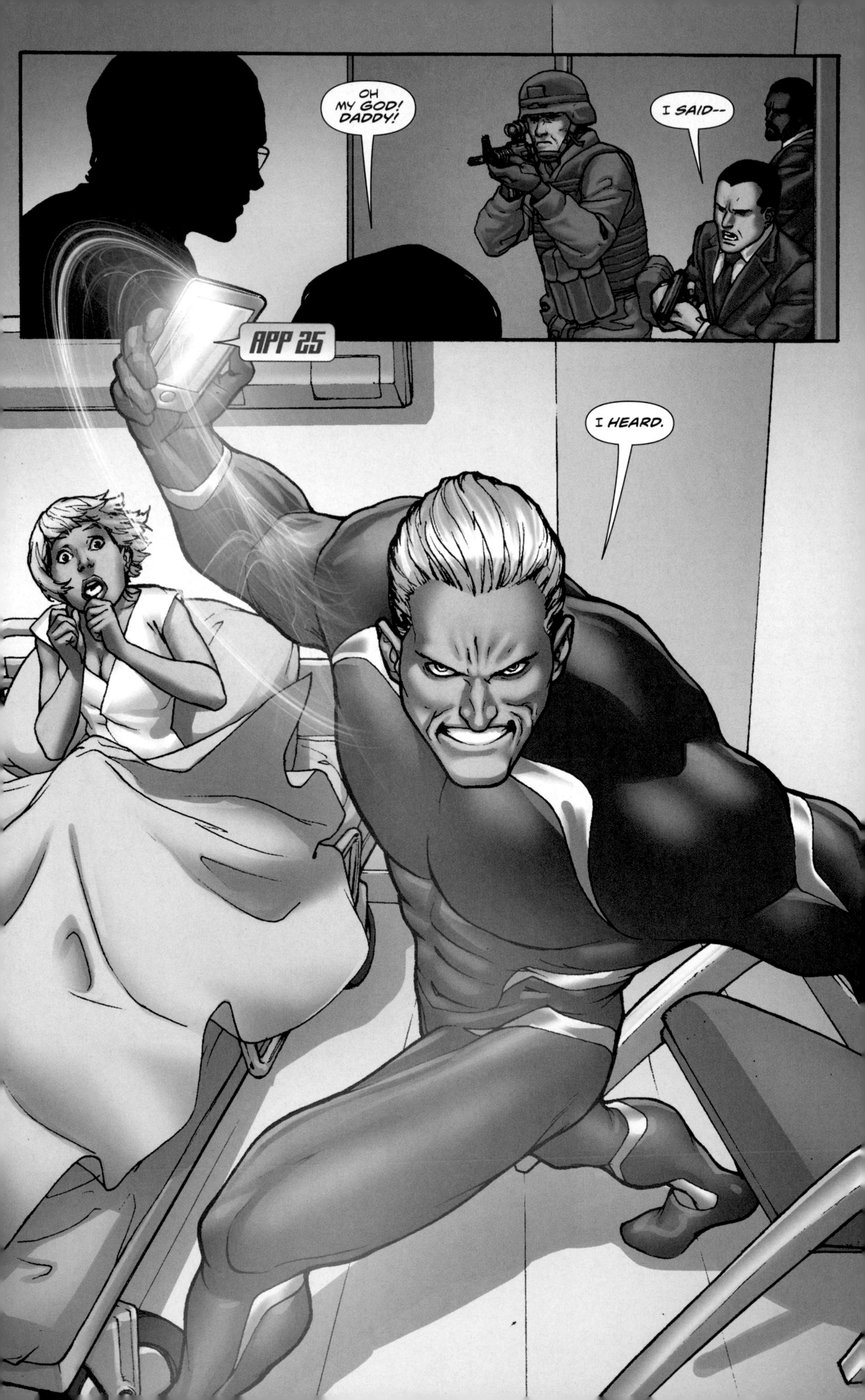
OH
MY GOD!
DADDY!
I SAID--
APP 25
I HEARD.

TO BE CONTINUED...BY SUPERSTAR WRITING TEAM
DAN ABNETT & ANDY LANNING IN

SOLDIER ZERO
VOLUME TWO COMING SOON!

Stan Lee